GIUSEPPE MAZZINI'S YOUNG EUROPE
AND THE BIRTH OF MODERN NATIONALISM
IN THE SLAVIC WORLD

Giuseppe Mazzini's Young Europe and the Birth of Modern Nationalism in the Slavic World

ANNA PROCYK

UNIVERSITY OF TORONTO PRESS
Toronto Buffalo London

© University of Toronto Press 2019
Toronto Buffalo London
utorontopress.com
Printed in Canada

ISBN 978-1-4875-0508-0

Library and Archives Canada Cataloguing in Publication

Title: Giuseppe Mazzini's Young Europe and the birth of modern
nationalism in the Slavic world / Anna Procyk.
Names: Procyk, Anna, 1937– author.
Description: Includes bibliographical references and index.
Identifiers: Canadiana 20190151412 | ISBN 9781487505080 (hardcover)
Subjects: LCSH: Mazzini, Giuseppe, 1805–1872 – Influence. |
LCSH: Polish people – Europe, Eastern – History – 19th century. |
LCSH: Youth – Political activity – Europe, Eastern – History – 19th century. |
LCSH: Youth movements – Europe, Eastern – History – 19th century. |
LCSH: Nationalism – Europe, Eastern – History – 19th century. |
LCSH: Europe, Eastern – Intellectual life – 19th century.
Classification: LCC DJK48 .P76 2019 | DDC 947/.07 – dc23

This publication was made possible in part by the financial support of the
Shevchenko Scientific Society, USA from the John and Elisabeth Chlopecky Fund,
the Ukrainian Academy of Arts & Sciences in the U.S., and the Ukrainian Studies
Fund.

University of Toronto Press acknowledges the financial assistance to its publishing
program of the Canada Council for the Arts and the Ontario Arts Council, an
agency of the Government of Ontario.

Canada Council   Conseil des Arts
for the Arts   du Canada

ONTARIO ARTS COUNCIL
CONSEIL DES ARTS DE L'ONTARIO
an Ontario government agency
un organisme du gouvernement de l'Ontario

Funded by the   Financé par le
Government   gouvernement
of Canada   du Canada

Canada

MIX
Paper from
responsible sources
FSC® C016245

To my father, Stefan Oleksiw

Contents

Illustrations

Acknowledgments

Research for this study was undertaken with the help of a generous grant received from the City University of New York, which enabled me to examine the archives and libraries in Italy (Milan, Rome, and Pisa), in the Slovak Republic (Martin and Bratislava), in the Czech Republic (Prague), and in Ukraine (Kyiv and Lviv).

A number of years of association, first as a student and subsequently as a research fellow at the Program on Soviet Nationality Problems at Columbia University, provided me with the necessary background for a deeper understanding of the central question under investigation in this study. I wrote my dissertation, published in 1995 under the title "Russian Nationalism and Ukraine: The Nationality Policy of the Volunteer Army during the Russian Civil War," under the guidance of the program's director, Edward Allworth. My mentor's objectivity, attention to documentary evidence and detail, as well as his beautiful, unadulterated English have been an inspiration to me for the years to come.

During my first year at Columbia University I had the good fortune to take a course with Peter Brock before this distinguished scholar of East Central Europe began his long teaching career at the University of Toronto. His numerous meticulously documented works on East Central Europe continued to stimulate my interest in this area of research. Fluency in several Slavic languages as well as an intimate familiarity with the multicultural character of East Central Europe would keep my research interests centred on the nationality question in this part of the world during my teaching and research assignments after completing my studies at Columbia. It was the very favourable response to my article "Polish Émigrés as Emissaries of the *Risorgimento* in Eastern Europe," which appeared in Harvard Ukrainian Studies that provided me with an incentive to expand this theme into a larger work. This monograph is the first attempt in English to trace the influence of the political thought of Giuseppe Mazzini on the Slavic nationalities in Eastern Europe.

According to my recollections, I first encountered what in college I recognized as Mazzini's ideals by listening to my instructors in post-war Czechoslovakia, who introduced me at a very early age to the political thought of their country's first president, Tomáš Garrigue Masaryk. For the initial inspirational lectures, I am especially indebted to Michal Chrtiansky, a pedagogue of distinction and dedication. This early interest in the political thought was deepened during my teen-age years through discussions with my father, Stefan Oleksiw, who also was an admirer of the celebrated twentieth-century Czech historian-politician. In my mature years I often pondered about the sources for the similarity of thought among individuals brought up in different cultures and under diverse political systems. It was only in the course of my research on this project that I realized that both my Lutheran teachers in central Slovakia and my father – who, though not an ordained priest, had studied at a Greek Catholic seminary in today's Ukraine – were educated by individuals whose mentors were the great-grandsons of political activists inspired in the first half of the nineteenth century by the ideals promoted by the emissaries of Young Europe.

While this manuscript was being prepared for publication, I received invaluable advice and constructive suggestions from a number of eminent scholars both on this continent and in Europe. Among them are: Maciej Janowski of the Institute of History in the Polish Academy of Sciences, Tomasz Stryjek of Collegium Civitas in Poland, Yaroslav Hrytsak of Ivan Franko National University in Lviv, Ukraine, John Merriman of Yale University, and Andrzej Kamiński of Georgetown University. I have also benefited from the multilingual talents of Grant Dawson, who had the goodwill to read the first draft of the manuscript, as well as the editorial expertise of Ian MacKenzie. A special thank you is due to Marta D. Olynyk for her assistance with transliteration. Vasyl Lopukh of the Shevchenko Scientific Society in New York provided technical help in the preparation of the illustrations. I am deeply indebted to Richard Ratzlaff and Stephen Shapiro of the University of Toronto Press for their invaluable professional guidance during the publication process. Needless to say, I take full responsibility for all shortcomings that critics may find in this study.

I also wish to acknowledge the assistance of a large number of librari-ans and archivists, especially in Europe, who have aided me in locating manuscripts and books during the years of research. I recall fondly the names of a few highly qualified professionals: Ksenya Kiebuzkinski of Harvard University (before she moved to the University of Toronto),

Lev Chaban of the Widener Library at Harvard, Robert Scott of Butler Library at Columbia University, and Lyudmila Shpileva of the New York Public Library and the Ukrainian Academy of Arts and Sciences in the United States. A number of individuals in the Slovak Republic have aided me in locating rare articles and books. For this I am especially thankful to Stefania Majerská Janičková and Marta Mišinová Abonyiová. My colleague Halyna Hryn of Harvard Ukrainian Research Institute has been always ready with helpful suggestions. Lastly, a special thank you is due to my daughter Motria Procyk and her husband Greg Snyder for not only having the patience to listen to my frequent impromptu lectures on Young Europe but also for occasionally surprising me with a rare edition of a work by Mazzini after a visit to Rome.

New York, 2019

GIUSEPPE MAZZINI'S YOUNG EUROPE
AND THE BIRTH OF MODERN NATIONALISM
IN THE SLAVIC WORLD

Introduction

The revolutionary fervour awakened by the events in France in July 1830 spread with lightning speed and asserted itself with resounding thunder across the European Continent. The subsequent uprisings that erupted in Belgium and Poland threatened to undermine the very foundation on which the terms of the Vienna treaty were painstakingly worked out by the conservative statesmen representing the victorious powers responsible for Napoleon's defeat in 1815. Would the Quadruple Alliance of Austria, Russia, England, and Prussia survive this rush of liberal and national-democratic insurgencies in Europe? Would the Holy Alliance of "legitimate" rulers withstand the quest for freedom of the subjugated peoples in the multinational empires of Austria and Russia? These were the unsettling thoughts of many a political leader at the helm of the authoritarian regimes clutching in his hands the destiny of Europe.[1]

These thoughts must have been especially vexing for one of the principal architects of the treaty of Vienna and the de facto director of the "Concert of Europe," Austria's iron-willed chancellor, Prince Clemens Metternich. A talented diplomat with consummate political skills, impeccable manners, and personal charm, Metternich dominated the political scene in post-Napoleonic Europe. Vehemently opposed to both liberalism and nationalism, he favoured a system in which a strong monarch would share power with traditional privileged groups of the realm. In order to strengthen and preserve a conservative political arrangement on the continent of Europe, the Austrian chancellor viewed the Quadruple Alliance as a convenient instrument for the suppression of revolutionary outbreaks wherever they threatened to occur. In the lands ruled by the Habsburgs as well as in regions in which Austria could wield its influence, he endeavoured to strengthen the local police, introduce close supervision of the universities, and establish strict censorship. With this reputation, there is little wonder that the Austrian chancellor became known as the architect of reaction and an arch-enemy of liberty in post-Napoleonic Europe.[2]

An uneasy, nervous atmosphere continued to prevail in the cabinets of conservative statesmen on the Continent, even when the dust of the revolutionary fury began to subside by the end of 1831. True, the revolutions did not prove strong enough to inflict a mortal blow to the reigning kings and emperors, but their impact proved sufficiently serious to necessitate revisions in the Vienna settlement – revisions that considerably undermined both the idea of legitimacy and the concept of balance of power, two important principles on which the peace agreement signed in Vienna had been built. With respect to the former, the conservative "legitimate" Bourbons were overthrown in France, with Louis Philippe, the new king of the Orleans dynasty, promising to rule in accordance with the principles of a liberal constitution. With respect to the second, a revision of the political map of Europe did become a fact when Belgium proclaimed its independence in November 1830.[3]

According to the decisions made at the Congress of Vienna, the Belgian provinces had been united with Holland into a single Kingdom of the Netherlands. Dutch was proclaimed the official language of the state, although the overwhelming majority of the Belgian population spoke French or Flemish. Experiencing both cultural and religious discrimination, the Belgian Catholic and Liberal parties concluded a provisional political alliance to struggle for the equalization of rights as well as for administrative, legislative, and financial separation of Belgium from Holland. Under the leadership of Louis de Potter and Charles Rogier, the idea of an independent Belgium gained momentum. On 25 August 1830 a revolt broke out in Brussels following a performance of Daniel Auber's patriotically inspired opera *La Muette de Portici*, in which a seventeenth-century Italian hero, Masaniello, leads a revolt in Naples against the Spanish rule. Following the performance, a large crowd of Belgians gathered on the streets of Brussels shouting patriotic slogans and occupying government buildings. The revolt spread quickly to the Belgian provinces. By the end of September almost all of Belgian territory was cleared of Dutch troops. A provisional government was formed and a Belgian national congress was convened. It proclaimed Belgium's independence and adopted a democratic constitution. To make matters worse from the point of view of Metternich and the absolute rulers of Europe, a constitutional monarch was placed on the throne of an independent Belgium.[4]

In other places, like the small kingdoms and duchies on the Italian peninsula ruled with a few exceptions either by foreign dynasties or

Austria's puppets, disturbances were suppressed one by one with relative ease. Yet the resulting flood of political émigrés from these territories to France, Switzerland, and Belgium – places in which the political climate was more conducive to spinning plans for the next round of revolutions – would prove especially troublesome for Metternich's police apparatus in Vienna in the following decades.

In Eastern Europe the liberal revolution in France and in particular the national uprising in Belgium ignited a year-long war of independence led by Polish patriots who after a number of failed attempts in the preceding century, still found it difficult to abandon their dream of restoring the glories of their dismembered commonwealth.[5] The uprising began on 29 November 1830 in Warsaw, when a group of young Polish officers led by Lieutenant Piotr Wysocki stormed the residence of the Russian regent, the brother of Tsar Nicholas I. During the ensuing struggle the insurgents were joined by thousands of Polish patriots as well as hundreds of foreign sympathizers who enthusiastically responded to the rebels' call to fight for "Your and our freedom." In spite of initial successes, the Polish national struggle was crushed by the numerically superior Russian Imperial Army. In the ensuing months, according to a decree issued by the tsarist regime, Polish lands under Russian rule lost the autonomy they formerly enjoyed and became an integral part of imperial Russia. The well-established, centuries-old policies of Russification applied to Ukrainians and other nationalities of the empire would now be extended to the territories inhabited by the Poles. In order to escape executions, oppression or exile to Siberia, over 8,000 Polish rebels, among them distinguished poets, writers, scholars and political activists, chose to flee to Western Europe.[6]

The suppression of the Polish revolution did not bring peace to the troubled imperial house of the Romanovs. Tsar Nicholas I could not easily erase from his memory the fact that the Polish uprising at its inception would have posed a serious threat to Russia's control of the empire's western domains had aid been extended to the insurgents by the champions of liberal causes in Western Europe. In fact, such assistance was eagerly anticipated by the Polish insurgents, because the opposition leaders in both France and Belgium were appealing to all European democrats to unite in order to put an end to absolutism so that through a joint effort a free homeland could be secured for everyone. Fortune, however, favoured the autocratic ruler of Russia, for the expectations of assistance to the Polish patriots failed to materialize, even though it was quite clear that the insurgency in Poland proved to be of considerable benefit to the pro-liberal cause in Western Europe. Few could overlook the fact that the determination of the Polish insurgents to continue fighting for their homeland's independence against over-whelming odds did actually prevent the despatch of Russian troops to suppress the revolutions in France and Belgium. In fact, on the eve of the Polish insurrection such a move was considered by Nicholas in order to restore to power in Western Europe the "legitimate" rulers in accordance with the terms of the Holy Alliance – an agreement initiated by the tsar's predecessor, Alexander I, and solemnly sealed with a pledge by most European monarchs in 1815. This pact of collective security among the ruling emperors and kings to aid each other in times of trouble was intended to reinforce the maintenance of the status quo in Europe based on the peace settlement of Vienna after the defeat of Napoleon.

The end of the Polish national uprising represented a singular victory for the autocrat in Russia, yet the revolution added fuel to the nervous paranoia of the tsar both because of the strength of revolutionary fervour exhibited by the insurgents and the triumph of liberalism in France and Belgium. It was only six years earlier, at his accession in December 1825 that Nicholas was confronted with a revolt of Russian officers whose political objectives bore the unmistakable imprint of liberal and radical thought.[7] The executions and deportations to Siberia that followed did not restrain the revolutionary fervour in the imperial lands, as the force of the Polish insurgency had clearly demonstrated. Consequently, after 1831 Nicholas became even more determined than before to quell all forms of opposition, especially in the western borderlands of his sprawling imperial domains. He saw to it that his police apparatus would be even more efficient in reinforcing its surveillance over all forms of unauthorized activity and even more repressive in its application of punitive measures against real and potential conspirators.[8]

An agreement among the three partitioning powers to share information regarding suspicious signs of political stirrings in the annexed territories from the Polish Commonwealth proved to be most advantageous to the security agencies of the imperial courts of Russia, Austria, and Prussia. Little thought was given to the fact that the intense police vigilance and harsh punitive measures were driving underground even the most innocent stirrings among the subjugated people. Thus, inevitably, the youthful Romantically inspired national awakeners in Eastern Europe were compelled to move in the direction of radical thought and action as the century progressed.

Was the Polish quest for independence and democracy a failure? If one approaches this question from the point of view of the insurgents' immediate objectives, it appears to have been so. But this certainly is not the case if the event is examined from a broader perspective of European history – in particular if we consider the revolution's impact on the intellectual stimulation and rapid politization of the emerging intelligentsia in Central and Eastern Europe.

This study explores the intellectual currents that stimulated the minds of educated young men and women in Eastern Europe after the upheavals of 1830–1. Its focus is on the political ideas brought to the Slavic world from the West, mainly by Polish émigré conspirators closely tied to Young Europe, an international revolutionary alliance of subjugated peoples established in the spring of 1834 by Giuseppe Mazzini, the leader of the Italian cause for unification and independence. While the motives of the principal players in this organization will be taken into consideration, they do not constitute the focal point of this investigation. What is considered important is the impact of Young Europe's ideals on the political awakening of the emerging intellectual elites in the Slavic world.

The principles articulated in Giuseppe Mazzini's program for Young Europe were universal and thus have been applicable to all subjugated nationalities that have manifested a desire to become independent. The right to self-determination did not depend on an explicit recognition of a specific nationality by the founder of Young Europe. Mazzini had a very active political career spanning over four decades and, depending on the geo-political realities of a particular moment in time, his position did not remain the same, yet the ideals guiding his organization have been constant. The principles contained in Young Europe's program, together with Mazzini's conceptualization of what constituted a nation, are discussed in chapters 2 and 3.

For a number of reasons, the Poles and the Ukrainians have been chosen as the focal point of this study – the former because they represented the strongest building block of Young Europe and from the start were recognized as such by the organization's founder; the latter both because of their numerical strength and the hope shared by some political activists that perhaps because of Ukraine's unique place in history, the pan-European democratic revolution of subjugated peoples would begin in their land. Furthermore, because of the geopolitical conditions, the influence of the Polish emissaries was bound to have the strongest impact on the emerging Ukrainian intelligentsia inhabiting the lands under the rule of the Habsburgs and the Romanovs. The Polish long-range political objectives as well as their immediate plans are discussed in chapters 3 and 5, while the Ukrainian political awakening in the Austrian and Russian Empires is investigated in chapters 4 and 6.

The dissemination of Young Europe's ideas by the Polish revolutionaries among the Czechs and the Slovaks and the reception of these ideas by the youthful intelligentsia in East Central Europe constitute an integral part of this study. The political objectives and tactics, as well as guidelines for action formulated and implemented during the 1830s and early 1840s by activists of these two nationalities are presented in chapter 3 and summed up in the first part of chapter 7. The documentary evidence contained in these sections as well as in chapter 4 make it quite clear that national awakening among the Czechs, Slovaks, and Galician Ukrainians had been political in nature as early as the mid-1830s, that is, several decades earlier than it has been assumed in most scholarly studies.

Romantic nationalism that swept through both Western and Eastern Europe at the end of the eighteenth and during the first half of the nineteenth century extolled the plurality of national cultures, viewed each nation's spiritual achievements as a unique, irreplaceable, and therefore highly valuable component in the collective treasury of human accomplishments. For a broad intellectual background that moulded the world view of the educated youth in Eastern Europe as well as the political atmosphere in which the key actors of this study have been reared, the numerous scholarly works written by Andrzej Walicki could serve as an excellent point of reference.[9] Also very useful in this connection are views on the dynamics of cultural nationalism presented in the writings of John Hutchinson and Anthony D. Smith.[10]

On the other hand, the theoretical works of twentieth-century "modernist" or "constructivist" writers such as Benedict Anderson, Ernest Gellner, Miroslav Hroch, and Eric J. Hobsbawm,[11] while of interest at times for reflection or comparison and contrast, contribute little to a better understanding of the prevailing spirit guiding the intelligentsia in Eastern Europe during the first half of the nineteenth century.[12] In a number of instances a careful analysis of the thoughts and actions of the young men and women of this period contradicts the theoretical framework proposed in studies cited above. For example, the first, so called preparatory or "heritage-gathering" stage stressed in the works of Myroslav Hroch, is either missing or is of little significance for the political awakening of some national elites in East Central Europe. In the case of the Ruthenians/Ukrainians[13] in Galicia, for example, the impact of the Polish Revolution of 1830–1, the broadly publicized ideals for which the Polish rebels fought and that they carried into the lands through which they passed on their way to Western Europe represents the determining factor in the politization process of young national awakeners. In East Galicia both the cultural and political phases of the national awakening were occurring at the same time. With respect to the Czechs and Slovaks whose intellectual elite had been involved in the heritage-gathering pursuits since the eighteenth century, the Polish uprising as well as intensive work exerted by Young Europe's emissaries speeded up the political awakening so that, as noted earlier, young students became involved in projects with well-defined political objectives almost immediately after the formation of Mazzini's international movement of national liberation. On this question, my research findings would be in agreement with Edyta Bojanowska's opinion that the "distinction between cultural and political nationalism is a false dichotomy"[14] as well as with Roman Szporluk's point of view that nationalism is "political *ab initio* – even when those engaged in nationalist activities denied any political intend, or insisted that their sole object was a scholarly understanding of political culture, folklore or local history."[15]

A closer examination of the prevailing ideas guiding the Slavic intelligentsia during the first half of the nineteenth century makes it quite clear that among the Czechs, Slovaks, and Galician Ukrainians the ideological roots of the "Spring of Nations" were inextricably linked with the revolutionary underground brought to life by Young Europe's conspirators in the 1830s. Even though both political and cultural undertakings were considerably toned down with the intensification of police surveillance in the 1840s, the smouldering embers of the revolution planted in East Central Europe a decade earlier exploded with full force when the first opportunity for action arose in the spring of 1848. All in all, the documentary evidence presented in this study provides compelling evidence for the argument that, contrary to the accepted version of history, all was not quiet on the East European front between 1831 and 1848. By concentrating on the political underground of the 1830s, this study contributes to a deeper understanding of forces that were responsible for the upsurge of revolutionary action sweeping through the European continent in 1848. It fills in the gap in East European studies which exists in scholarship today.

Because of the extreme caution and secrecy required in the work of clandestine organizations, not too many documentary records such as minutes of meetings or guidelines for action have survived until our day. However, on the basis of a few well-preserved political programs, public appeals, police records, memoir literature, and correspondence of the key figures tied to Young Europe, sufficient evidence can be assembled to trace the organizational structure and to determine the essence of aims guiding the political underground before the revolution of 1848.

For a number of reasons Austria's province of Galicia figures prominently in this study.[16] First, Galicia was highlighted by some of the
most influential personages connected with Young Europe and its main
agent among the Slavic peoples, Young Poland, as the centre of political
action and as a region through which revolutionary ideas could be best
distributed to the territories under the rule of the two imperial regimes.
It was through Young Europe's conspirators concentrated briefly in
the free Polish city of Cracow and subsequently in the Galician capital,
Lviv, that contacts were established with the Czech and Slovak activists
and through the mediation of the latter with the leaders of the southern
Slavs as well. It was through Galicia that émigré conspirators tied to
Mazzini's Young Europe were smuggled into the western provinces of
the Russian Empire in the mid-1830s, among them Szymon Konarski,
the organizer of underground operations in the lands controlled by the
Romanovs. Throughout the period under investigation, Galicia was
viewed as a cauldron of the most dangerous conspiracies by the police
authorities in Vienna. Thus in the early 1840s one of the most celebrated
trials of the radical underground tied directly to Young Europe took
place in the Galician capital.

Furthermore, the majority of the inhabitants of Galicia consisted
of two Slavic nationalities, Poles and Ukrainians. Both national
groups were overwhelmingly Catholic, but the Ruthenians belonged
to the Eastern or Greek Catholic Rite administered by Rome through
a separate church hierarchy. Since the first partition of Poland in
1772, both groups were governed by the Habsburgs, but because of
several centuries of Polish rule, at the time of Galicia's absorption by
Austria, the two nationalities were far from equal in the economic,
political, and cultural sense. Therefore it was in Galicia that Young
Europe's ideals of brotherly love and cooperation among nations
underwent one of the most critical tests. Thus both the successes
and failures of the movement can be brought to light on the basis of
the Galician experience.

As the developments presented in this study will show, in spite of
the disadvantages of the Ruthenian/Ukrainian inhabitants in this easternmost province of the Habsburg lands, because of the proximity and
dynamism of the Polish political underground as well as the availabil-
ity of Young Europe's revolutionary literature in the Galician capital,
the most successful recruitment to the revolutionary cause in Eastern
Europe during the 1830s was among Ukrainian Greek Catholic seminarians. In fact, one of the most balanced and politically mature statements
during the revolution of 1848 came from the pen of a Greek Catholic

cleric who earned his revolutionary training during the preceding decade in an organization directly tied to Young Europe:

> Nothing can restrain us from pursuits common to the whole of Europe,
> and we shall not be silent unless Europe becomes silent. We all want to
> be free together with other European nations and are patiently yearning
> to attain this goal. We want to be a nation and without doubt will become
> one, because the voice of the people is the voice of God.... We Ruthenians
> fervently believe in the resurrection of a free, independent Ruthenia.
> Will this be realized in the near future or later is of no great significance.
> Distance in time does not trouble us because what does a century repre-
> sent from the perspective of a nation's existence?[17]

The documentary evidence related to this theme will also bring to
light the fact that in spite of some deep-rooted differences between
the Poles and Ukrainians during the period under consideration, the
more enlightened political activists of both groups became keenly
aware that their two nations bound together by the forces of history
and political necessity ought to find a workable, mutually beneficial
solution, because their interests were best served when they cooperated
with one another, as they did in the 1830s. It was during that decade
that Mazzini's emissaries were most active in spreading the message
of brotherly love and cooperation among nations. Even though the
Mazzinian ideal of brotherly love and peaceful co-existence among
nations was overshadowed by a new brand of nationalism at the turn
of the century, Young Europe's ideals re-emerged at the end of the First
World War and asserted their presence in Western Europe with even
greater force after the conflagration caused by the second world con-
flict. These ideals have not lost their relevance and vibrancy in both
Western and Eastern Europe in our day, even though not too many are
aware of their deep nineteenth-century roots. What is also frequently
overlooked is the fact that the first wave of theoretical nationalism in
Eastern Europe was democratic, that is, strictly Mazzinian at its core.
This constitutes one of the underlying themes of this study.

Young Europe as an Idea: The Impact of Exile on the Revolutionary Thought of Giuseppe Mazzini

I think that above a Pole, a German, a Frenchman, or an Italian there is something higher – a Human Being – and that among all groups and all nations there exists something far more sacred, the fatherland of fatherlands: humanity, which ought to bring them together and without which a nation has no aim and democracy has no meaning.[1]

Giuseppe Mazzini, the founding father of Young Europe and the leader of the Italian movement for unification and independence, traced the birth of his grand design for the reconstruction of Europe on democratic principles to his imprisonment in the fortress of Savona. The two-month confinement at the end of 1830 for his involvement in the Carbonari conspiracies in his native Genoa provided this youthful, intellectually gifted activist with an occasion to reflect on the reasons for the failure of the numerous uprisings that had taken place on the Italian peninsula in the course of the preceding decade.[2]

A first-rate educational background in classical and contemporary literatures, a good knowledge of European history, philosophy, and languages, as well as a law degree from the University of Genoa equipped the Italian patriot with the necessary tools for an intelligent critical analysis of the European political developments in the distant and not too distant past. History fascinated this precocious young man of twenty-five but he found the discipline meaningful only if it could provide lessons for the times to come. It was from this perspective that he began to search for a key to a new path leading to a brighter future for Italy within a reconstructed democratic Europe.

Partly because of a growing disillusionment with the aging leadership of the Carbonari – the Haute Vente – and partly because his highly imaginative, inquisitive mind was always searching for new ideas and new ways for their realization, Mazzini already at this early stage of his political career intuitively sensed an urgent need for the creation of a new revolutionary organization.[3] The international Carbonari movement had its headquarters in France, and even though the organization's principal leader, Filippo Buonarroti, was an Italian by origin, after a lengthy imprisonment and long years of residence in France it was becoming apparent that the old man's outdated ideas and unconcealed Francophile leanings had little to offer to the new generation of Italians who wished to liberate their homeland not only from conservative regimes but also from foreign domination. It was becoming clear to the more astute thinkers engaged in conspiracies against the existing autocratic regimes in Europe that equality for all members of the underground, especially those desiring to liberate their nations from foreign oppression, could not be assured if primacy of the French was an accepted tenet in the revolutionary underworld centred in Paris. Furthermore, the Carbonari ideology rooted in the cosmopolitan thought of the Enlightenment no longer appeared to provide ideas that could inspire young people nurtured in the Romantic spirit of Johann Herder, Johann Goethe, or Lord Byron. If everything was not as yet satisfactorily clarified in the mind of young Mazzini, of one thing he was confident: brand new ideas and innovative ways had to be found in order to attain the main object of his generation's yearnings: a democratic, unified, and independent Italy.

An independent Italy, however, was not viewed as an end in itself, even at the very inception of the Italian thinker's conceptualization of the national idea. This was partly because a keen awareness and appreciation of the commonality of elements existing in different European cultures predated Mazzini's involvement in politics. This awareness manifested itself when Mazzini, while still in his teens, immersed himself in the study of literature. In one of his first published essays he argued forcefully that national literary styles ought to develop not in isolation but through a dialogue with literatures of other European nations, because all peoples of Europe shared a common cultural background and all seemed to be heading towards similar goals. The common background was the classical literature of Greece and Rome, and the common goals were the Christian moral ideals of universal brotherhood and love. It was from these roots of the classical and Judeo-Christian heritage that he thought a European literature would continue to blossom, becoming ever richer through the diversity and unique qualities of each national literary style.[4] A decade later in one of his most important political statements of belief, "Fede e avvenire" (Faith and the future), Mazzini expressed his concept of a national and at the same time European culture most clearly and succinctly: it would be "European in substance, national in form."[5] It is of interest to note that for students of Soviet nationality policy, the phrase has a familiar ring, for it was adopted, with the suitable changes, of course, by Soviet ideologues in the twentieth century to read as "socialist in content, national in form." Thus we see that not only Marx had borrowed from Mazzini[6] – also with appropriate changes – but his followers in Russia have done so as well.

Steeped in the Romantic literature of his day, the Italian revolutionary readily assimilated writers' notion of national missions and embraced with enthusiasm the idea that his country with its long history and rich cultural traditions was bound to become the initiator of a new life, a new, great union of the nations of Europe in the general pan-European struggle for democratic ideals and independence. Thus, even before Mazzini plunged into the whirlwind of international conspiratorial politics, the concept of nationhood was evolving within the context of a supranational idea: a loose European union in which independent, sovereign nations cooperated with one another for the mutual enrichment and growth of their individual cultures.[7] His thoughts on this question contained echoes of Herder's ideas: "By its own efforts not a single nationality of Europe was raised to the level of culture,"[8] or "The essence of human nature encloses a universe whose motto is: 'Nobody for himself alone, all for one. Therefore, let us all be happy and valuable for each other. An endless variety tending towards unity is in all and advances all.'"[9]

For Mazzini, as for Herder, culture constituted one of the most important components of nationhood. To both thinkers a nation represented a community of people bound by an evolved culture whose uniqueness constituted an important component in the treasury of world civilizations. For Mazzini, a nation was not an imagined community built on transient expectations of material progress, but a real, spiritual entity either already conscious of its existence or – in the case of unfavourable historical circumstances – waiting to be awakened in order to manifest itself. In other words, Mazzini envisioned nationality as an intrinsic reality based not on blood but on spiritual and cultural values that in many instances remained dormant until awakened by enlightened leaders. Through education or upbringing, those "apostles of the people" were fortunate to become acquainted with the wealth and depth of their nation's heritage. Viewed from this perspective, all inhabitants of the peninsula were Italians: all those who had gathered and mingled there in the course of centuries to produce a nation that "combined southern vivacity and spontaneity with the seriousness and steadfastness of the northern nations."[10] The determinant of a person's national identity was not racial distinctiveness based on blood lineage but one's affinity with or "rootedness" in a particular culture. A nation thus was neither primordial (in the racial sense) nor imagined, but so to speak, historically evolved and congealed and in this sense perennial.

Confronted with the harsh reality of Austria's presence in northern Italy and Metternich's influence at the courts of Europe, Mazzini understood very well that Italians alone would have no chance to attain their national goals until the centres of despotism in Europe were demolished. And this formidable task could be accomplished only through the concerted efforts of all oppressed peoples in the vast multinational empires of the Habsburgs and Romanovs. A Holy Alliance of independent nations in opposition to the Holy Alliance of kings – Mazzini would refer to the latter as "the accursed compact ... of the stagnant sophists of old Europe"[11] – appeared to be the logical answer. These must have been some of the thoughts and musings that passed through Mazzini's mind at the time of his release from the Fortress of Savona in January 1831.

Giuseppe Mazzini and the Exiled Revolutionaries in France

Freed from confinement but forbidden to reside in his native Genoa, Mazzini had little choice but to join the ranks of exiles finding a refuge in countries in which autocracy was only a bad dream of the past. Early in 1831 he left for France where, after the July Revolution, the political climate for the attainment of his goals appeared to be most promising. After establishing contacts with prominent Italian intellectuals and revolutionary leaders – including Buonarotti – in Paris and Geneva, young Mazzini chose to settle in Marseilles, a Mediterranean port at that time brimming with Italian, Hungarian, and Polish political refugees. Here he found an ideologically stimulating and politically hospitable environment for the realization of his pan-European project.

If indeed the idea of Young Europe was born in the prison cell at Savona, as he claimed in his reminiscences, Mazzini's conviction of the efficacy of his grandiose plan for a renewed democratic Europe of free independent nations was considerably strengthened during his journey through France and Switzerland, especially in the course of his meetings with the eminent historian Jean Charles Sismondi, whose work on the *History of the Italian Republics in the Middle Ages* he greatly admired. His thoughts on the practical steps for Italy's path to independence and the reconstruction of Europe on democratic principles[12] also greatly benefited from the close bonds of friendship he was able to establish with the highly respected Italian revolutionary Count Carlo Bianco di St Jorioz, the leader of a secret organization known as the *Apofasimeni* (those who have vowed to die). Since the principal objectives of this group, "to make Italy one, independent and free" coincided fully with his own aims and ideals, Mazzini joined its ranks with enthusiasm. Bianco's anonymously published *Della guerra nazionale d'insurrezione per banda applicata all'Italia* (Of national insurrectionary warfare by bands applied to Italy) also appealed to him because it contained concrete directives on the manner in which unification and independence was to be achieved.[13] Many of Bianco's ideas, such as "war of all nations striving to emancipate themselves from foreign rule," were incorporated into Mazzini's thoughts and writings. Their impact was especially strong on the Instructions (*Istruzione generale per gli affratellini nella Giovine Italia*), which Mazzini was preparing for his new organization, Young Italy.[14]

In this document, later to become broadly circulated in the form of a pamphlet among revolutionaries throughout Europe, Mazzini explained that all nations desiring to free themselves from foreign rule were bound to resort to guerrilla warfare, because, in the absence of a regular army at the beginning of each insurrection, this was the only option available to them. Furthermore, guerrilla combat had certain significant advantages. First, it made the military art accessible to all segments of the population. In addition, guerrilla units were able to utilize new tactics not familiar to the men in the regular army – tactics through which they could entrap the enemy with ease. Thus, the argument continued, guerrilla warfare, if planned carefully and conducted skilfully, could make a nation fighting for freedom virtually invincible.[15] For this type of struggle, the youthful, enthusiastic revolutionary was preparing those who would choose to follow his call, first in Italy and later in the rest of Europe. The military tactics outlined in the *Instructions* would be read with great interest by conspirators interested in spreading revolutionary ideas in Eastern Europe. A prime example is Szymon Konarski, a young Polish revolutionary tied to Young Europe who would become the leading conspirator in Ukraine, Belarus, and Lithuania in the second half of the 1830s.[16]

The Birth of the Risorgimento

In July 1831 Mazzini and his close associates in exile formed an organization that the founder called a federation but would become known in history as Young Italy. It was conceived as a federation because Mazzini wished to keep Young Italy's door open to all political groups that desired to bring about his country's unity and independence. Furthermore, Young Italy's members were free to belong to or cooperate with other associations that pursued similar goals. Not surprisingly, the first to provide an example and merge with Young Italy were members of Bianco's *Apofasimeni*. Recognizing his debt to the elder revolutionary leader, Mazzini referred to the two groups "as two wheels in the same cart."[17]

A youthful, enthusiastic missionary spirit pervaded the organization's instructions, programmatic statements, and publications. Young Italy was viewed as an apostolate of young people who through their exemplary moral qualities and persistent, undaunted efforts would bring about the regeneration of the Italian people, reinvigorate their culture, and in this manner weld the masses of the peninsula into a nation conscious of its existence and of its mission in the European community of peoples. Education through publications disseminated by means of a network of dedicated emissaries and insurrections through conspiratorial work were the principal means through which the organization hoped to attain its aims.

Initially, only a few dozen, mostly youthful Italian political exiles in southern France joined the organization. Among them were sons of prominent Italian aristocratic families from Lombardy, Reggio Emilia, and the Duchy of Modena who, like Mazzini, were forced to flee the warmth and comfort of their homes because of their involvement in revolutionary, mostly anti-Austrian activity, and who subsequently could not help but be inspired by their young colleague's idealism, enthusiasm, and above all, determination to make Italy one, independent, and democratic. Among Mazzini's principal financial backers were young men and women of titled families such as Carlo Bellerio and his sister Giuditta Bellerio Sidoli, Emilio Belgioioso and his estranged wife Princess Cristina Trivulzio Belgioioso, Marquise Gaspare Rosales, and others.[18] They were willing to extend generous financial help for Mazzini's efforts to liberate Italy both by means of written word and revolutionary action. Others who joined Mazzini's organization were of a more modest background similar to that of the founder: well-educated sons of minor gentry, doctors, professors, and lawyers brought up by patriotic, well-educated, intelligent mothers whose roots could often be traced to lesser nobility. Among these stand out Mazzini's close childhood friends Jacopo, Agostino, and Giovanni Ruffini. Young Italy's devout supporters who remained close to their leader throughout his long years of exile were Angelo and Emilio Usiglio, two Italian patriots of Jewish background from Reggio Emilia. Most members of Count Bianco's *Apofasimeni*, on the other hand, were sailors, dock workers, and farm workers. Irrespective of their background, Young Italy's enthusiasts tended to have one thing in common: they all desired to make Italy free from foreign rule and democratic at the core. In a letter to his friend Giuseppe Giglioli, Mazzini described the small but idealistic and passionately patriotic band of his followers as a "brotherhood of the young who have joined together for a common cause with courage, sincerity and faith."[19]

With this multi-layered social fabric, in which the weakest link had been, incidentally, the representatives of the bourgeoisie, it was only natural that when Young Italy began to spread its roots in the countryside of the Italian provinces, members from all strata of the population were encouraged to join. Only through a cooperative effort of all inhabitants, Mazzini believed, could Italy become morally transformed into "a great nation – one, independent, sovereign."[20] To encourage his educated compatriots to form closer bonds with the common people, Mazzini observed – no doubt as a result of his recent interaction with the *Apofasimeni* – that the clasp of a labourer's hand could be more beneficial than the cold work of the intellect.[21] In order to facilitate recruitment among the uneducated and impoverished masses, Mazzini established a special section within Young Italy called the Societa di propagazione de'lumi (Society for the propagation of enlightenment). Moral decline among the Italians of all social backgrounds, Mazzini believed, was caused by the degradation of the national culture, a development that he viewed as an inevitable by-product of long years of foreign domination. And the attainment of moral regeneration he viewed as essential for the realization and maintenance of true freedom and democracy for all nations. In his appeals Mazzini called upon his fellow countrymen to form a unified community aiming at high moral standards: "Be neither people of Tuscany, nor of Piedmont nor of Romagna; be Italians! Nations do not experience a renaissance without a moral rebirth. Contribute to enlightenment through publications, example, and word. Revolutions are realized by the people and for the people."[22]

In accordance with his convictions formed early in his intellectual development, Mazzini viewed Young Italy as a part of a wider European movement. "Young Italy is aware that revolutionary Europe awaits a signal."[23] The role of Young Italy was to provide the spark for an international insurgency of all the oppressed peoples. These thoughts were reiterated again and again in Mazzini's writings: "Young Europe. There is the camp of liberty in the nineteenth century. And us? – We should try to point the way by ... being affiliated with it. Italy must carry its standard into the common camp."[24] In an article, "Fratellanza de' popoli" he observed confidently that the people were "yearning toward a European fraternity."[25]

On the basis of these convictions, Mazzini issued appeals to all sub-jugated people to respond to Young Italy's call. In *La Giovine Italia*, the organization's journal that began its publication in March 1832, the Italian leader implored, "My young brothers, have courage, aspire to greatness. Have faith in God, in what is right, and in us. That was Luther's call, which stirred half of Europe. Raise that call and go forward."[26]

According to the rules of the organization, only young people below forty were to be admitted as members, and even though this princi-ple was not strictly enforced, Young Italy and the subsequent Young Europe attracted primarily young activists. Members were required to take an oath to work by means of word and action to wipe out tyrants, to disseminate the organization's ideals, and to stand prepared at any moment to join the struggle for Young Italy's objectives. As noted above, the organization's aims included, in addition to Italy's inde-pendence based on republican principles, self-determination for all the nationalities of Europe.

Both men and women constituted Mazzini's immediate circle of friends and supporters in the early period of emigration and through-out his more than thirty years of exile. The large contingent of women who supported Mazzini's cause proved to be of invaluable assistance not only financially but also morally and spiritually. Especially helpful, in addition to the two above-named women from distinguished titled families, Giuditta Bellerio Sidoli and Cristina Trivulzio Belgioioso, were the patriotic ladies in Mazzini's native Genoa who, because of their aristocratic background, had the education and the means to provide concrete support for Young Italy's struggle for independence.[27] In the years that followed, recruitment of women was encouraged when simi-lar associations were formed by Mazzini's followers in Eastern Europe.

Reliance on women would not only continue but substantially in-crease during Mazzini's later years as an exile in England. Being a sensitive man with a highly developed ability to delve into the deeper recesses of human nature, he could not overlook the fact that while his close friends in London, among them John Stuart Mill and Thomas Carlyle, responded to his expressions of unshakable faith in the libera-tion of Italy with polite scepticism, their wives, Harriet Taylor Mill and

Figure 1.1 Giuseppe Mazzini at the time of the founding of Young Europe. From *Edizione Nationale*, vol. XIII (Cooperativa Tipografico-Editrice Paolo Galeati of Imola, 1912–1924).

Jane Carlyle, offered their assistance with enthusiasm and a genuine commitment to Young Italy's cause. In fact, it was primarily through women that Mazzini was able to reach the ear of influential figures in political and intellectual circles in Britain. Mazzini attributed these differences in attitudes between the two genders towards national liberation to the fact that women's subordinate status in society made them more open and sensitive to the plight of the subjugated peoples of Europe.[28] To the end of his life he admired and valued highly the support of his devoted, patriotic mother Maria Drago Mazzini, as well as of the woman whom he often called his "second mother," Emilia Curlo Ruffini. Both Genovese ladies were of minor gentry background who ensured that their sons were provided the best education and subsequently, without reservations, dedicated their lives to Italy's freedom from foreign rule.[29]

If Mazzini's organization gained prominence first among Italians and soon thereafter among a small but intellectually polished and highly influential group of European revolutionaries, it was largely thanks to the resourcefulness, intelligence, and magnetic personality of its leader, his untiring energy and perseverance, as well as his keen understanding of the spiritual needs and aspirations of the young men and women coming of age in his day. A well-documented and insightful study of the Italian leader's political thought and action sums up this point very well: "Mazzini was a tireless and resourceful organizer who took the high road and appealed to the ideals rather than to material interests, stressed the need for unity and discipline, expressed political concerns in the emotional language of religion, demanded principled behavior from its members, spoke of duties as well as rights and delivered a positive message of victory through action and education."[30] For many idealistic young men and women in the post-Napoleonic era it was difficult to resist this call.

The Risorgimento and the Great Polish Emigration: A Pact Sealed in Heaven or a Marriage of Convenience?

In his plans to destroy Austria – the principal block to Italy's unification – the Slavic cause was of the foremost importance. This was the main reason for his [Mazzini's] great interest in Poland, this was the reason for his indefatigable efforts to propagate Poland's missionary role among the Slavic peoples oppressed by Austria and by tsarist Russia.[1]

If at the inception of his exile Mazzini had only a vague knowledge of the Slavic world, after his arrival in Marseilles, the mecca of political exiles of Europe, he became keenly aware that the erstwhile enemy of his country's national aspirations, the conservative regime in Vienna, was also the oppressor of a large number of Slavic nationalities. The Poles, having lost their independence only a few decades earlier, were expressing the strongest desire and determination to resurrect their fallen, partitioned land. There was little doubt in the revolutionary circles in Western Europe that the Polish war of independence of 1830–1 demonstrated far greater patriotic fervour, tenacity, and perseverance than any other revolutionary event of that day.

Becoming a political exile himself and thus no stranger to the emotions, yearnings, and passions permeating the vibrant clusters of émigré community in France, Mazzini sensed that the chief reason for the mass exodus of the Polish patriots in 1831 was their fervent desire to search for new ways to resume their national struggle.[2] He was pleased to observe that the faith of the Polish patriots in this possibility was greatly buoyed by the display of support and fanfare with which the exiles were greeted by German, Belgian, and French liberals and radicals throughout Western Europe. Their military songs were translated and sung by German revolutionaries as if the Polish cause were their own.[3] Their strong belief in the inevitability of a Polish upheaval in the near future was further reinforced by the widespread anticipation in the émigré circles of a general conflagration that was expected to erupt at any moment in the stultifying atmosphere of Metternich's Europe. In fact, it is believed that Poland's most prominent poet, Adam Mickiewicz, wrote the highly celebrated *Księgi narodu polskiego i pielgrzymstwa polskiego* (Books of the Polish nation and of the Polish pilgrims) in the wake of this anticipation.[4]

Among the more than 8,000 Polish émigrés who found a haven in France, Switzerland, Belgium, and England in 1831, the preponderant majority consisted of men connected in one way or another with the military, but there was also a large contingent of eminent political thinkers and activists among them. When a group of émigré civilians – politically implicated intellectuals, writers, and students – requested through the mediation of one of Poland's strongest backers in France, the elderly but still active and influential Marquis de Lafayette, that the French government grant them permission to continue their scholarly pursuits at French institutions of higher learning, the patriotically charged Polish legionnaires branded this move as nothing less than shameful "egoism."[5] From the point of view of the military patriots, a political refugee – irrespective of whether he was an officer or civilian – should steer clear of all distractions in order to be fully prepared at any moment to resume the struggle on behalf of the fatherland. Such a stand could not but earn admiration of Mazzini who himself, while being intensely interested since his early years in literature and music, placed effort on behalf of Italy's independence above all other pursuits, no matter how lofty, noble, or alluring they might have appeared. If during the years of exile Mazzini occasionally published works of literary criticism in French and English journals, it was mainly to supplement the meagre allowance he was secretly receiving from his mother.

The widely held belief among Polish émigrés disseminated through the writings of Mickiewicz that an individual without a sense of national consciousness or identity was an incomplete human being, reinforced some of Mazzini's own convictions on this subject.[6] For Mazzini, as for the Polish bard, a nation represented an intermediary between an individual and humanity and thus constituted an essential stepping stone in the march of men towards progress. Mazzini believed, as did the Polish Romantic writers, that each nation was endowed by God with a mission, and therefore, in its essence, the nation was sacred. In order to be able to fulfil this mission, each nation possessed an inalienable right to an independent existence. At the same time, however, a nation was viewed not as an end in itself, an entity to which an individual owed the highest allegiance, but only as a means to a loftier ideal, which was understood to be the brotherhood of nations united by love, a community of peoples frequently referred to in Mazzini's essays as humanity. But while Mickiewicz and his Polish compatriots viewed the question of independence as an indisputable right of nations that were considered "historical," those that at present or in recent past represented independent political entities, Mazzini believed that this right applied to all nationalities, irrespective of whether they were considered "historical," or not, if they possessed a culture moulded through a shared path in history and demonstrated a will to struggle for their nation's independence. Mazzini's understanding of the concept of nationhood was close to what the German scholar Friedrich Meinecke defined as a cultural nation: "Despite all the obvious reservations that can be made, we can still divide nations into cultural nations and political nations, nations that are primarily based on some jointly experienced cultural heritage and nations that are primarily based on the unifying force of a common political history and constitution. A standard language, a common literature and a common religion are the most important and powerful cultural assets that create a cultural nation and hold it together."[7] Considering the history of the Italian people in medieval and modern times, Mazzini's emphasis on culture rather than on statehood is not at all surprising. It is his cultural conceptualization of nationhood that made his political views especially attractive to the stateless nationalities in Eastern Europe, which, with the exception of the Poles, had to search for traces of their political existence in the distant medieval past.

By the nineteenth century, as a consequence of the long periods of domination by the Habsburgs and the Romanovs, most nationalities within the Austrian and Russian realms were reduced to cultural communities. The historical path of the Italian people was somewhat different, yet their symbol of unity too was first and foremost a common historical path and cultural heritage. It was because of the absence of a unified state existence among the Italian people that Metternich, a determined advocate of Austria's imperial dominance and expansion, brazenly announced that the designation "Italy" was a mere geographical expression! It is of interest to note that a similar designation would be used in reference to Ukraine by the imperial defenders of Russia's unity and indivisibility throughout the twentieth century.

A cultural nation, in Mazzini's view, could become a political one if a group of nationally conscious men and women who were aware of the historical past of their people resolved to gain their country's independence. In his works the Italian leader was especially emphatic in stressing the importance of the role of national "awakeners" to whom he reverentially referred to as the "apostles of the people." At the same time, it is important to note, that whenever Mazzini wrote about independence as a national goal, he always emphasized the fact that a sovereign state was not the ultimate goal of humanity but only a stepping stone to a higher ideal. Thus, like his views on literature and culture, his concept of nationalism included both an element of national uniqueness or national individualism and cultural and political universalism or internationalism.

Political nationalism within the Polish intellectual community continued to be strong in the post-Napoleonic era, both because the wounds inflicted in the struggles for the recovery the lost statehood were not as yet completely healed and because ideas of the Enlightenment lingered somewhat longer among the members of the Polish Carbonari underground. Most émigrés with leftist leanings saw the Polish national cause as a struggle against the Holy Alliance of absolute monarchs and, as the historian Andrzej Walicki points out, "were inclined to think that it would be in the interest of all-European progress" if the territory of the former Polish Commonwealth would not only be restored to its pre-partitioned boundaries but actually expanded. The Polish Left in particular, "like the French Jacobins," explains Walicki, "sometimes too easily identified Polish territorial claims with the universal cause of liberty."[8] This type of reasoning under different guises has been almost universal in the liberal and radical circles of the imperial nations of the past and at times continues to resurface in the present. Thus, one can understand why many Poles were unaware – just as members of the liberal intelligentsia of the dominant nations even in the twentieth century continued to be unaware – that their nationalism or internationalism in its essence represented nothing less than great power imperialism.[9]

Mazzini acknowledged that while protection of individual rights was a significant achievement of the revolutions in the preceding century, civic liberties could guarantee full protection only to those peoples who were already enjoying the advantages of an independent existence. For those nationalities that were still subject to foreign rule, civil rights could offer only partial protection, because they could not fully guarantee their national-cultural rights. An individual, if not part of a politically unified national collective, stood helpless in confronting the governments of multinational empires whose leadership had been promoting the interests and culture of the ruling nation for centuries. There were many examples, even from the not too distant past to support this argument: the patronizing attitude of the French towards other nations, both "historical" and "non-historical," while fighting under the slogan of liberty, equality, and fraternity; Russia's assertion of hegemony in what had been formally the constitutional Kingdom of Poland; or the browbeaten position to which the Irish had been reduced in constitutionally governed England. In the preponderant majority of cases, modern history bears witness to the fact that only a sovereign state could fully guarantee the permanent protection of an unhindered national development in the cultural, political, and economic sense. On the issue of the right of every nation to self-determination Mazzini stood firm, because early in life he came to the realization that under foreign rule the people would sooner or later experience not only a cultural decline but also moral degeneration. This belief dated back to his youthful ventures into literary studies, in particular to his immersion in the works of Dante, a writer who may have served as an inspiration for his life-long preoccupation with the idea of nationhood, culture, and moral regeneration.[10]

While on the question of national independence both Polish and Italian political thinkers and activists were in full agreement, they differed on the subject of what represented the fundamental principle of a nation's independence. With some exceptions, the Polish patriots understood the restoration of their recently lost statehood within what they viewed as Poland's historical boundaries. Mazzini, on the other hand, provided theoretical arguments for the right of every nationality to sovereignty in order to safeguard its unique national identity. This would include the right to self-determination for the Ukrainians, Belarusians, and Lithuanians – nationalities inhabiting a large part of the territory the Poles claimed as rightfully belonging to historical Poland, not on ethno-cultural but on purely political considerations.

In spite of this divergence of views on this vital issue, the Italian leader never wavered during his long political career in his support of the Polish cause. Perhaps, like some of his Polish acquaintances, he hoped that with the passage of time most Polish democrats would be persuaded to adopt a more conciliatory attitude towards the interests of the non-Polish inhabitants of the former commonwealth, signs of which were already in evidence in the writings and discussions within the large Polish émigré community. But the most important reason for Mazzini's tolerance of what could have been interpreted as a sign of Polish great power imperialism was the fact that from the early days of his exile, the Italian leader considered the Poles the strongest and therefore the most important force in revolutionary Europe. Thus, he was willing to tolerate or even overlook issues that were not entirely consonant with his vision of a democratic Europe representing a union of free, independent, and equal nations.

The Italian leader's concern with the fate of Poland was reflected in his numerous essays, speeches, and, above all, in his letters, both private and official.[11] According to a Polish study, about 40,000 letters of Mazzini's voluminous correspondence dealt in one way or another with the Polish question.[12] A twentieth-century Polish historian explained Mazzini's inordinate interest in the fate of the Slavic peoples – the Poles in particular – very well: "In his plans to destroy Austria – the principal block to Italy's unification – the Slavic cause was of the foremost importance. This was the main reason for his great interest in Poland, this was the reason for his indefatigable efforts to propagate Poland's missionary role among the Slavic peoples oppressed by Austria and by tsarist Russia."[13]

The element of mutual advantage undoubtedly played an important role in the creation of a firm Polish-Italian alliance in the community of revolutionary exiles, but this explanation alone is not sufficient to account for the intensity of the bonds of friendship and for the longevity – in different forms and under different guises – of the union. A closer look at the two national groups of émigrés reveals that, in addition to the advantages to be derived from a Polish-Italian alliance against Austria's domination in Europe, there existed a striking affinity in the two groups' political and cultural backgrounds – the Carbonari connection with respect to the former and a deeply imbedded Catholic tradition with respect to the latter – that welded the Italian and the Polish émigré communities into a closely knit association. It was also the strikingly similar philosophical and political currents of thought and anguished soul-searching that both groups were experiencing during the first years of exile that fertilized the soil on which their solidarity and comradeship would flourish. As an example of the depth of these bonds, both political and personal, it is sufficient to cite the case of Stanisław Worcell and the leader of the Italian Risorgimento. When, after almost three decades of exile, the highly respected Polish aristocrat and once radical social thinker became acutely aware that his end was near, he asked for Mazzini, and it was to the Italian patriot that he chose to dictate his political testament. The last request of the dying Polish émigré leader in England was that Mazzini take a solemn oath not to forget Poland during the forthcoming rebirth of nations in Europe. Alexander Herzen, the influential Russian émigré thinker and activist present during this emotionally charged moment, with sensitivity penned the details of this unforgettable scene: "Mazzini took a pen, wrote a few sentences and read them to the sick man. Overcome with emotions, the old man was incapable of uttering a word ... the features on his face became transformed, his eyes once again became illuminated with an expression of happiness – through them and with a silent smile, the dying man was expressing his gratitude to a friend. It seemed that now it became easier for him to leave his post."[14] Such bonds of friendship between the Poles and Italians could not have been sealed on merely pragmatic, purely politically calculated grounds.

As already noted, during the first phase of their life as émigrés, both the Poles and the Italians were undergoing a profound disillusionment with the ideology, organizational structure, and leadership of the Carbonari movement with which many of them had had close ties in the preceding decades. What the Romantically inspired youthful political thinkers and activists sympathetic to Young Italy's objectives found especially objectionable were the older conspirators' cosmopolitan world outlook, their organization's strong centralizing tendencies, their indifference to religion, and most of all their pronounced Francophile leanings, which often prevented some of them from acting decisively and honestly in their country's national interest.

What caused the ultimate break between Mazzini and the leaders of the organization in the ranks of which he as a youth underwent his political apprenticeship was the aloofness displayed by the Carbonari centre during Young Italy's first important military undertaking, the raid on Savoy in February 1834. It was in the course of the difficulties experienced during the preparations for this bold venture that, while Mazzini's ties with the Carbonari centre in Paris were reaching a breaking point, intimate bonds of comradeship and brotherhood were being forged with Polish revolutionaries. During this brief and unfortunate – with respect to its immediate outcome – campaign,[15] the Italian patriot had an opportunity to witness first-hand the patriotism, enthusiasm, and passionate desire of young Poles to fight for their ideals – ideals that had been part of his own constitution ever since he left the prison at Savona.

Mazzini showed an interest in the Polish émigré community soon after his arrival in Marseilles. In fact, as early as 1832 he wrote a letter to a left-wing Polish émigré group, the Towarzystwo Demokratyczne Polskie (Polish Democratic Society), with an offer of Italian-Polish collaboration.[16] Not discouraged by the lack of interest on the Polish side, a year later Mazzini wrote directly to one of the most eminent figures in the Polish democratic circles, the highly revered historian and politician Joachim Lelewel. In his letter the Italian leader focused on the need of an all-embracing preparation for the future revolutionary war, the initiative of which, he suggested, ought to come not from France (obviously a reference to Buonarotti's Carbonari leadership) but from Italy. The main fault of the Carbonari centre, Mazzini explained, was the fact that it attempted to monopolize all revolutionary initiatives.[17] The Polish leader, most likely because he was immersed in the preparations for a new campaign against Russia sponsored by a Polish Carbonari group, did not respond.[18] By no means would this be Mazzini's only attempt to contact the Polish scholar-conspirator. Even though bonds of an intimate friendship between Mazzini and Lelewel would never be solidified, the two men treated each other with respect and would carry on, as will be shown later, an intellectually stimulating correspondence in the years to come.

Direct personal ties between the Italian political thinker and Polish revolutionaries developed only in Switzerland where, as the result of persistent pressures of Austria's ambassador in Paris, Mazzini and his close compatriots were compelled to flee in the summer of 1833. It was also at this time that several hundred Polish officers, after their involvement in a revolutionary uprising in Frankfurt ended in failure, sought a haven in the Alpine retreats. Contact with the Polish exiles was established through the mediation of a Polonophile Italian revolutionary, Colonel Jacopo Antonini. This seasoned soldier, whose ties with Polish patriotic causes dated back to Napoleon's campaigns, found time in emigration to become involved not only in Polish-Italian émigré politics and various petty Carbonari intrigues, but also in the intricate web of French Masonry.[19] Another active individual who served as an intermediary between the Poles and the Italians was the German poet Harro-Harring who, in the course of a few years, chanced to participate in the struggle of Greek independence, as well as the national rebirth of Poland, and in 1833, under the influence of Mazzini, not surprisingly, he became an ardent partisan of the Italian cause.[20]

It was through Antonini and Harro-Harring that Mazzini met Karol Stolzman, Franciszek Gordaszewki, and Feliks Nowosielski, three Polish officers soon to be actively involved in Mazzini's planned attack on Savoy, as well as in preparations for the establishment of what was soon to become the Polish counterpart of Young Italy.[21] It was also through Antonini and his new acquaintances that Mazzini succeeded in persuading over a hundred Polish legionnaires stationed in Switzerland to participate in a raid on Savoy, an undertaking that the organizers hoped would trigger revolts in the Kingdom of Sardinia and from there spread not only to the rest of the Italian peninsula but also to other parts of Europe.

Among the Polish participants actively involved in the campaign's preparations was Szymon Konarski, an idealistic man who at the age of twenty-seven had already made a name for himself in a number of insurgencies and conspiracies.[22] He would become one of the most ardent admirers and devoted followers of Mazzini in his brief but exploit-filled life. While the two revolutionaries had much in common, they also complemented one another: Mazzini was a brilliant political thinker and Konarski was a soldier of unbridled energy and fearless action. Both were endowed with charisma as well as exceptional organizational skills. On 29 June 1833, just a few months before his first meeting with the Italian leader, the idealistic Polish soldier-patriot made the following entry in his diary: "O my Fatherland, my ill-fated Poland! The circumstances of my exile make me realize how precious you are to me, what sacrifices I am prepared to make on your behalf. The surrounding reality has convinced me that each one of your sons and even many of your daughters are capable of holding you in the same high esteem as I do and would be ready to offer the same sacrifices as I am willing to make, but no one is capable of loving you more than I do."[23] It is no wonder that bonds of friendship between the two conspirators would be sealed for life.

It was in the course of the Savoy preparations that Konarski became acquainted with Mazzini's *Instructions* on guerrilla warfare, lessons that he would put to practice when conditions permitted him to do so a few years later in Eastern Europe.[24] With the same zeal that he fought on behalf of Poland's freedom on the battlefield in 1831, Konarski undertook the task to aid Mazzini in the formation of Young Poland. He found time to campaign with great energy and passion for this cause among his fellow exiles while the preparations for the raid on Savoy were still underway. A few years later, in the second half of the 1830s, as the principal emissary of this organization, he was instrumental in spreading Mazzini's message among the Poles and Ukrainians inhabiting the multinational Austrian and Russian imperial domains. One wonders to what degree this encounter with Konarski – relatively brief but filled with intense emotions – deepened Mazzini's lifelong fascination with and commitment to Poland and set in motion his belief that the Slavic peoples were the harbingers of a new democratic Europe in the days to come. Mazzini's thoughts on Konarski were expressed ten years later in a moving speech delivered on the occasion of the fourth anniversary of the Polish patriot's execution by the Russian authorities. In it the Italian leader spoke with conviction and passion of the need to carry on Konarski's cause "with a spade in one hand and a pen or a book in another," to unite action with an apostolic zeal in order to achieve victory of democracy over tyranny and bring to realization the dreams of freedom of the oppressed nations.[25]

In spite of the enthusiasm of the Italian, Polish, German, and some French participants and the generous financial backing from Princess

Belgioioso, Giacomo Ciani, and Marquise Gaspare Rosales,[26] the Savoy expedition proved to be a failure almost from the start.[27] The aloofness of the Carbonari during this operation shocked the revolutionaries and, since it became quite obvious that the authorities in Savoy knew beforehand about the planned raid, some suspected the Carbonari leadership of betrayal. After the Savoy disaster, Mazzini's relations with the Carbonari centre were irrevocably severed. Ties between the Carbonari and some Polish revolutionaries continued to linger a bit longer, but through Mazzini's power of persuasion, a large part of the democratic segment of the Polish emigration was brought to the orbit of Mazzini's Young Europe, an organization that was in the process of formation while the preparations of the Savoy expedition were under way. For the final rupture between the Poles and the Carbonari, a Polish source gives Mazzini the lion's share of credit: "Mazzini snatched away the Polish conspiratorial movement from the Carbonari centre and [from the centre's] strong communist leanings propelling it in the direction of the mystical revolution of Young Europe and its daughter – Young Poland."[28] A number of years later in the Polish periodical *Orzel Bialy* Mazzini himself recalled that it was he who declared war on the Carbonari leadership, because it favoured the interests of French conspiracies at the expense of Italy and other oppressed nationalities.[29]

As the ideas of Romanticism and nationalism captivated the imagination of the youth among the Polish émigrés, it was becoming more and more evident, even to the members of the older generation, that the spirit of the Enlightenment dominating the Carbonari world view, with its emphasis on the general and material rather than the particular and spiritual, did not favour the interests of the people fighting for their nation's independence. Many of them were becoming convinced that the right path to universal progress was not "through mankind to Poland," as the men of Enlightenment had thought it ought to be, but rather "through Poland – or through Italy for that matter – to mankind." A Polish convert to Mazzini's national idea, Walenty Zwierkowski, expressed succinctly the reason for this transition from one ideological camp to another in a letter to his mentor, Joachim Lelewel. Zwierkowski explained that he chose to sever his ties with the Carbonari in order to work on behalf of Young Poland because he believed that the interests of "the fatherland" ought to be placed higher than the interests of "cosmopolitanism."[30] He implored Lelewel in the name of a still small but determined group of enthusiasts inspired by Mazzini to lend his support to the recently formed Preliminary Committee of Young Poland: "We entreat you not to deny us your participation in it. After all, this group consists of your friends, your students, your followers."[31]

Not only Mazzini and his steadily growing group of followers but also some Polish democrats not as yet acquainted with the aims of the organization promoted by Mazzini's supporters began to question the role of the French as the indisputable standard-bearers of progressive revolutions in Europe. But unlike the Italians, the Polish political leaders, Lelewel among them, were becoming more and more convinced after a number of failed uprisings in Western Europe in which Polish legionnaires took an active part that it would be best to steer clear of international entanglements and concentrate exclusively on Poland's immediate needs and interests. This was the position most resolutely defended by Colonel Józef Zaliwski, one of the leaders of the upheaval of 1830–1 and thus a highly respected and influential figure both in the Polish revolutionary underground at home and in the democratic circles of the émigré community. Through a mutual acquaintance in Belgium where Lelewel was organizing his headquarters, after he, together with a number of Polish activists of the Democratic Polish Society, was forced to move by the French authorities, Zaliwski made a special effort to impress on the eminent Polish émigré leader his conviction that national interests demanded concentration exclusively on the immediate needs of the fatherland. The Polish patriot insisted that no effort be spared to prevent the scattering of Polish men into faraway corners of the world such as Portugal or Tunisia – where some of them had indeed been sent by the French – "because there was enough work for them at home." Polish military units, Zaliwski stressed, should be in the service "neither of thrones nor of nations." Rather, their efforts should be concentrated strictly on the reconstruction of their homeland.[32]

The experienced soldier wrote this note after the aforementioned abortive expedition into Russian-controlled territories sponsored by Polish Carbonari units from the Austrian province of Galicia in the spring of 1833. In the preparations and execution this venture Zaliwski knew that he had Lelewel's full support; nevertheless, he considered it prudent to impress on the mind of the émigré political leader that the scattering of Polish legionnaires on behalf of various international causes was the chief reason for the unfortunate outcome of the campaign. Zaliwski's message was plain: Polish émigrés should steer clear of all international involvements.[33]

Zaliwski's advice to stay away from adventures on behalf of foreign causes was directed at Young Italy's call to form an international alliance of subjugated nationalities, an idea that was receiving wide publicity through Mazzini's *Giovine Italia* as well as through other closely related publications. Mazzini had already appealed to the Poles for cooperation as early as 1832 and, as noted earlier, personally initiated correspondence with Lelewel with this idea in mind. By the second half of 1833 it became evident that these appeals were not just dreams of a small group of Romantically inspired Italian visionaries. Concrete steps towards realization of Mazzini's plan for an international alliance of peoples were clearly evident after an Italian contingent of political activists arrived in Switzerland in the summer of 1833. The time and place for Mazzini's project was providentially most auspicious, as one contemporary sympathizer aptly observed: "Switzerland was crowded with German, Polish, French, and Italian fugitives. All were motivated by the most fervent hatred against their suppressors. All had been chased away by their governments, haphazardly thrown together in little Switzerland; what else could they do but conspire."[34] What was probably most important was the fact that this international enclave of hounded conspirators harboured in its midst a leader with a ready-made well-thought-out program designed to propel Europe into an international revolutionary upheaval spearheaded by the oppressed nationalities of Europe.

Intimate contacts and passionate political debates among these clusters of political fugitives hiding from the watchful eyes of Metternich's agents culminated not only in the creation of a modest yet symbolically significant international force that boldly marched on Savoy, but also in cementing a political group from which Young Europe would soon emerge. The Italian and Polish revolutionaries brought together in Switzerland by Antonini and Harro-Harring were soon to be joined by a small cluster of German radical conspirators also seeking refuge in Switzerland. Thus, during the preparations for the Savoy expedition, in addition to the Temporary Committee of Young Poland mentioned in Zwierkowski's letter to Lelewel, a similar group of activists was formed by the exiled Germans whom Mazzini befriended and who, through the mediation of the Poles, were slowly being won over to the idea of Young Europe. These two temporary committees, together with Young Italy, became instrumental in bringing to life Mazzini's dream: an international alliance of subjugated peoples designed to spearhead a struggle against the existing alliance of kings and emperors. It was on account of this accomplishment that Mazzini considered the Savoy expedition – in spite its unfortunate military outcome – an event of singular importance. In his writings he would refer to it as "the Holy Crusade of humanity [that] ... has put the foundation stone to the future edifice, has given baptism to Young Europe."[35]

Mazzini's skill in recovering speedily from even the most crushing defeats, together with his talent for discerning a glimmer of the positive even in what most may have perceived as an irreparable disaster, explains his ability to persevere and remain true to his ideals throughout his long, tortuous career as a revolutionary leader. This undercurrent of optimism is brought to light in one of his meditative observations: "The same calculating coldness that makes me feel the desperate state of our condition as individuals also makes me feel the silent progress of humanity. Would I be here otherwise? Progress is continuous, like the improvement of the majority, even when it seems otherwise."[36]

Mazzini's Introduction to the Slavic World

Ever since he established intimate ties with the Polish exiles in Switzerland, Mazzini had closely followed their heated debates in émigré publications concerning the reasons for the failure of the revolution of 1830–1. His interest in the Polish question became so intense that he occasionally included in *Giovine Italia* lengthy excerpts from the Polish journals with personal commentaries on what was becoming, as generally is the case with every group of political exiles, a highly fragmented émigré community. Divisiveness and friction, he knew, did not augur well for the anticipated European revolution.[37]

It was in the course of this interaction with Polish émigrés that Mazzini's thoughts on Eastern Europe broadened and matured. His sanctuary in Switzerland, which shielded him from the watchful eyes of Metternich's police – at times for reasons of safety he and his Polish colleagues were confined to their quarters for months – provided Mazzini with an opportunity to immerse himself in the study of Slavic history and culture. During the initial stages of investigation, the Italian thinker relied primarily on sources that were readily available: Polish works published in French journals or materials translated for him by his Polish comrades-in-hiding. He was especially impressed by Mickiewicz's aforementioned *Księgi narodu polskiego i pielgrzymstwa polskiego* (Books of the Polish nation and of the Polish pilgrims), which was available in French translation soon after its publication in 1832. From this work, as well as from Félicité Robert de Lamennais's *Paroles d'un croyant* on Catholicism and democracy – a work highly popular among Polish émigrés – Mazzini drew inspiration for his most important statement of beliefs "Fede e avvenire," published in 1835.[38] He was an avid reader of the Polish paper *Le Polonais, journal des intérêts de Pologne*, which began appearing in Paris in 1833.[39]

In years to come, Mazzini would further draw information on Eastern Europe from the publications of the British polyglot scholar John Bowring on Czech, Polish, and Serbian literature, as well as from the Paris lectures on Slavic literatures and cultures delivered by Mickiewicz at the Collège de France in the early 1840s. The fact that the Italian revolutionary became genuinely interested in Slavic literature, in particular in the works of Polish Romantic poets, deepened his understanding of the spiritual world of this part of Europe, which was still practically unknown to most intellectuals in the West. Mazzini's infatuation with the Polish poet Zygmunt Krasiński continued throughout his lifetime. Krasiński's highly esteemed view of the nation as the embodiment of God's thought on earth found reflection in Mazzini's political writings. In the pantheon of European giants he placed Mickiewicz higher than Goethe and Byron and devoted a number of his literary essays published in French and English journals to popularize the works of Polish writers.[40] He himself translated Mickiewicz's poem "Do Matki Polki" (To a Polish mother) from French to Italian, expressing the wish that Italian mothers be guided by the courage and fortitude of Polish women.[41] His feverish political activity did not leave him time to add a Slavic language to his impressive repertoire of foreign tongues, but his fervent desire to read more of the literature that captivated his imagination did not deter him from looking for ways to do so. In the closing years of his life, for example, he attempted to persuade a young friend, the British poet-translator Harriet Hamilton King, to study Polish so that she could translate Mickiewicz into English. In order to encourage her to undertake this task, Mazzini confided that it was his firm belief that the Slavic nationalities were destined to become the dominant power in Europe and that eventually "these younger people would regenerate the older" nations of Europe.[42]

In view of his obvious infatuation with Polish literary achievement and deep admiration for the exiled Poles' revolutionary élan, one would assume that the Italian leader inevitably viewed Eastern Europe from a strong pro-Polish bias. This was true but in part only primarily because Mazzini's principal sources on the Slavic world were perhaps the best and most objective that one could find at that time in Europe. Mickiewicz's broad world outlook, his familiarity and personal acquaintance with Russian poets and enlightened political thinkers, with Czech and Slovak scholars, as well as the fact that he relied heavily in the preparation for many of his works, including his celebrated *Books of the Polish Nation*,[43] on materials gathered by individuals genuinely interested in the cultural reciprocity of the Slavic peoples, like the Romantic poets Bohdan Zaleski and H.N. Bonkowski, made his survey of the Slavic cultures broad in scope and balanced in content. For example, in addition to his familiarity with the literature of the Czechs, Serbs, and Croats, Bohdan Zaleski was a lifelong admirer of Ukrainian Cossack history and culture. Together with Seweryn Goszczyński and Michal Czajkowski, among others, he belonged to what became known as the Ukrainian school of Polish literature. This group of writers tended to present a highly idealized view of Ukrainian-Polish relations in their works, especially with respect to the comradeship and solidarity of the two nations during the Cossack era.[44]

This idealized interpretation of Ukrainian history by Polish Romantic poets and writers was reinforced by an occasional discussion in the Polish émigré circles of the not too distant past when the Polish patriots in their zeal to restore their fallen homeland sought different paths towards the achievement of their goal. During the Napoleonic wars, for example, some Polish émigré leaders approached influential French politicians like Talleyrand, as well as members of the French military, with various plans to bring about the defeat of Russia, their common enemy. In their suggestions they often spoke of the freedom-loving "Ukrainian Cossack nation," which, even after long years of Russian despotism, "continued to nurture in its bosom sentiments of freedom."[45] The radical Polish political activist Hugo Kollątaj, for example, in an attempts to persuade the French military to form a regiment of Ukrainian Cossacks during Napoleon's Russian campaign, emphasized the profound chasm that separated the Ukrainians and the Russians, and in order to make his argument better understood in the West, he compared the relationship between the two nations to that of the Irish under the British rule: "The Cossacks hate the inhabitants of Great Russia almost as much as the Irish [hate] the English." The Polish radical praised the Ukrainian Cossacks as "a brave and spiritual nation that intensely resents the heavy burden of the Russian yoke and has no greater desire than to put an end to it."[46] Thus, without question, asserted the Polish revolutionary, the Ukrainian participation in the struggle against Russia could deliver a mortal blow to the imperial might of the northern colossus. One of Kollątaj's compatriots, Michal Sokolnicki, guided by similar considerations, spoke of the advantages for Europe if an independent Ukrainian state were to be established: "The Cossack state could become one of the mightiest barriers, a buffer principality against Russia."[47] These proposals presenting the Ukrainians as a formidable force in the struggle against Russian imperial expansionism, as well as the advantages to be derived from a resurrected Ukraine as a buffer state against the dangerous "northern colossus," could not have been overlooked when the Polish revolutionaries within Mazzini's milieu began to search for ways to bring down the bulwark of autocracy and conservatism in Europe.

The mythical, highly Romanticized view of East European history publicized in France by Polish émigré writers strengthened Mazzini's belief in the desirability of stirring up revolutionary enthusiasm in that part of Europe, and the Polish Romantics' vision of brotherly love and republican spirit in the land of the Ukrainian Cossacks may have inspired the Italian political thinker to consider the new nations, unspoiled by conquests, as the nucleus of an international revolutionary upheaval of peoples fighting for national freedom and republican ideals.

Evidence of Mazzini's intimate acquaintance with Polish views on this subject are contained in the aforementioned important essay "Fede e avvenire":

> Remember Grochow, Wawer, Ostrolenka [places at which battles between Polish insurgents and Russian forces took place during the revolution of 1830–1] and tell me to what straits Russia would have been driven if Poland had wasted no precious time begging support of the diplomacy that had stabbed her for a hundred years; if her armies had at once shifted the active revolutionary movement to its natural centre beyond the Bug [the Buh River]; if the great idea of people's freedom had called to insurrection the races whose secret thoughts Bogdan Chmielnicki revealed in 1648; if, while enthusiasm was dictator and terror paralyzed the enemy, while the masses of Lituania, Galizia, and Ucraina were quivering with hopes of liberty, the insurrection had flown from the Belvedere [the Russian viceroy's residence in Warsaw from where the insurrection began] to Lituania.[48]

In his writings, correspondence, and, as already noted, even in private conversations, Mazzini often expressed the opinion that a young nation could serve as a better candidate for the role of an initiator of the new European epoch of freedom and brotherhood than an old nation that may have been great in the past but "as a result of the cult of materialism and pride in its acquisitions entered the path of moral decline."[49] The French, by their unconcealed desire for pre-eminence and their inclination to hold on to power and leadership – a tendency that could be detected even among members of the French radical elite – were for Mazzini the prime example of a nation that had already entered the road of moral degeneration. The cause was undoubtedly hubris, excessive pride in the country's material wealth and cultural achievements. One of Mazzini's ponderous observations on this question was that "in France one is accustomed to regard Paris as the cradle of French destinies. In Europe one is accustomed to regard France as the cradle of human destinies. One is wrong; grievously wrong."[50] A penetrating and highly intuitive judge of human nature, the Italian political thinker was perhaps the first to perceive and bring to light the dangers associated with what in the twentieth century has become known as the "elder brother" syndrome, not only among

imperial officialdom but also among democrats and radical revolutionaries of the ruling nations in Europe. A number of years later, a Czech
political activist, Josef Václav Frič, came to a similar realization regarding two leading Russian émigré revolutionaries, Alexander Herzen
and Mikhail Bakunin.[51]

On the basis of what he learnt from the émigré press, as well as
from information brought to his attention by his Polish colleagues,
Mazzini became convinced that the principal reason for the failure of
the recent Polish uprising was the fact that "the theory of cast [rule] has
supplanted the people's idea of the emancipation of all by efforts of
all,"[52] alluding to the egoism of the unenlightened Polish feudal lords.
This conviction was the chief reason why Mazzini failed to show any
interest in establishing ties with the Polish émigré conservative centre in Paris presided over by the "uncrowned king of Poland," Prince
Adam Czartoryski,[53] even though with Polish individuals of aristocratic background like Stanisław Worcell who dedicated their lives to
the welfare of the common people, he developed the most intimate ties.
Among his chief Italian supporters for the cause of Italian unification
and independence were titled aristocrats whom Mazzini held in high
esteem because they were able to submerge their personal and class
interests for the higher cause of a united and independent Italy.

The Italian thinker's persistent emphasis on the need for a concerted action of all peoples – irrespective of their class background,
irrespective of whether they were viewed as historical nations or not,
irrespective of the level of their cultural maturity and/or political
viability[54] – contributed to the strengthening of those groups within
the Polish émigré community that favoured a more sympathetic attitude towards all peoples, including those inhabiting the territories of
"historical Poland." Among the individuals who were inclined to favour a more conciliatory approach was a group of writers and political
activists close to the aforementioned Ukrainian school in Polish literature, among them the poet Bohdan Zaleski and his intimate circle of
friends, which included among others his somewhat older, politically
active colleague and namesake Józef Bohdan Zaleski.[55] Closely associated with this milieu was a polonized Ukrainian political thinker, Piotr
Semenenko, who in 1834 published in the Polish radical journal *Postęp*
an article entitled "On Nationality," a subject obviously close to the
heart of the members of the circle. In it Semenenko argued that in the
pre-partitioned commonwealth the Polish nation had been represented
by the Polish-speaking gentry. The Poland of the future, however,
should be a people's Poland – a regenerated and resurrected nation,
a nation in which the dominant role would be played by the common

people. Since the majority of the inhabitants in pre-partitioned Poland spoke Ukrainian, this group, Semenenko's argument continued, should enjoy pre-eminence in the future national life of the regenerated and restored commonwealth.[56]

Another interesting personality close to Zaleski's circle for whom the question of Ukrainian-Polish nationality became an integral part of his personal life was Hipolit Terlecki. He was a Pole by education and culture, but unlike many of his compatriots from the province of Volynia, he was very much aware of his family's Ukrainian roots. One of his ancestors was Kyrylo Terletsky, the Orthodox bishop of Lutsk who had been instrumental in bringing about the Union of Brest in 1596, an agreement with Rome that established the Uniate or Greek Catholic Church in Ukraine. A Roman Catholic upbringing, an excellent education at the Lyceum in Kremenets – an institution known for moulding young minds in the spirit of Polish patriotism – as well as a medical degree from the University of Kraków did not prevent Terlecki from choosing to become a Uniate priest with a firm commitment to bring about the union between Orthodox Christians and Catholics, Ukrainians, and Poles. He translated Zaleski's poems and Thomas à Kempis's *Imitation of Christ* into Ukrainian. His most original work was a programmatic pamphlet, *Słovo Rusina ku wszech braci szczepu słovianskego o rzeczach słowiańskich* (Address of a Ruthenian to all brethren of the Slavic origin on Slavic matters), which he wrote in Polish in order to reach a larger public. In it he focused on the important role of Ukraine in the future Slavic world, advancing the idea of a Ukrainian-Polish alliance as an axis of the future federation of free and independent Slavic republics.[57]

No important Polish émigré intellectual, even in Bohdan Zaleski's circle, was ready to support Semenenko's vision of a resurrected Poland with the Ukrainian language as the official tongue, nor accept the idea of an independent Ukraine as an equal partner in the future federation of the Slavic nations as proposed by Terlecki. Yet many of them were deeply concerned with what they viewed as an unenlightened, selfish attitude of the Polish gentry during the revolutionary upheaval of 1830–1. What some intellectuals may have found especially disturbing was the fact that, in spite of the opinions so forcefully expressed during Napoleonic campaigns by such influential revolutionary thinkers as Kollątaj regarding the Ukrainians as potential partners in the struggle against Russia, in the period between 1815 and 1830 the issue of the non-Polish nationalities of the pre-partitioned Poland was a subject largely ignored in the discussions and programs of Polish or predominantly Polish secret societies that mushroomed in the territories under the Russian rule in the post-Napoleonic era.

Among these clandestine groups, two are of special interest, since the question of Slavic cooperation or Slavic unity, on the basis of the names selected, appears to have been of principal concern: the Masonic lodge Jedność Słowiańska (Slavic unity), founded in 1818 – which included among its members Poles, Russians, and Ukrainians – and the Society of United Slavs, established in 1823. Neither of these secret circles considered it necessary to pay special attention to peoples other than the Russians and Poles on the territory of the Russian Empire. The program of the Society of United Slavs spoke of "eight Slavic tribes" inhabiting Russia, Poland, Bohemia, Moravia, Dalmatia, Croatia, Hungary, Serbia, Moldavia, and Wallachia. It is of interest to note that at the meeting during which the issue of the "Slavic tribes" was discussed, the Polish Ukrainophile poet Tymko Padura – a precursor of the writers of the Polish school of Ukrainian literature – reminded his colleagues, tongue in cheek, that in their deliberations they forgot the national interests of their hosts, the inhabitants of the territory on which the meeting was taking place, the Ukrainians![58]

The neglect of this issue became painfully evident during the Polish national uprising of 1830–1, when, partly as the result of class interests of the Polish landlords, partly because of the ideological obfuscation so common in provincial centres to which the philosophy of Romanticism was a late arrival and to partly just out of plain ignorance – of which the program of the Society of United Slavs was a striking example – the political rights and social interests of the non-Polish inhabitants in the territories of the former commonwealth were almost completely ignored. True, the Polish rebels during the uprising of 1830–1 were issuing calls for a united front of all democratic forces wishing to fight for freedom, but this appeal was addressed only to those peoples who were regarded as members of the "historical nations." Thus the celebrated slogan under which the Polish revolutionaries fought, "For Your and Our Freedom," referred to the Poles and the Russians, since it was only in those two languages that this slogan was publicized in the territories through which the insurrection spread. Practically no attention was paid to the national interests of the Lithuanians, Belarusians, and Ukrainians in the propaganda literature, even though some of them sympathized with the ideals of the Polish rebels and a number of them, inspired by the slogans and personal heroism of the freedom fighters, even joined the Polish rebels in their struggle against Russian rule.[59]

The leading members of Young Poland were well aware that the principal cause for the failure of the November uprising was the neglect of the rights of the nationalities in the western provinces of imperial Russia. Among them the Ukrainians constituted the largest group, and it was principally in the territories they inhabited that Young Poland made plans for the forthcoming revolution.[60] Therefore it was essential that the Ukrainians be induced to cooperate. For this task Konarski was very well prepared because of the close ties he maintained with Polish Ukrainophile writers and poets.

The poet Bohdan Zaleski's home near Paris was known as a mecca for literary and cultural travellers from Eastern Europe who were passing through France during their sojourns abroad. Among the guests from the Russian Empire to be welcomed by Zaleski in the mid-1830s was the future celebrated writer Nikolai Gogol. To the host, the visitor represented first and foremost his "fellow countryman," a "fellow Ukrainian." Zaleski was deeply touched by Gogol's profound attachment to Ukraine and was intrigued by a manuscript the writer shared with him during the visit. In it Gogol wrote with disdain about the "hated Muscovites" (a commonly used appellation for the Russians by both Poles and Ukrainians) and emphasized the cultural differences between the Russians and other Slavic peoples, Ukrainians in particular.[61]

Bohdan Zaleski's group maintained direct contacts with Ukraine through the good will of Joseph Zaleski's wealthy niece Countess Dionizja Poniatowska, known in literature as the "Ukrainian muse" of the poet Bohdan Zaleski. Countess Poniatowska and her husband were frequent visitors to southern France on account of their frail health. Bohdan was impressed and deeply moved by Countess Poniatowska's sensitive nature and her remarkable knowledge of Ukrainian folklore, culture, and history. Deeply interested in Ukraine's past, encouraged in this pursuit by a historian from Kyiv, Konstant Świdziński,[62] Countess Poniatowska not only collected Ukrainian folklore but wrote a study in French on the psychological and cultural differences between Ukrainians and Russians. The two Zaleskis awaited her visits with great anticipation, not only because of her intelligence and charm but also because she and her mother, Felicia Iwanowska (Józef Zaleski's sister), always brought with them news from Ukraine, letters from family members, friends, and political activists, as well as the much-needed financial aid collected by Polish patriots in Ukraine for the support of the Polish revolutionary cause abroad.[63]

The letters from home that Bohdan Zaleski appreciated especially were those written by his godson Ludwik Jankowski. What interested Zaleski in particular were Jankowski's vivid descriptions of the national awakening among the Ukrainians, about a highly talented, idealistic group of Ukrainian writers, some of whom were the descendants of the freedom-loving Cossacks whose exploits Zaleski celebrated so glowingly in his poetry. In his godson's messages, the poet mused in a letter, one could hear "the voice from home, the voice of those still living and those who were dead, the voice of the steppes, the Dnepr, the towns and mounds, everything that took place there in the past and who knows, perhaps of what was yet to come."[64] In his correspondence the poet encouraged his godson to remain always as genuinely pure as he sounded in his letters, to nurture those qualities that were instilled in him "by mother Ukraine."[65] He advised him and the younger generation of Poles living in Ukraine, "Love the people there and always show willingness to treat them with justice, with an all-encompassing justice. For this you will be rewarded with recognition as leaders in the sacred rebirth of the Slavic community of peoples."[66] While showering praises on Ukraine and its inhabitants in this lengthy epistle, Zaleski did not entirely overlook Poland, even though his comments addressed to his fatherland had a formal, somewhat detached ring. In the concluding sentence the young man was advised "Lift your soul toward God, toward Poland, toward everything that is dignified, good, and beautiful."[67]

Zaleski's correspondence, perhaps even with greater force than his poetry, reveals the dichotomy in the poet's consciousness, a division of loyalties between Ukraine and Poland, a phenomenon that was not uncommon among sensitive young Poles born and reared in Ukraine in the nineteenth century. Even though it must have been difficult for Zaleski to acknowledge that emotionally he was becoming more than just a Ukrainophile Polish poet, one wonders whether he sensed the possibility that the younger generation of Poles whom he was attempting to guide with his epistles and poetry would not only learn to love Ukrainian history, folklore, and people like he did, but actually adopt the language and customs of the land in which they were born and reared. Not even a generation later, the future Ukrainian historians and writers of Polish descent like Volodymyr Antonovych (Włodzimierz Antonowicz) and Tadej Rylsky (Tadeusz Rylski), young men close to Jankowski's age, would indeed immerse themselves wholeheartedly in Ukrainian folklore, history, and culture and in the end dedicate themselves almost exclusively to the cause of the Ukrainian national rebirth. Few men among the Polish émigrés, including Bohdan Zaleski, were psychologically prepared in the first half of the nineteenth century to take the radical step chosen by the next generation of Polish activists, but the love they expressed towards the Ukrainian people was genuine, and the concern they were expressing for Ukraine's future seems to have been authentic. The presence of individuals who were familiar with the work of Zaleski as well as other Ukrainophile writers, and those who shared their sentiments regarding the Ukrainian people facilitated the preparatory work of Konarski when conspiratorial activities in the Ukrainian, Belarusian, and Lithuanian territories began to unfold during the second half of the 1830s.

The Pivotal Role of Polish Émigrés in the Birth of Young Europe

Opinions differ among students of the Great Polish Emigration on the question of the exact date and place of Young Poland's birth.[68] This is partly because of the secrecy under which Mazzini and his Polish comrades had to operate before and especially after the Savoy expedition, and partly because such details were not considered to be of the utmost importance in the highly secretive conspiratorial day-to-day reality of the revolutionaries. What mattered at the start and in the immediate future was not the name under which an organization was operating, the place and the exact day of its formal coming into being, but rather the acceptance and endorsement of the ideals Mazzini was propagating through his writings in *Giovine Italia*: liberty, equality, and brotherhood among all nations.

As noted above, the first clusters of enthusiasts for Young Poland appeared in Switzerland shortly before the Savoy venture. It was in the Swiss city of Bienne at the end of 1833 or in the first days of 1834 that a section within an organization called the Rights of Man and Citizen adopted the name Young Poland. Among its members were individuals with close ties to Mazzini: Karol Stolzman, Józef and Aleksander Dybowski, and Tadeusz Żabicki, as well as the Italian Polonophile Jacopo Antonini.[69] Some of these men would figure prominently in the formal establishment of the future organization.

With the intention of organizing similar groups of Young Poland's sympathizers in France, Mazzini dispatched Szymon Konarski to Paris where the young man won Walery Piętkiewicz, Karol Rożycki, Bohdan Zaleski, and the aforementioned Walenty Zwierkowski to the Mazzinian cause. Not every one of them formally joined the ranks of the organization but all worked assiduously on behalf of its objectives. The principal task of these early activists was to enlist new members from the clusters of Polish émigrés in France. After a month's stay in Paris, Konarski rushed back to Switzerland to join the Italian, Polish, and German regiments in the march on Savoy. Undaunted by the campaign's disappointing end, the Polish patriot returned to France in order to complete his work on behalf of Young Poland and to co-edit the leftist Polish émigré journal *Północ* with Jan Czyński. This periodical, though not officially an organ of Young Poland, publicized many of the organization's ideals.[70] Konarski's indefatigable efforts through recruitment and publicity undoubtedly contributed to the successful

Figure 2.1. Joachim Lelewel. Courtesy of Wikimedia.

DYONIZYA PONIATOWSKA

* 1816 † 1868.

Figure 2.2. The Countess Dionizja Poniatowska.

Figure 2.3. Jósef Bohdan Zaleski (the poet). From *La Pologne historique, littéraire, monumentale et illustrée ... Rédigée par une Société de littérateurs*, 1839. British Library HMNTS 10291.f.9. Courtesy of Wikimedia.

completion of the preparatory work for the formal establishment of Young Poland in mid-March 1834.[71]

If there are conflicting reports regarding the details of Young Poland's beginnings, all sources are in agreement on Mazzini's vital role in the organization's creation. It was in the period after the Savoy misadventure that the Italian leader turned his undivided attention to the Polish question, acknowledging with a heavy heart, no doubt, that the Poles and not the Italians were destined to play the central role in the future Pan-European democratic revolution. By this time Mazzini became fully aware that since the summer of 1833 – the time of the decimation of Young Italy in his homeland – from the broader pan-European perspective, the organization no longer represented an effective force, at least for the time being. Suffering enormous losses, both organizational and personal – among the Italian casualties during the sweeping repressions of 1833 was his closest friend Jacopo Ruffini – Mazzini saw the Polish political exiles as the key players in the future alliance of nations. Their vigour and patriotic enthusiasm instilled in him confidence that the idea of Young Europe could be brought to a successful completion, in spite of the seriousness of Italian losses. Writing at this time to Luigi Melegari, the head of what remained of Young Italy in Marseilles, Mazzini acknowledged that he considered the future Young Poland as a sine qua non of Young Europe.[72] A few weeks later, on 16 March 1834, the Italian leader elatedly informed his compatriot in Marseilles that Young Poland had indeed become a reality.[73]

With this most important task accomplished, Mazzini moved with resolute speed to work on his international European project. Not even a month had passed after the founding of Young Poland when on 11 April 1834, in Bern, Switzerland, in a small inn by the name of Zum Adler, the Italian leader succeeded in bringing together some seventeen enthusiasts of Young Europe, representing Italians, Poles, and Germans. After three days of deliberations and discussions of the statutes and other documents that Mazzini had carefully put together, on 15 April 1834 the assembled delegates were ready to affix their signatures to the Pact of Brotherhood, the formal covenant of Young Europe. In addition to Mazzini, the Italian signatories were well-known activists in his organization from the beginning: G.O. Rosales, A. Ghiglione, L.A. Melegari, G. Ciano, and the two younger brothers of the martyred Jacopo Ruffini, Agostino and Giovanni. The Polish group included, in addition to the already mentioned close friends of the Italian leader, K. Stolzman, F. Gordaszewski, F. Nowosielski, Józef Dybowski, and Konstanty Zaleski. The German signatories were Dr August Breidenstein and his brother F. Breidenstein, Jerzy Peters, F. Stromeyer, and the journalist Karl Theodor Barth.[74]

The Pact of Brotherhood was written in the three languages of the signatories (Italian, German, Polish) as well as in French, the customary language of international agreements and the language in which the deliberations were conducted.[75] It is not without significance, considering the nature of the association, that this was the first instance in modern history that a text, other than agreements between governments, was drawn up in languages of all the participants.

The chief objective of Young Europe was the promotion of happiness among all people. In order to achieve this goal, all members were expected to become actively involved in efforts leading to the attainment of liberty, equality, and brotherhood for all nations. Liberty was declared to be a right to which every individual was entitled in order to be able to fulfil one's mission in life. This mission had to conform to the universal aims of humanity. With respect to the second principle, it was explained that the idea of equality embodied both rights and duties. Since every privilege violated the right of equality, similarly every egotistical action on the part of an individual violated the idea of brotherhood. The word *brotherhood* signified mutual respect and love among individuals and among nations.

Every member was obliged to fight all forms of violation of liberty, equality, and brotherhood. Similarly, every nation was expected to defend the rights and freedoms of other nations wherever sovereignty was threatened or violated. In other words, the association was seen as a defensive alliance designed to promote national liberation of the nations represented by the signatories, but other nationalities were invited and expected to join the association as well. An ivy leaf, symbolizing rapid growth and eternal bonds among the association's members, was chosen as the organization's emblem. The motto inscribed on the emblem read, "Nunc et semper."

In the association's statutes, articles focusing specifically on nationalities (seventeen) and the nationalities' relations with the future European union of nations (twenty) stated, "Every nationality has its own special mission, which would contribute towards the fulfillment of the general mission of humanity." This unique individual mission constituted the nation. Nations were declared sacred. The terms on which relations among the constituent nationalities were based were to serve as a model for the future reconstructed, democratic Europe. This involved the harmonization of aims of the two fundamental entities that comprise humankind: fatherland and humanity.

This international association was headed by a central committee consisting of one delegate from each of the national committees. There were two categories of members: the initiators and the initiated. A special position of an organizer was created for the coordination of larger regional units.

With respect to economic issues, everyone had the right to own property, and each individual was entitled to use goods held by the community in common according to the amount of work contributed to the community's welfare. Finally, it was explained that all nations have a special mission within the realm of the universal mission of humanity. "This mission constitutes the Nation. Nationality is sacred."[76] The document explained that a truly happy human community could be realized only after every nationality attained its sovereignty and each sovereign nation joined the future federation of republics. The aim of this federation was to strive for and safeguard national sovereignty and happiness of all.

In the meantime, before independence of all the nations in Europe was achieved, the subjugated nationalities were to form associations. Members of each of these national associations would elect committees that would become the constituent parts of the Central Committee of Young Europe. Members of each association would be governed by two statutes: that of Young Europe and that of a particular nationality. But the statute of the latter had to be confirmed by the Central Committee of Young Europe. Activists representing nationalities that, because of existing political conditions, were not able to form associations, would be supervised by an initiator who would be responsible to the Central Committee of Young Europe. The initiator's responsibilities included keeping detailed information about the members and coordinating activities of the regional units. Irrespective of whether they were members of an association or of a unit headed by an initiator, all were required to adhere faithfully to the principles on which Young Europe was founded and to work towards the realization of the organization's objectives. In order to succeed in this task, all members had to strive for personal growth so that each would be better equipped to contribute towards the attainment of the organization's objectives. Before being accepted, each candidate had to take a solemn oath promising to live in accordance with the motto inscribed in the Pact of Brotherhood: "One God; the only authority: his law; the only interpreter of this law: humanity." Adhering to the principle of God's law, the highest penalty for treason within the organization was not execution but expulsion. There were some variations in the statutes of Young Europe's constituent members. Young Germany, for example, representing the radical wing of the association, kept the death penalty as the punishment for disloyalty.[77]

Mazzini, the principal author of the Pact of Brotherhood, summarized his vision of the organization eloquently:

Young Europe ... is a vast association of men from all countries who acknowledge one banner, that of the human fraternity, the solidarity of all
suppressed [nationalities], the alliance against the oppressors whoever
and wherever they might be; equality, liberty, and humanity and the mission of each man to fight for these concepts.... [But] Young Europe will
do more ...; it will transform individual beliefs into a general belief: in
this respect it is a piece of religion, the religion of the future.... It organ-
izes a propaganda [in the sense of propagation or dissemination of ide-
als] above all – and for all; it institutes a great apostolate, a vast political
and social education, ... the harmonization between rights and duties, the
emancipation of all people, ... the principle of action substituted for that
of conspiracy.[78]

The question of youth, inscribed in the very name of the organization, was explained by the founder: "Europe ... is at the threshold of an
entirely new development. She tends to rejuvenate.... In one world the
Young Generation knows how to rid itself of the past and enter freely
upon the roads towards the future.... That is the Young Europe of the
Peoples, which will superimpose itself on the Old Europe of the kings.
That is the struggle of the Young liberty against the old slavery; the
struggle of the young equality against ancient privileges; the victory of
the young ideas over the old beliefs. Everywhere it is the same war, the
one and yet such a multifaceted war that feeds the efforts of the young
generation against the old."[79]

What were the thoughts and opinions on Young Europe expressed
by other members of the association? Karol Stolzman – one of the
initiators of Young Poland and the staunchest supporter of the
Mazzinian idea in the years to come, perhaps because of his awareness of the prevailing opinion among Polish democrats that it was
important to steer away from international entanglements – made
an effort to justify his entry into the new international association
purely on pragmatic grounds: "Our aim is to fortify the cause of
Polish democracy upon a formidable basis, to ensure the collaboration of foreign democrats, all the more disposed to help us because
they find themselves held in check."[80] He attempted to allay the
fears of his compatriots in the Polish National Committee with a
firm declaration of loyalty to the Polish cause: "Brothers! You may
think that our alliance with Young Italy will result in the defection
of a considerable number of democrats, but Young Poland will not

denounce either the ancient organization of its mother society or its previous obligations."[81] A new member recruited to Young Germany embraced the idea of an international alliance of nations without apologies or reservations: "The Association of Young Europe aspires to ... the emancipation of all nations.... Without the expansion of our European association, without the cooperation of the patriots from all countries ... the freedom of an individual [nation] will either not be possible or always be endangered."[82]

Mazzini and Lelewel: An Uncomfortable but Workable Team

In the spring of 1834 Mazzini had no doubt that most of his Polish associates actively involved in the creation of Young Europe were resolutely committed to the organization's objectives. As a perceptive political thinker, however, the Italian leader knew that for Young Poland to become a truly powerful, dynamic organization and the pivotal partaker in Young Europe, it had to have the endorsement of the most authoritative figure among the Polish democrats, Joachim Lelewel. When the efforts of the Polish enthusiasts of the Mazzinian idea did not prove persuasive enough to win over the strong-willed, cautious, if not always practical political leader of an important segment of the Polish émigrés, Mazzini resolved to apply the full force of his extraordinary epistolary talents to attain this objective.

In his letters – the only means of communication for the two prominent émigré leaders, because of the strict police surveillance imposed upon their whereabouts – the Italian revolutionary described in glowing terms the role that he believed the Slavic nations were destined to play in Europe's future, imparting to Poland the important task of bringing about the political renaissance in Europe's north, the same role he envisaged for Italy in the southern part of the continent. He stated forcefully his firm conviction that the time had arrived for the young nations to take the torch from the hands of the old, egoistical nations, so that the struggle for freedom could become more effective,[83] referring obviously to the disappointments that both the Italians and the Poles had experienced in their relations with the French or Francophile revolutionary leadership. "Don't you think that the initiative in civilization's development is undergoing transformation? Don't you think that the nature of events propels with ever greater force the idea that the present epoch must be an epoch of nations in exile, an epoch of rehabilitation of the downtrodden races?"[84]

When flattery and cajoling did not prove strong enough, Mazzini appealed to lofty ideals, to the need for selfless commitment on behalf of the righteous cause: "The present mode of thought is drenched in individualism. Let us provide an example, let us begin; our task is difficult but it is holy. Let us not look back in order to see how many are following us. Let us march forward. Let us chart new territories."[85]

To make sure that his high esteem of the national idea would not be construed as an elevation of the state into the highest ideal – the Italian leader was always critical of Hegel's worship of the state – Mazzini stressed what he considered to be the kernel of his beliefs: "I think that above a Pole, a German, a Frenchman, or an Italian there is something higher: a human being and that among all groups and all nations there exists something far more sacred, the fatherland of fatherlands: humanity, which ought to bring them together and without which a nation has no aim and democracy has no meaning."[86]

In December 1835, after two years of untiring appeals both to the mind and the heart, Mazzini finally persuaded Lelewel to officially become a member of Young Poland.[87] By this time Lelewel had executed to perfection what appears to have been his original plan since the time he was first approached to join Young Poland. First, he was able to disentangle the Polish Carbonari units from the French centre – a task that he began to work on in earnest after the ill-fated Zaliwski campaign. Second, he weaned away at least some members of Young Poland from Mazzini's overpowering influence, something he was secretly working on since Zwierkowski's plea to come to the support of Young Poland at the organization's beginnings. Most of his confidants, including Zwierkowski, knew that at least from the end of 1834 Lelewel was keeping a close watch on the developments surrounding Young Poland, viewing many of its declared objectives with approval.[88] For example, as early as the end of 1834 he responded to a letter of invitation to join the organization from one of the central figures of Young Poland, Konstanty Zaleski, in language that left no doubt about his sympathies: "Where the national thought is alive and where it appeals to the right principles, I am there with you."[89] A year later he confided to Walery Piętkiewicz, one of his most trusted colleagues, that he envisaged Young Europe as an accessory of Young Poland.[90] By the end of 1835 the scrupulously cautious Polish leader felt sure that taking full control of Young Poland was within his reach.

Mazzini must have sensed Lelewel's calculated intentions, but he was in no position to pose objections. He knew that Lelewel, just like most members of Young Poland and of Young Italy, for that matter, believed that one could work best for the higher ideal of humanity by working first on behalf of one's nation. The Polish political leader, just like Mazzini, was also convinced that only through the concerted effort of all segments of the society, in particular with the full cooperation of the common people, could victory be achieved in the struggle against the autocratic regimes.[91] Should one wonder, therefore, that Lelewel wished to take full control of an organization that promised to be best equipped to bring about national liberation for Poland, an organization that had an international connection but with practically no strings attached? This was not entirely contrary to Mazzini's plans. The Italian leader's high hopes for a popular upheaval in Eastern Europe were expressed as early as his celebrated essay of 1834, "Fede e avvenire." Lelewel's plans also were in full agreement with Mazzini's thoughts on the occasion of the establishment of Young Poland's Permanent Committee in October 1834, in which the Italian leader ponderously asked, "Could it be possible that in Paris they know and love Poland better than in Poland?... You have Polish objectives, Polish obstacles, Polish resources, Polish interests. Approach them from the point of view of what best suits Poland, for I know that only you hold in your hearts the secret of the Fatherland, the concept and the sense of your mission, knowledge of the means which ought to lead you to rebirth."[92] Of course this meant the recognition of full autonomy for Young Poland within the international organization. The fact that Lelewel was a democrat and a firm believer in the necessity of gaining the support of the common people helped a great deal in making possible this tacit agreement between the two strong-willed leaders.

In the stultifying atmosphere of Metternich's Europe of the mid-1830s, any kind of revolutionary activity was greeted by Mazzini and his compatriots as sign of hope, a window of opportunity for the attainment of Young Europe's ideals. Everything was not lost, in spite of a series of setbacks in the preceding two years, Mazzini firmly believed, so long as the spirit of the rebirth was kept alive in the hearts of the subjugated nations of Europe. In view of the international situation, he had no choice but acknowledge that Young Europe could indeed be viewed as an ancillary of Young Poland rather than the other way around.

A Polish authority on this subject did not exaggerate too much when he observed that, from the end of 1835, "Young Poland became an instrument in Lelewel's political game both in the emigration and at home. A new phase of conspiratorial activity inspired by Young Poland began in Polish lands. Lelewel assumed his leadership under exceptional émigré conditions, acting with forethought and in accordance with carefully prepared tactics."[93]

Chapter Three

Reception of Mazzini's Ideas
in East Central Europe

It was through his [František Kampelík's] efforts that national consciousness was awakened at the faculty of philosophy and at the theological seminary in Brno from where it would spread through the land of Moravia. After being ordained as priests, we were sent to various corners of the diocese.... This was the mustard seed planted among the graduates that later grew, as you can see, into a mighty tree.[1]

Mazzini's patient but persistent efforts to recruit Joachim Lelewel into Young Europe proved invaluable for the dissemination of the organization's ideals in the Slavic world. Soon after joining the Permanent Committee of Young Poland, the Polish intellectual-conspirator began to work on an elaborate plan for a national revolution among the Slavic peoples with Poland, as the pivotal player, of course. Remaining true to his solemn pledge not to interfere in the internal affairs of the constituent parts of Young Europe, Mazzini prudently chose not to become directly involved in the planning process, even when he learnt from Karol Stolzman, the official representative of Young Poland in Young Europe, that Lelewel was conducting consultations with a small cluster of trusted individuals, some of whom were not members of the organization. In fact, very few members of Young Poland were aware of Lelewel's secret advisory group operating under the name of Związek Dzieci Ludu Polskiego (The union of children of the Polish people). The union's charter, signed on 23 February 1835 by Lelewel, Zwierkowski, and Wincenty Tyszkiewicz, made no mention of Young Poland. Nevertheless its guiding principles conformed fully to the statutes of Young Europe. The organization's aim was to bring together all Polish patriots who supported republican ideals and wished to establish close contact with their brothers at home for the purpose of liberating Poland from foreign domination, establishing civil and political freedoms, granting land to rural inhabitants, abolishing all privileges, and bringing about humanity's great mission to establish the reign of liberty, equality, and brotherhood for all nations.[2] This cluster of conspirator-advisors consisted mainly of members of a defunct Polish Carbonari unit known in the past as the Zemsta Ludu (People's vengeance), who, together with Lelewel, were actively involved in the preparation and execution of the ill-fated Zaliwski campaign in 1833. Like Mazzini after the Savoy expedition, as well as Lelewel after the Zaliwski campaign, these men too chose to sever ties with the leadership of the Carbonari centre in Paris. This step by members of Lelewel's secret council reassured Mazzini that he could rely on Poland's most eminent leader and his chosen group of advisors.

Because the Zaliwski campaign had its centre in Galicia, members of Lelewel's chosen advisory council were better equipped than any other émigré group to re-establish links with the remnants of the revolutionary underground in this strategically located Austrian province, from where, once again, revolutionary operations would most likely begin. Of great assistance in this connection was Count Wincenty Tyszkiewicz, on account of his familiarity with the political climate in East Galicia gained during the Zaliwski campaign, even though some of the council's more radical members looked with suspicion at this prominent aristocrat in their midst. For Lelewel, who generally tended to steer clear of titled nobility, pragmatic calculations proved more important than personal likes or dislikes. In this instance, the example of Young Italy could teach the Polish democrat a valuable lesson: among its supporters, Mazzini's organization had a significant number of wealthy, titled aristocrats who provided invaluable financial aid and sound advice to the cause of Italy's struggle for independence. Furthermore, Mazzini's idea that, in order to be successful, a national movement had to include in its ranks members of all social groups, was beginning to gain acceptance among the left-wing former Carbonari members of the Polish émigré community, even though in its official publications it was customary to blame the aristocrats and unenlightened members of the gentry for Poland's past and present misfortunes.

The Polish leader also thought it prudent to co-opt into his secret enclave Piotr Kopczyński, the chief organizer of the November uprising in Ukraine, whose contacts could be of particular importance in the territories under the control of imperial Russia.[3] Another valuable recruit was Karol Różicki, a respected member of the Polish Democratic Society who headed an émigré military unit at that time. The fact that Różicki never formally joined Young Poland, in spite of Lelewel's efforts to co-opt him, did not seem to matter, so long as the high-ranking officer endorsed the organization's aims. Highly regarded and loved in the secret enclave was its youngest member, Szymon Konarski, admired by most Polish democrats, Lelewel in particular, for his inexhaustible enthusiasm, undaunted courage, and unique conspiratorial talents.[4] At the age of twenty-eight, Konarski was already a veteran of the November uprising, the Zaliwski campaign, and Young Italy's Savoy expedition! Furthermore, he had been one of the most energetic recruiters for Young Poland during the initial stages of its formation. Konarski, on his part, considered Lelewel as the un-disputed leader of Poland's national cause. In September 1833, when he was returning – as did many of his compatriots – low-spirited and dejected from the Zaliwski campaign, he penned a glowing description of the historian-revolutionary: "In the evening I visited Lelewel, and a flash of hope that it would still be possible to sacrifice one's life for the fulfillment of one's spiritual yearnings interrupted my plans for a quiet retirement.... My entire being became literally consumed by an electrifying fire."[5]

In addition to those listed above, among the members of the secret advisory council were the two Zaleskis: Józef the soldier, and Bohdan the poet. This choice on Lelewel's part could not have been better cal-culated. Both Zaleskis were on excellent terms with Różicki, and both were highly regarded among the members of the Polish Democratic Society, Józef for his military accomplishments and valour and Bohdan for his inspirational poetry. It was with Józef Zaleski that Lelewel first shared his comprehensive plan for the forthcoming upheaval. In or-der to be successful, the future revolution had to represent a broad popular uprising, with all segments of the population actively taking part in it, the Polish leader wrote: "The more the masses are stirred to action, the stronger, the more real, the more violent and effective it will be."[6] In order to make this possible, special attention had to be de-voted to a carefully planned propaganda campaign designed for both Polish-inhabited and non-Polish ethnic territories. This undertaking, Lelewel thought, could be carried out most effectively by local activ-ists who had a good grasp of the terrain and knowledge of local con-ditions and who would not easily fall under suspicion of the police. The role of the emigration in this effort was to maintain contacts with the underground at home through emissaries, or in Young Europe's parlance, which Lelewel adopted, carefully selected group of "apos-tles of the people," whose task would be to spread enlightened dem-ocratic ideas among the inhabitants of the countryside. In return, the patriotic groups at home were expected to be involved in fund-raising campaigns designed to aid the émigrés in Western Europe in the publication and dissemination of propaganda and the promotion of Poland's cause abroad.

Lelewel's program was almost an exact replica of the plan of action that Mazzini outlined for Young Italy in 1831, including the stress on the significant role envisaged for the "apostles of the people." Likely Lelewel had Mazzini's approval, irrespective of whether the Polish leader chose to share this plan with the organization's centre. The fact that the role of Young Europe would be reduced to no more than an ancillary organ participating mainly in the dissemination of propaganda could have been easily interpreted as a realistic assessment of the political situation in Western Europe. By the end of 1835 even Mazzini had to acknowledge that what was most important in those politically stressful times was not so much a coordinated effort of all the constituent parts of Young Europe to act in unison for the attainment of the common goal, but rather to focus attention on the particular national group that appeared to be best equipped to begin a revolution.

By sharing his thoughts with Josef Zaleski on what was to be done in order to assure success in the impending all-embracing upheaval in Eastern Europe, Lelewel hoped to induce the seasoned veteran of numerous conspiracies and battles to join him at his headquarters in Brussels. Zaleski, while declaring his confidence in Lelewel as the leader among the Polish democrats, politely declined this invitation. After participating in the Napoleonic wars, the November uprising, and the recent Zaliwski campaign, he chose Paris as his permanent residence in emigration. In addition to the deep bonds of friendship that tied him to Bohdan Zaleski, the poet, this hardened yet highly sensitive individual preferred the stimulating literary milieu of his soul mate's in the French capital, which included among others the celebrated Polish bard Adam Mickiewicz. Fresh from a failed campaign and not as yet certain of what role would suite him best in the émigré world, Zaleski exercised caution before committing himself again to another risky venture. This guarded attitude was reflected in an appeal addressed to "Do przyjaciół galicyjskich" (Friends in Galicia), written in 1833 and signed by members of the Zaleski literary circle. The appeal counselled the Polish patriots in that province to act independently of the émigrés, to concentrate on working out their own plan of action, which, the signatories advised, should focus primarily on bringing enlightened, democratic ideas to the people in the countryside. Above all, the appeal warned against isolated, uncoordinated, poorly prepared uprisings.[7]

These guidelines for action coincided with the main features of Lelewel's plan: all activities had to be thoughtfully planned and carefully supervised. Thus, when in the early months of 1835 Young Poland began in earnest to spread its conspiratorial net in the home territories, Józef Zaleski often hastened with helpful words of advice. It was partly through the two Zaleskis that the émigré leadership of Young Poland kept abreast of important developments at home, and it was through their well-established channels of communication that a good part of the organization's correspondence passed. This was made possible by the numerous contacts the two charismatic Zaleskis maintained by opening their residence on the outskirts of Paris to visitors who passed through the French capital during their sojourns abroad. It was also partly thanks to them as intermediaries that the much-needed funds from generous donors at home – such as the Zaleski, Iwanski, and Poniatowski families residing near Kyiv, and the Count Uruski family in Galicia – found their way to Young Poland's coffers.[8] Of special importance in this connection were the visits of Józef Zaleski's close relatives, especially his wealthy niece, Countess Dionizja Poniatowska, and her husband.[9] Because of their intimate knowledge of the local conditions and the first-hand news items brought to them by their numerous guests, the two Zaleskies served as an invaluable source of information about the political developments in territories in which the preparatory stage of the revolution was expected to occur.

Both Zaleski the poet and Zaleski the soldier represented the enlightened, broad-minded segment of the Polish intelligentsia always open to the sensitive issue of the non-Polish inhabitants of Galicia, Belarus, Lithuania, and Ukraine – provinces of the pre-partitioned Polish Commonwealth in which the Poles constituted a minority. By the mid-1830s most educated political émigrés realized that gaining the trust of the local people in the above-named regions was essential to realization of a resurrected Poland. Even the Polish conservative circles in emigration who, in contrast to the democrats, tended to focus on the establishment of diplomatic contacts in their effort to promote the Polish cause, were not altogether oblivious to the question of non-Poles in their former homeland. Elaborate plans for a workable resolution of the nationality question were being prepared with utmost care at Hotel Lambert, the headquarters of the conservative groups in Paris presided over by Prince Czartoryski.[10] The Polish democrats gathered in Lelewel's circle, who embraced Young Europe's ideals regarding the right of all nationalities to self-determination, understood the importance of this complicated question very well.

Polish Perceptions of the Nationality Question
in a Resurrected Poland

If the program of Young Poland was to be interpreted in the spirit of the ideals of Young Europe, it would be logical to assume that the Poles within or closely associated with the organization would support self-determination of the non-Polish nationalities living in the eastern territories of pre-partitioned Poland, including the Ukrainians, who represented the majority of inhabitants, not only in some provinces of the former commonwealth's eastern borderlands now under the control of Russia, but also in the eastern part of Galicia. Article 28 of Young Poland's statute corresponded closely to article 18 of Young Europe's. It stated that the same spirit of brotherhood that guided the relations between individuals should apply to the relations among nationalities: all nations were required to mutually aid one another in both the attainment and in the defence of independence.

Lelewel's professional training and populist interpretation of history prepared the Polish scholar-politician well for a comprehensive assessment and a possible solution for this complex question. As a descendant of a family with a highly mixed ethnic background, he had a personal interest in attempting to unravel the mystery of one's national identity and political allegiance. To the surprise of many, while he was revered by his fellow countrymen as one of the most trusted leaders of Poland, some referred to him as "the best of all Polish men, a wise educator of the Polish nation."[11] the historian himself did not shy from admitting with a touch of irony and impish glee, "There is not a drop of a Lach [*Lach* was a term commonly used to designate a "pure" ethnic Pole] in my blood. My mother's father was a Rusyn [a term commonly used in the nineteenth century for Ukrainians] Szeluta by name, my father is a son of a Prussian father and a Saxon mother of the Sas coat of arms, and, to complicate it further, she was born of a Swiss mother; peas mixed with cabbage."[12] But in spite of this wide web of ethnic connections, there appears to have been no question in Lelewel's mind that he was a Pole: a Pole by culture, education, upbringing, and personal conviction and choice. From his point of view, it was the milieu in which one was born, raised, and educated that determined one's nationality. This was generally the conviction held by many of Lelewel's contemporaries – in particular those gathered in Mazzini's Young Europe. It should be noted that it would be only in the last decades of the nineteenth century when social Darwinism, with its emphasis on blood or race, had rudely thrust itself into the realm of the national idea, that the liberal and highly individualistic understanding of national identity – root-edness in the culture in which one was reared – was superseded by an exclusive, strictly deterministic racial doctrine.

Choosing this personal approach, according to which one's cultural and political environment and not one's blood determined a person's national identity, many Poles like Lelewel were convinced, or at least attempted to convince themselves, that once a democratic Polish republic came into being with guarantees of freedom and equality for all, irrespective of religion, language, or class, most inhabitants would inevitably – through education and other forms of assimilation – become part of the Polish nation. This line of reasoning was reflected partly in a patriotic manifesto Lelewel wrote in 1834 on the occasion of the fourth anniversary of the November uprising. It received wide publicity among the émigrés and was distributed by the agents of Young Poland in the home territories. In this document the Polish patriot bemoaned the erosion of ancient Polish rights of freedom and equality as a result of the centuries-old aristocratic-gentry domination in the commonwealth. In the anticipated resurrected Poland, he envisaged full guarantees of equality and freedom for every inhabitant, irrespective of social class, irrespective of language or religious denomination, because the future existence of the nation was possible only through a concerted effort of all inhabitants: "The strength of the nation resides in the people," announced the manifesto.[13]

Would the principles of equality and freedom guiding the social relations of the elites in the Polish Commonwealth during the Middle Ages be applicable to the society in modern times? Would the promise of equality and freedom satisfy the needs of Ukrainians, Lithuanians, and Belarusians in an age in which the "non-historical nations" were beginning to emerge from their enforced political slumber? In the case of the Ukrainians, whose daring bid for independence took place only a little more than a century earlier – when their leader, Hetman Mazepa concluded a secret alliance with Charles XII of Sweden against Peter I of Russia – the memory of an independent national existence still lingered in the minds of many educated and not-so-very-educated individuals. Historically attuned men and women of both nationalities were aware that a number of influential Poles involved in the Napoleonic wars spoke glowingly of a Ukrainian nation whose independent existence was in the interests of Europe, because it could form a mighty bulwark against the despotism and expansionism of Russia.[14] The more astute political thinkers, especially those with a good background in history, sensed that an independent Ukraine would be an asset, not a hindrance, to a resurrected Poland. On the other hand, very few of Lelewel's compatriots in the emigration, not to mention the politically less enlightened members of the gentry at home – irrespective of whether they were of conservative, liberal, or radical persuasion – were ready to renounce Poland's claims to its historical lands, gathered by Polish kings through intermarriages and conquests in the Middle Ages. Furthermore, the success of the forthcoming revolution depended to no small degree on the leadership of the Polish nationally conscious intelligentsia, the composition of which consisted predominantly of gentry with small and medium landholdings. Even liberally inclined populists like Lelewel had to acknowledge this fact. Perhaps a mere promise of equality for all nationalities and freedom for all religious denominations would prove satisfactory for the multitude of socially and culturally oppressed non-Polish inhabitants in the lands viewed as historical Poland. After all, at the beginning of the nineteenth century, the signs of a national awakening appeared from a distance, at least, to be weak, even among the Ukrainians, in spite of the lingering memory of a heroic Cossack past among the elite. Perhaps it was sufficient – Lelewel and many of his likeminded compatriots might have thought – to demonstrate that the Polish revolutionary leadership was attentive to the religious, cultural, and social needs of the non-Poles, an attitude that was practically non-existent during the revolutionary upheavals of the most recent past. It was with the objective of correcting this blunder of the Polish leadership during the November uprising that Lelewel felt obliged as the head of Young Poland to prepare a series of carefully worded appeals that addressed the nationality question.

Targeting Galicia as a pivotal territory of Young Poland's operations, Lelewel prepared two separate appeals to the population of this ethnically divided territory, with the Poles inhabiting the western region and the Ukrainians constituting a majority in the larger, eastern part. The first was addressed to the inhabitants of the city of Lviv, "Do obywateli miasta Lwowa)."[15] Like many of the provincial capitals of the Austrian Empire, this commercial centre, with roots dating back to the Middle Ages, was known for its multinational composition: Poles, Ukrainians, Jews, Germans, and Armenians living and working side-by-side for centuries under different dynasties and regimes. The future great national upheaval, Lelewel explained, would be brought about not for the benefit of dynasties or the privileged inhabitants, but in the interests of all people. All residents of the city were promised full equality and freedom. "Brothers of Lwów," the appeal solemnly intoned, "your celebrated city from ancient times has represented the congregation of a variety of peoples and religions, and up to the present day it has not ceased to be a centre of national diversity. You have been selected by Providence to promote brotherhood: you have the capacity to bring together and unify this diversity so that at every level cooperation could be achieved."[16]

The second appeal was addressed to the Greek Catholic clergy, representing the elite of the Ukrainian population in that province. As in the first document, Lelewel approached the question from the point of view of a historian, by calling attention to the long tradition of interaction and cooperation between the Greek Catholic and the Polish Roman Catholic priesthood. These relations, he pointed out, were based on firm foundations, because both branches of the church had been drawing their spiritual sustenance from the same sacred texts. He called attention to the persecution in the Russian Empire of all Ukrainians, irrespective of whether they belonged to the Orthodox or the Greek Catholic denomination. Therefore, Lelewel pointed out – now approaching the issue from a perspective of a politician – the Greek Catholics should consider the nationality question just as important as the religious one.[17] The subtext of the message was that the Ukrainians of both religious backgrounds would fare much better in a free democratic Poland, enjoying full religious and cultural freedom, rather than languishing in despotic Russia, where the last vestiges of Ukrainian national identity were being systematically erased, irrespective of creed.

Detailed information about the political and religious climate in the eastern part of Galicia supplied by the participants in the Zaliwski campaign, in particular Józef Zaleski and Wincenty Tyszkiewicz, instilled confidence in Lelewel that the future emissaries of Young Poland could count on the support of the Ukrainian clerical circles in that province. Expressions of genuine sympathy and assistance extended to the Polish patriots by the Greek Catholic clerics during and after the November uprising were not uncommon. For example, Ukrainian parish priests, often at great personal risk, issued false birth certificates to Polish insurgents fleeing from Russian-controlled territories in order to protect them from deportation by the Austrian imperial police.[18] It was a known fact that Austrian law enforcement agencies in the post-Napoleonic era cooperated closely with their Russian counterparts in ferreting out and arresting revolutionaries seeking a refuge in Galicia. In this easternmost province of the Austrian Empire, through which so many different armies and regimes had passed in the preceding turbulent decades, neither the Greek Catholic clergy nor the civilian population could remain oblivious to political and military matters. Some Greek Catholic seminarians, inspired by the Polish call to action on behalf of equality and freedom during the November insurrection, joined the uprising or expressed eagerness to do so.[19] It was probably with the intention of reminding the local Ukrainian intelligentsia of these acts of brotherly assistance, rendered to the Polish revolutionaries only a few years earlier, that Lelewel personally affixed Józef Zaleski's name to the appeals. "I figured that your signature would not be without significance," Lelewel explained apologetically to Zaleski, in a note attached to a copy of the appeal.[20] The Polish leader requested that Zaleski prepare a similar document addressed to the Czechs,[21] hoping, of course, that with the assistance of Bohdan Zaleski, who was known not only as a poet but also as a scholar with an interest in the literature of the Czech national revival, such a call would be based on sound historical foundations.

Lelewel's appeals conveyed the spirit of Young Europe, stressing the ideas of brotherhood and cooperation among nations, even though, aside from vague promises of freedom and equality, no mention was made of national political rights for the non-Polish inhabitants in territories claimed as "historical Poland." That the Ukrainians, Lithuanians, and Belarusians inspired by the ideals of Young Europe and the Polish struggle for independence would demand their right to a separate political existence did not appear to be one of Lelewel's immediate concerns. Perhaps there was an undercurrent of hope in the mind of the historian that, as in the past with respect to the assimilation of the Ukrainian elites, a similar process would take place naturally within the ranks of Ukrainian educated classes and subsequently, with the spread of universal literacy, embrace the masses as well. If this had been the case with respect to the Ukrainian upper classes under very different political and social circumstances in the distant past, could the course of assimilation also absorb the majority of the inhabitants in modern times? Would efforts in this direction be consonant with the ideals of democracy and national freedom that Lelewel so fervently preached and as the leader of Young Poland had the obligation to promote? Lelewel and most of his educated countrymen may have placed this question on the back burner because of a conviction consciously or unconsciously perpetuated among the elites of the ruling nations, especially by individuals still under the influence of the rationalistic thought of the Enlightenment, that an underdeveloped nationality would greatly benefit from an assimilation that would bring it into the bosom of a culturally and politically more advanced nation.[22] This, it was believed, constituted a natural process and therefore was consistent with the march of human progress.

A number of other documents intended for the popularization of Young Poland's program among the émigrés and among the politically active intelligentsia at home were soon to receive broad circulation as well. Among these was a Wyznanie wiary Młodej Polski (A declaration of faith of Young Poland) modelled closely on Mazzini's Instructions for Young Italy of 1831. If there were departures from the Italian document, they represented mainly differences in emphasis prompted by the changes in the political climate of the day, to wit, the waning of hope for the anticipated popular upheavals in Western Europe. Great stress was placed in the declaration on the attainment of Poland's independence, with the question of extending assistance to other nationalities relegated into the background.[23] On this account the document drew criticism from the more orthodox members of the organization residing in Switzerland. Wojciech Darasz may have been expressing both Mazzini's and Stolzman's point of view when he criticized the document for devaluing "the ideal of the solidarity of the nationalities."[24] If Lelewel chose to act independently of his compatriots in Switzerland, it was largely because he suspected Stolzman of leaning a bit too much towards the organization's international commitments. Lelewel did not ignore this commitment completely, but he viewed the question of international obligations towards the non-Poles primarily as an ancillary factor in the quest of Poland's fight for freedom. Furthermore, he knew that his collaborators in the secret advisory council supported Zaliwski's opinion that at present all efforts ought to be concentrated on the home front in defending the interests of Poland.

A second version of the declaration attempted to clarify the meaning of "the Polish people," a designation frequently used in the printed propaganda materials of the day. It explained that the Polish people were "all true sons of the Fatherland," i.e., all the inhabitants of historical lands of Poland, irrespective of what religion they professed, what language they spoke, or whether they considered themselves Poles, Lithuanian, or Ruthenians. In other words, in the sphere of nationality, the non-Polish inhabitants were considered Polish people and thus promised the enjoyment of equal rights. This pledge of equality was reinforced by assurances that Young Poland stood for the eradication of all class privileges. In order to achieve this aim, it was necessary to bring together all "righteous and enlightened sons of the Fatherland," so that they could disseminate ideas of equality and freedom among the "most numerous class," that is, the rural inhabitants. Every young Pole was expected to solemnly promise to show his readiness to sacrifice his property for the welfare of the majority and to actively participate in the dissemination of the ideals of Young Poland among the masses.[25]

Another appeal written in the name of Young Poland and addressed to brothers at home (Młoda Polska do braci swych w Polszcze) was authored most likely by Konarski, because it contained echoes of the radical views he frequently expressed in his editorials and articles in Północ, a journal, as already noted, he edited in Paris with Jan Czyński. It differed from the documents penned or edited by the much more cautious hand of Lelewel, by squarely placing the blame for all of Poland's misfortunes not only on the shoulders of the aristocrats – the principal culprits from the point of view of even moderate Poles – but also on the bulk of the less prosperous but far more numerous gentry. Every Polish defeat in the recent past, the appeal claimed, was due to the total indifference towards Polish national aspirations of the poverty-stricken peasantry, and this was the consequence of the fact that the gentry never sincerely wished to extend freedom and equality to the common people. It was of the utmost importance, therefore, to gain the confidence of the masses because – borrowing an idea from Mazzini's *Instructions for Young Italy* with which Konarski was well acquainted – there was no military force that could equal the might of the people under arms.[26]

What would be the reaction to this declaration among members of the Polish gentry who were expected to play the key role in the preparatory stage of the forthcoming revolution? In principle, on social issues Lelewel most likely agreed with many ideas held by Konarski, but for tactical reasons he preferred to exercise prudence and caution by not antagonizing both the Polish aristocrats and gentry.

Young Europe's Emissaries in Action

Even though Lelewel did not consider it necessary to consult with Stolzman in Switzerland on such issues as the content of appeals and other materials intended for propaganda purposes, both leading figures of Young Poland thought it proper to coordinate their efforts on the important question of selection of emissaries to be sent to the territories of the former Polish Commonwealth. Because of the strict rules of secrecy applied to all clandestine operations, the first envoy of the organization has not been identified, even though circumstantial evidence and future developments lead us to believe that it was either Seweryn Goszczyński or Lesław Łukaszewicz. A local branch acquainted with the program of Young Poland was already in the process of formation when the first documented emissary, Tadeusz Żabicki, arrived in the free city of Cracow in March 1835.[27]

In contrast to the secrecy surrounding the first emissary, there is a great deal of documentation about Żabicki's mission, yet ironically not due to the agent's organizational skills and accomplishments but because of his bad luck. Shortly after fulfilling his mission, which consisted mainly of delivering Young Poland's charter and Lelewel's appeals into the hands of Teofil Januszewicz, the organization's main contact in Cracow, Żabicki's identity was uncovered by the police. He was promptly arrested and, as a subject of Congress Kingdom, handed over to the Russian authorities in Warsaw. The interrogations that followed forced some general information about the activities of the underground out of the hapless emissary, but his knowledge about the conspiratorial world both at home and abroad was limited. Neither Stolzman nor Lelewel with whose knowledge and approval he was sent on the mission had confidence in the emissary's conspiratorial talents, even though he had been one of the original members of Young Poland and, at the same time, Lelewel's close relative. Both leaders of Young Poland, it seems, simply wanted to take advantage of Żabicki's personal wish to visit his family at home. In a letter written to Januszewicz, Lelewel prudently warned not to involve Żabicki in matters of major importance.[28] Thanks to this precautionary note, the only serious political consequence of Żabicki's arrest for the Cracow conspirators was the fact that information about his trial was sent from Warsaw to A.D. Guriev, the imperial governor general of Kyiv. In this manner the Russian authorities were made aware of the possibility of the resumption of Polish revolutionary activity months before Young Poland began to spread its wings over Belarus, Lithuania, and Ukraine.[29] The possibility of another Polish revolt must have appeared to the lethargic bureaucrats in Kyiv so unrealistic that the governor general did not deem it necessary to order any precautionary measures, which could have easily nipped the emerging conspiracy in the bud. This oversight would later have serious consequences for the careers of the imperial officials in Kyiv, when the full scope of the conspiratorial work of Young Poland was uncovered three years later.[30]

The designated emissary on whose shoulders the task of organizing and overseeing the preparatory work for the future revolution rested was Lelewel's and Mazzini's trusted soldier-conspirator Szymon Konarski. This selection may have been suggested by Mazzini, whose close ties of friendship with the Polish revolutionary dated back to the days of the Savoy campaign. The cautious Lelewel was a bit wary of Konarski's youth and lack of restraint in voicing his radical opinions on social and economic issues, but he endorsed the candidacy on account of the young man's conspiratorial talents and deep commitment to the cause. Konarski's charisma, unbridled energy and exceptional organizational skills, his infectious youthful charm and extraordinary courage overshadowed his shortcomings in the sphere of political foresight and diplomatic discretion. Furthermore, not too many members of the organization were ready to undertake this highly dangerous mission so soon after the debacle of the Zaliwski campaign. To both Mazzini and Lelewel the young man appeared to be the very embodiment of an ideal emissary-conspirator of Young Europe.

Before his departure, Konarski received instructions from Lelewel, which were prepared in consultation with Young Europe's headquarters in Switzerland and with the advice of his secret council. First, the emissary was to consolidate all Polish underground cells into a single organization whose authority would encompass the entire territory of pre-partitioned Poland. This undertaking was considered necessary in order to set up a more effective network of conspiratorial units pursuing Poland's all-encompassing national aims outlined in Young Poland's program. Simultaneously, this underground activity was to be expanded into the neighbouring lands inhabited by the Slavic peoples of East Central Europe. Second, the instructions stressed the importance of appropriate propaganda work among the rural masses, so that they too could become active participants in the forthcoming upheaval. This work was to be accomplished through the efforts of enlightened members of the gentry and clergy. Third, weapons were to be collected and stored in preparation of the forthcoming uprising. Last, Konarski was expected to assess the income of local property owners for purposes of taxation so that funds could be collected for the needs of the revolution.[31]

The unification of all clandestine groups into a single organization would mean in practice the severance of ties of all patriotically inspired underground cells still connected to the Carbonari centre in Paris. The question of international cooperation in the planned revolution was touched upon, but it seems to have been limited only to the Slavic peoples, in particular the Czechs, Slovaks, and Ukrainians. The stress on the necessity to gain the confidence of the rural population meant that the landlords would have to be willing to give up at least part of their property and that the cultural and religious rights of the non-Polish population would be treated with respect.

Together with the instructions, Konarski also received copies of Lelewel's appeals addressed to the Lithuanians and the inhabitants of the Ukrainian provinces of Volynia and Podolia. They were written in spirit similar to that of the historian's appeals to the inhabitants of Galicia but contained explicit calls to revolutionary action. The Lithuanians were reminded of their past support for the Polish cause and urged to show their readiness to sacrifice their lives for the fatherland. In the appeal designated for the provinces of Volynia and Podolia, the need for intensive propaganda work among the predominantly Ukrainian population in the countryside was stressed.[32] This emphasis on the work among the masses would be later repeated in a number of proclamations that were to follow. It figured prominently in one addressed specifically to women of gentry background. The ladies were exhorted to turn their attention to the needs of the country people so that through their compassionate maternal care they could gain the peasants' confidence. It was stressed that this type of activity could be of vital importance in convincing the rural inhabitants that "a Pole fighting for freedom and independence will not deny freedom to his poorer brethren."[33]

In the months preceding Konarski's arrival at the end of July 1835, the members of the Cracow headquarters of Young Poland were already involved in the work of bringing to life the local branch of Young Poland by shaping the formal aspects of the organizational structure. Besides Januszewicz, into whose hands Young Poland's program was entrusted, especially active in this endeavour were his two closest assistants: Seweryn Goszczyński, a popular poet with a strong Ukrainophile bent, and Lesław Łukaszewicz, a specialist in legal studies and the editor of a journal on Slavic literatures, a position that provided him with an excellent opportunity to establish contacts with the emerging Czech, Slovak, and Ukrainian national awakeners. Both were actively involved in the November insurgency, had spent some time in emigration, and thus had ties with prominent individuals among the Polish émigrés.

Lesław Łukaszewicz: An "Apostle" of Young Poland among the Czechs, Slovaks, and Galician Ruthenians

Lesław Łukaszewicz was a political activist of many talents: like Mazzini, he was a conspirator with seemingly inexhaustible energy and imagination, as well as an indefatigable master in the art of persuasion. While working on Young Poland's charter for the home territories, recruiting members to the new organization among the youth in the city of Cracow, corresponding with Mickiewicz and Bohdan Zaleski regarding a new work about the Czech fifteenth-century national hero Jan Žižka, and editing a journal on Slavic literatures and cultures under the title *Powszechny Pamiętnik Nauk i Umiejcnosti*, the Polish revolutionary found time to maintain close ties, through correspondence and clandestine meetings, with his Czech, Slovak, and Ukrainian national awakeners with whom he shared both literary and political interests.[34]

The world of Slavic cultures and Slavic reciprocity was opened to Łukaszewicz at an early age in Buchach, a small town in the eastern part of Galicia, by N. Hamorak, a Ukrainian classmate in the local gymnasium. He continued to keep in touch with his Ukrainian colleague after he left the town to pursue a legal career, and after Hamorak went to Vienna to begin his theological studies at a Greek Catholic seminary in the Austrian capital. A number years later, it was through Hamorak that Łukaszewicz established direct contacts with Czech national awakeners František Cyril Kampelík and Karel Slavoj Amerling, among others.[35] Only a few documentary sources regarding these first inter-Slavic political encounters have been preserved, but on the basis of correspondence, memoir literature, and police records, sufficient material has been compiled by

Figure 3.1. Michal Miloslav Hodža. Courtesy of Wikimedia.

Figure 3.2. Jozef Miloslav Hurban. *Slovensko v obrazkoch: Historia.* Juliana
Krebesová, ed. (Martin: Vydavatelstvo Osveta, 1990).

Figure 3.3. Ľudovit Štúr. *Slovensko v obrazkoch: Historia.* Juliana Krebesová, ed. (Martin: Vydavatelstvo Osveta, 1990).

students of this period to present a fairly good description of the emerging political underground in East Central Europe during the 1830s.[36]

Three letters written by Łukaszewicz to František Cyril Kampelík on 1 February, 8 May, and 22 May, and preserved among Kampelík's papers in the Literary Archive in Prague,[37] serve as a good example of these not numerous but rich in content sources. The correspondence was taking place precisely at a time when the formation of Young Poland's branch in Cracow was being brought to completion in anticipation of the arrival of Young Europe's most important emissary to the home territories, Szymon Konarski. The letters convey the earnestness and zeal with which Polish activists of Young Poland were prodding their Slavic brothers (the appellation "brother" was the most common address in the correspondence of the Slavic national awakeners) to become involved in an all-embracing revolutionary cause against the existing autocratic regimes in Europe. At the same time, they show how closely political and literary matters were intertwined in those days. Lastly, they reveal with unmistakable clarity that more than just literary reciprocity was on the mind of the members of the youthful Slavic intelligentsia when they held their first official meeting in August of 1834, that is, only a few months after the founding of Young Europe.

In all three letters Łukaszewicz makes numerous allusions to a secret meeting that had taken place in August 1834 in Brno, a centrally located city in the primarily Czech-inhabited Austrian province of Moravia. Besides Łukaszewicz and Kampelík, the meeting was attended by Czech and Slovak cultural activists in most cases tied to one another through their studies at the University of Vienna. The meeting was initiated and hosted by Kampelík, a former theology student both at Brno and at a Lutheran seminary in Bratislava (then known as Possony, Prešpork, or Pressburg) and subsequently a student of medicine in Vienna. From the beginning of his student days, Kampelík's interests centred on Slavic literatures and cultures as well as on the political ideas of equality and freedom. At least one of the attendees of the secret conclave, the promising Slovak writer Samo Chalupka, had participated three years earlier as a volunteer in the Polish November insurrection. His relations with Polish and Ukrainian students in Vienna had been most cordial during his student years. Among the other Czechs present, Václav Svatopluk Štulc aided the Polish rebels as they were fleeing to France in 1831–2 and was so moved by their heroism that he promptly began to study the Polish language in earnest.[38] All of the participants were familiar with and to no small degree inspired by the Polish struggle for independence.

In all three letters Łukaszewicz makes cryptic references to solemn pledges made by those attending the gathering during an excursion to a mountain in the vicinity of Brno which he calls at times Myslivska hora (Hunter's hill) or as a hilltop bearing the name of Perun, the Slavic pagan god of thunder.[39] These pledges involved a promise that all would work closely together until national freedom for all Slavic peoples was attained. According to the projections suggested by the Czechs and Slovaks, at least ten years of preparatory work would be required to accomplish this objective. For Łukaszewicz and his Polish co-conspirators in Cracow, according to the letter, this time span was much too long. The work had to be speeded up, the Polish conspirator repeatedly stressed.

Łukaszewicz made very few references to names, but from other sources it has become known that in addition to the four names already mentioned, among the Czech participants were Karel Slavoj Amerling and Jan Oheral. The Slovak contingent was represented by a brilliant law student, Aleksander Boleslavín Vrchovský, and his and Chalupka's colleagues from Vienna, Adam Špaček and Jaroslav Matúška.[40] In the following years, all present would become directly involved in activities that reflected the aims pursued by Young Europe, even though the Czech national awakeners never adopted a name for their group, while their Slovak colleagues officially called their underground cell Vzájomnosť (Reciprocity). At the end of the Brno conclave it was agreed that the conspirators would meet periodically in order to coordinate their activities. The next meeting was scheduled for 25 June 1835 in Trenčín, a resort town in northwestern Slovakia, then part of the Habsburg-ruled Kingdom of Hungary.

Because of a much tighter police vigilance in Cracow in 1835, Łukaszewicz informed Kampelík in the first letter that it would be impossible for him to attend the June meeting in Trenčín. He explained that while in 1834 [a Pole] still could arrange trips to Brno or Vienna on a false passport,[41] such risky undertaking would be too dangerous in 1835. He added, however, that perhaps a Ruthenian[42] would be able to come.

The Polish conspirator was eager to report that he had become well acquainted with the situation in the eastern part of Galicia, because he had visited Czerwona Rus' (Red Ruthenia)[43] a few months earlier. He was overjoyed that the situation there appeared to be much more promising than he had anticipated and found it most encouraging that the Greek Catholics were considering the possibility of adopting the Latin alphabet (instead of the Cyrillic script then in use), implying that, if implemented, the reform would bring the Ukrainian inhabitants in the eastern part of the province closer to their Polish neighbours as well as to other western Slavs.

The main purpose of the correspondence, however, was not to provide information about the most recent developments in Cracow and political and cultural conditions in the province of Galicia but to persuade the Czechs and Slovaks to change the location of the scheduled meeting from Trenčín to Cracow. If that would not prove possible, Łukaszewicz insisted on seeing at least Kampelík before the end of July. Selection of this time period may have been connected with Konarski's anticipated arrival and ceremonies involving the formal establishment of a local branch of Young Poland. "Do whatever you wish, but you must be here no later than the end of July. If you do not come, you will bring upon yourself the harshest form of condemnation not only by me but by all the generations to come. This is a very important moment for me." The first letter ends with this strong, earnest plea as well as with a playful comradely warning: "I entreat you in the name of everything [we hold] sacred to respond as soon as possible because otherwise you'll become the target of Perun's deadly thunderbolts." This threat was followed by expressions of deep friendship and brotherly love.[44]

In his response the Czech correspondent wrote (Kampelík's letters have not been preserved, but the gist of their content can be reconstructed from the details of Łukasewicz's subsequent letters) that because of a journey he had already arranged with Amerling for the summer to visit the national awakeners among the Southern Slavs, his trip to Cracow would not be possible. Łukaszewicz expressed deep disappointment but refused to give in. In fact, he continued to stress even with greater urgency the importance of the meeting in Cracow, especially now that he had learnt of Amerling's and Kampelík's plans to visit their South Slavic brothers: "I entreat you in the name of the most holy *Slávy dcéra*[45] to come without delay.... Otherwise you will never be forgiven.... Your refusal would remain on your conscience forever.... If you love me, you will respond immediately upon the receipt of this letter. I beg you to show me this act of courtesy. I always keep my word, and you must do the same, because without reciprocity life would not be possible."[46]

These earnest entreaties and comradely, playful cajoling could not but elicit a positive answer from a reluctant but obviously intrigued Kampelík. We can assume this because after he received Kampelík's reply, Łukaszewicz was so certain of his colleague's arrival that in the letter that followed on 22 May he enclosed twenty zlotys to cover the expenses for the journey. Just in case Kampelík was not as yet fully committed to undertake the journey, Łukaszewicz once again stressed the importance of their seeing each other in the Polish city:

I fervently entreat you to come to Cracow as soon as possible in order to complete an undertaking that later would not be possible to bring to realization. My friends and I have been working in earnest. We fervently desire that the task on which the welfare of Slavdom depends could be completed. Your [planned] trip [to the southern Slavs] this year would be of little value if first you would not meet with me. I assure you that this is not a mere whim or a child's game but a well thought out and thoroughly prepared plan. If you sincerely have the cause of humanity in mind, then come as soon as you can ... because it is important that you come here first before you go there [to meet the southern Slavs].

Regarding the question of primary concern, Łukaszewicz once again cryptically referred to the issues raised on Perun's mountain in August of the previous year. The meeting in Cracow would be imperative for the realization of plans discussed at that time. *"Today* or *never!* [emphasis in the original.] You must see me." The Polish conspirator explained that because of delay or neglect, the ten years spoken of earlier could turn into twenty or thirty, or perhaps everything would be lost forever. The entire cause could suffer, and "the ideas that we have talked about on Perun Mountain would be blown away by the wind forever. They would die for all times to come, and the past would come back again." At the end, once more in a playful jest but not without a touch of seriousness, the impatient Polish conspirator warned Kampelík that if he failed to keep his promise, the most dreadful punishment would come crashing upon him from above. At the end, Łukaszewicz pleaded once again: "Cyril! For the last time I entreat you, do not deny me this favour.... I am waiting for you every day. Every hour." After reading these passionate pleas, Kampelík had little choice but to comply. He postponed his and Amerling's visit to the southern Slavs and began preparations for what for him too could prove to be a perilous journey to a Polish city under strict police control.

In addition to political issues, a good deal of space in the letters was devoted to matters of literary nature, an area of singular interest to Kampelík and Amerling. What is of interest, however, is the fact that among the more important literary works highlighted, all could be directly or indirectly linked to political concerns. In the first letter Łukaszewicz discussed his contacts with the Polish émigré writers Adam Mickiewicz and Bohdan Zaleski regarding the preparation of a work on the Czech heroic figure of the Hussite wars during the fifteenth century, Jan Žižka (referred to in the letter as Jan from Trocznov). In the second letter Łukaszewicz elatedly reported that the work on Žižka had reached the final stages of preparation and should soon be in his possession. Kampelík's family, incidentally, traced its roots to one of Žižka's followers, and thus it is most likely that Kampelík provided Łukaszewicz with the source materials on the fifteenth-century Czech revolutionary leader. What would have been more inspirational for the Czech political conspirators than a work by a well-known contemporary writer about one of their national heroes?[47]

Another work singled out by Łukaszewicz was the second edition of *Marya*, a novel on a Ukrainian subject by Antoni Malczewski, one of the first works in Polish literature to focus on the lives of the common people. Such literary works, Łukaszewicz noted, were essential to bridge the gap between the gentry and the peasantry in Galicia. In return for Mickiewicz's national epic *Dziady* (The forefathers), which he promised to send to his Czech colleagues, Łukaszewicz requested new works by Czech and Slovak contemporary writers. These and other literary writings, especially new works by Ján Kollár, he promised to translate and publish without delay in the journal he edited.

Promotion of Slavic studies and literary reciprocity had been of great interest to Czech and Slovak scholars in the preceding decades, but among the older generation of national awakeners, few felt prepared to openly challenge the authorities. It was in the mid-1830s that cultural endeavour was openly used as a means to another end: a resource for drawing the Slavic intelligentsia closer together with a political objective as the ultimate aim.

As noted earlier, Łukaszewicz invited Kampelík to Cracow at a time when, together with his fellow conspirators, Januszewicz and Goszczyński, he was immersed in work on the construction of a home-based branch of Young Poland. In view of the organization's international affiliation, any reference to Young Europe would have immediately aroused suspicion in the capitals of the partitioning powers. By then it was well known that Metternich considered Mazzini the chief enemy of the status quo in Europe. Membership in a political group tied to Young Europe would have been considered by the authorities in Vienna, Berlin, and St Petersburg as an act of treason punishable by death.[48] For that reason, an innocuous sounding name, Stowarzyszenie Ludu Polskiego (Association of the Polish people) was selected to serve as a cover name for Young Poland, both in the Austrian and Russian Empires, but the fundamental principles on which the association's charter was based conformed to those espoused by Young Poland. Of this fact Januszewicz assured Lelewel in a letter written in mid-April 1835: "We share fully your principles ... even earlier [i.e., before Żabicki brought Young Poland's Charter to Cracow] our activities have been guided by them. The organization will use caution and vigilance in order to assure safety and peace of mind."[49]

On account of the critical need for vigilance, a good number of the association's rank-and-file were not aware of the organization's émigré connection or international affiliation, and in popular literature the association's activities became known as Konarszczyzna (the Konarski movement), especially in territories controlled by Russia. Partly because of the requirements of secrecy and partly because of a common tendency of local historians to emphasize indigenous roots and local initiatives, Young Europe's influence has been consistently minimized or sometimes completely ignored in works on the association, as well as similar political organizations inspired by Young Europe's political program.[50] In this study the two names, Young Poland and the Association of the Polish People, or just association, will be used interchangeably.

A "Geological Expedition" to Brno and the Political Awakening of Two Nations

As already noted, the secret Brno meeting in August 1834 was not the first encounter between the Polish conspirators and the members of the Czech and Slovak intelligentsia. In fact, the Brno participants differed from the majority of their educated contemporaries by the fact that most of them had been either inspired by the Polish patriots as they were passing through Slovak and Czech lands after the November uprising in 1831 or had met the uprising's sympathizers at the various institutions of higher learning in Vienna. Even though, as in the case of Kampelík, they continued to pay homage to the renowned bard of Slavdom, Ján Kollár, for his literary accomplishments, after 1831 all had moved beyond the confines of purely cultural pursuits.

The organizer and coordinator of the Brno meeting, Kampelík, came from a family of very modest means. Partly because of serious pecuniary problems – as a young man he was forced to interrupt his studies twice because of a dire need of funds – and partly because of his dedication to clandestine political work, his student years spanned almost two decades. He began as a student in the Lutheran theological seminaries in Brno and Bratislava, then for a brief time moved to Prague, and finally ended his student days in Vienna, where he earned a medical degree in 1843 at the ripe age of thirty-eight! It would be difficult to imagine that one could have survived such a lengthy student career without being surrounded by devoted colleagues and supportive acquaintances, and with both Kampelík was blessed from his first years in Brno. Among his intimate associates we find predominantly, even though not exclusively, young men and women of Slavic background – Czechs, Slovaks, Ukrainians, and Poles – and in later years he had contacts with practically every important figure tied in one way or another to the Slavic national renaissance.[51] The Czech activist kept in touch with them through travels and correspondence, deriving from both enormous pleasure and personal satisfaction, as one of his letters testifies: "It is my habit to visit by means of correspondence sincere souls, passionate Slavs, so that friends acquainted with one another could form an association and in this manner through deeper knowledge of each other establish a tighter union."[52] Kampelík's early mentor and in later years close friend from Vienna, the Polonophile lawyer Josef Dvoráček, sketched the Czech activist as "a zealous youth with deep commitment to the propagation of native history and patriotic books."[53]

A lifelong interest in Slavic languages and cultures was awakened in Kampelík in his youth during the time he studied in the Lutheran theological seminary in Bratislava, for even when he later pursued other objectives in earnest, one of his favourite pastimes during the summer months continued to include travels through the Slovak countryside and an occasional visit to Ján Kollár in Budapest.[54] The young student must have made a strong impression on the author of *Slávy dcéra*, for Kollár devoted a few lines in that celebrated poem to Kampelík. His early acquaintances in Bratislava were students at the Lutheran Lyceum, where it was customary to be a member of a study group known as Spoločnosť Česko-Slovanska (The Czekho-Slavic society, referred to from now on as Spoločnosť). Under the guidance of its conscientious, law-abiding Lutheran pastors, this group was preoccupied almost exclusively with reading and memorizing verses from Kollár's *Slávy dcéra* as well as conducting discussions about the wonders of linguistic and cultural affinities among the Slavs. The students and their mentors adhered scrupulously to the apolitical course advocated by Kollár, for whom strict loyalty to the European political order was the abiding rule.

Next to Kampelík, the best-known figure among the Brno attendees was the future Slovak poet Samo Chalupka, who, as already noted, participated as a volunteer in the Polish November insurgency. Before his actual involvement in combat, this young seminarian underwent a period of military training in eastern Galicia, in the course of which he befriended a number of Polish patriots as well as their Ukrainian sympathizers. His fascination with Polish literature and Ukrainian ballads lasted throughout his lifetime. Even more than fifty years after the Polish uprising, the ageing Slovak bard was fond of reminiscing about those unforgettable days of his youth, especially while conversing with young students who periodically came to pay their respects to the celebrated poet.[55] That it had been his favourite topic of discussion in his youth with his trusted friends goes without saying. Furthermore, as will be shown later, Chalupka, as well as his fellow Slovak countrymen Jaroslav Matúška and Aleksander Vrchovský, maintained close ties with a student circle of Polish patriots in Vienna as well as with Ukrainian students in the Greek Catholic seminary and the medical college.

With respect to Czech interaction with Polish conspirators, émigré emissaries had begun visiting Prague and Vienna, as well as other cultural centres in central Europe, almost immediately after the founding of Young Europe. Names of trusted individuals were supplied to members of Young Europe by František Zoch, a Czech participant in the Polish November revolution who, together with his comrades-in-arms, fled to France, where he joined the ranks of Young Poland. The immediate concern of these secret emissaries involved the establishment of reliable channels of communication to transmit underground literature for revolutionaries active in the territories of both imperial realms. Kampelík and Amerling were drawn into the political underground by Polish political activists tied to Young Europe.[56]

During the initial stages of the process of politization of the Slovak intelligentsia, Samo Chalupka's role was undoubtedly of primary significance, but the pivotal figure in the transformation of the purely cultural national awakening initiated by the works of Ján Kollár into a political movement was Alexander Vrchovský. Just as Chalupka and the other participants of the Brno meeting, Vrchovský was drawn into the sphere of revolutionary politics by a group of Polish patriots pursuing their studies in Vienna. In a brief biographical sketch, with unusual candour and uninhibited sincerity, Vrchovský describes his metamorphosis from a self-absorbed, apolitical, ambitious young man interested in little else than the attainment of a successful legal career, into a nationally conscious patriot committed wholeheartedly to the service of his downtrodden Slovak nation.[57] His experience undoubtedly mirrored the lives of many talented individuals of the emerging Slavic intelligentsia gathered in the Austrian capital during the 1830s.

Discriminatory practices against the Slovaks in his native land, even in elementary schools, contributed to the fact that, upon arriving in Vienna in the early 1830s, Vrchovský immediately plunged into his legal studies and, in order to assure success in his future profession, he worked diligently on perfecting his German, while also acquiring a good grasp of French, Italian, English, and Latin, while completely neglecting his native Slovak tongue. This single-minded pursuit of a career continued until he met a group of students he refers to as the "Viennese Slavans." It was under the influence of these young men that for the first time he became interested in Slavic studies. At the beginning, both Chalupka and Matúška, as well as Ukrainian theologians, among them Anton Dobriansky, were helpful in acquainting Vrchovský with the world of Slavdom, but most influential of these "Viennese Slavans" proved to be a group of patriotically inspired Poles. Vrchovský singles out "an outstanding young fellow" by the name of Zajączkowski who in the course of lengthy conversations unravelled before him in vivid colours the sad fate of the Polish nation and painted with passion a panorama of heroic deeds performed by Polish revolutionaries in their struggle to regain Poland's independence. During these meetings Zajączkowski often spoke of the obligation of educated men towards the common people who, in his view, represented the foundations of the nation. Thus, acknowledges Vrchovský, it was through a Polish patriot that he became a nationally conscious Slovak. and it was through conversations with his new acquaintances that he acquired a sense of human dignity, thus echoing Mickiewicz's belief that a man without a national consciousness is not a fully developed human being. As their friendship solidified, Zajączkovski offered to give Vrchovský lessons in Polish and in this process acquainted him with works of the great Polish poets and historians. It was from Mickiewicz's "Oda do Młodosci" (Ode to youth) that Vrchovský was fond of quoting a popular revolutionary motto: "Gwałt niech sie gwaltem odciska!" (Force should be countered by force!, or in Slovak, "Moc at' se moci odtíska!"). After his spiritual rebirth, Vrchovský relates that there was "only one guiding star illuminating my path," and this star continued to be a guide to the end of his life.

Among the leading figures of the Polish group was Nikodem Bętkowski, well known among his contemporaries as a passionate rebel with radical views. When discussing revolutionary events – a subject often talked about within these circles – the Poles often spoke of the treachery of the nobles, warning their comrades not to trust them in the forthcoming upheaval: "Always remember that it was our nobles who were responsible for our defeat and be on guard not to be victims of a similar failure."[58] In late summer 1834, as already noted, Lesław Łukaszewicz paid a visit to Vienna in order to establish closer ties with this strategically located contact group for Young Europe's underground activities. Relations among the students of practically all Slavic backgrounds, except Russian, were maintained by means of correspondence, even after their studies in Vienna were completed or interrupted. This group of young men provided the circle of young Slovak and Czech students of Bratislava literary works in different Slavic languages as well as pamphlets with revolutionary content. While passing through Bratislava when returning home, Polish students frequently stopped in this small but charming city to provide advice and encouragement to the young Czechs and Slovaks as they were embarking on the path of their political awakening.

If indeed a ten-year period of preparatory work for the anticipated revolution was a reasonable estimate by the Czech participants at the Brno meeting, this certainly was not the belief held by Alexander Vrchovský. Otherwise it would be difficult to understand the extraordinary energy and enthusiasm with which he launched a campaign of political education at the opening of the academic year in 1834–5. The program that he prepared for the small group of Slovak and Czech students in neighbouring Bratislava could be viewed as nothing less than a plan to transform a cluster of apolitical, peace-abiding seminarians into a cohort of Mazzini's "apostles of the people," i.e., dedicated missionaries single-mindedly pursuing the task of awakening the national consciousness among the people and stirring them to political action.

In order to understand the magnitude of this task, it would be of interest to take a look at the young men who were Vrchovský's targets of attention. They consisted almost exclusively of students in the Lutheran Lyceum, where it was customary to become a member of a study group known since 1827 as Spoločnosť. The group was preoccupied mainly with reading and memorizing verses from Kollár's *Slávy dcera* and conducting discussions about the cultural affinities of the Slavs. Guided by their law-abiding mentors, in most instances admirers of the Lutheran pastor and poet Ján Kollár, the students scrupulously adhered to the apolitical course advocated by the author of *Slávy dcera*. For Kollár, strict loyalty to the European political order was considered a *sine qua non* for the maintenance of a safe ground for what he considered to be of primary importance: an unhindered cultural development and growth through mutual enrichment among the Slavs, with Russia as the pre-eminent member among them. His idea of *vzájomnosť* (reciprocity) among the linguistically and culturally related Slavic groups could be compared to "a quiet, innocent lamb, which would not be posing any danger to the existing political authorities because it would not be concerned with state boundaries, it would not question the dependence of the commoners on the feudal lords nor be bothered with any other similar political or social matter. He expected full subordination and loyalty to the authorities of his day."[59] In other words, Spoločnosť was conceived as a body of educated men focusing exclusively on cultural advancement of the Slavs through mutual contacts and cooperation. When Chalupka returned after his Polish venture to resume his studies in Bratislava in 1831, he attempted to turn the students' attention to political matters, but with practically no success. It was the support of his colleagues who attended the Brno conclave, in particular the energy and determination exerted by Vrchovský, that led to the radical transformation of the students' mentality in the mid-1830s.

Through Chalupka's good judgment and persuasive abilities, the Lutheran study group Spoločnosť acquired a highly talented secretary by the name of Ľudovít Štúr, a former theology student at the Bratislava Lutheran Lyceum, and thus well acquainted with the seminarians' abilities, inclinations, and shortcomings. In the years following the Brno meeting, with diligence and care, Štúr implemented Vrchovský's instructions delivered by a special courier from Vienna. With a lawyer's caution and foresight, Vrchovský did not deem it necessary – at the incipient stage of what he saw as the formative stage of a political organization – to formulate a written program with statutes and rules for the students to follow or even to change the name of the study group. The name Spoločnosť sounded as innocuous as Stowarzyszenie did to the Polish underground activists in Cracow. Through highly inspirational sermon-like epistles, Vrchovský worked out a plan of action by means of which he intended to transform the passive group of the Bratislava theology students into what he saw as a *"centrum gravitatis"* of young people, whose task would be to unite and lead the emerging Slovak intelligentsia towards a political and social emancipation of their nation.[60]

In his first letter-epistle Vrchovský appealed to the Slovak youth to turn their attention to the needs of the people, instead of concentrating their energy on perfecting their oratorical skills in the mother tongue. Not that he considered the native language unimportant, but he viewed this instrument of communication mainly as a means to an end rather than an end itself. From his perspective as a lawyer, he saw language merely as a tool through which one would be able to reach the masses in order to awaken their national consciousness. For this reason, the language used had to be the tongue spoken by the people, which they easily understood and comprehended. Otherwise the political ideas disseminated in the countryside would fall on deaf ears. He advised the seminarians to set aside the trivialities of their day-to-day existence and focus on the great ideas of the age, because humanity, "especially our nation [*národ náš*] is on the threshold of a great undertaking." Therefore the present was not the time for recreation and amusements but for serious work designed for the attainment of an objective "that in the future will bring happiness to millions."[61] He stressed that the Bratislava Spoločnosť must become a Slovak centre of learning, from which "the young people, the blossom of the nation," could draw that great life-sustaining force and living fire that could provide nourishment for the days to come, so that while working for the welfare of their nation, the young men would abandon their trivial personal concerns and derive satisfaction from what was truly great and important. Furthermore, the Bratislava Spoločnosť was to serve as a model for other Slovak centres of learning, which, in Vrchovský's estimation, were still leading a vegetative existence and therefore were in great need of transformation. Before this could take place, the members of Spoločnosť "must be inspired with the flame of pure fire kept burning by a profound love of one's nation and the light of heroic dedication."[62] The young men in Bratislava were exhorted to make every effort to get to know their people; they ought to make the masses aware of the wrongs committed against them by their oppressors; they must be persuaded to rid themselves of their old habit of "perpetual patience" instilled in them in centuries past by the clergy; lastly, no effort ought to be spared to prepare the masses for a struggle to bring down tyranny and oppression. The first letter ended with a passionate call to action: "Have we been created to be a nation of slaves? Have we been destined to writhe forever under the whips of our enemies? Force is to be resisted by force."[63]

To strengthen his arguments, Vrchovský occasionally referred in his letters to the courage and dedication of great heroes of ages past, such as the selflessness of the Gracchi brothers in Rome, the courage of Martin Luther in his struggle against the corrupt Church authorities, or the valour of the Irish hero O'Connell, reminding the Slovak and Czech students in Bratislava that they too possessed a power within them that could be awakened if they became conscious that they were the sons of their nation.[64]

While endeavouring to inspire young minds through passionate appeals for sacrifice on behalf of their nation, appeals echoing ideas found in the writings of Mazzini, Mickiewicz, and Konarski, as well as other activists connected with Young Europe, Vrchovský was also very specific in his instructions to the members of Spoločnosť:

1 They were to organize themselves into a number of scholarly groups in accordance with their individual aptitudes and talents. Every member was to choose a particular area of specialization, because only in this manner would the nation be able to acquire the needed specialists and not just dilettantes.
2 Religious segregation among the Slovaks was to come to an end with the Lutheran members of Spoločnosť inviting their brothers from the Catholic Academy in Bratislava for a joint action.
3 Special attention was to be given to young students in the lower grades in order to sow in their minds the seeds of national consciousness while the ground was still tender.
4 Study of other Slavic languages was to be pursued instead of an exclusive concentration on West European languages.[65]

Even though the letters do not make any direct calls to revolutions and revolts, the reference to the "great task facing our people" and the directive to focus one's attention on the idea "that will bring happiness to millions," together with a reminder of the duty to sacrifice one's life for the good of the nation, were nothing less than instructions for a systematic preparation for a national revolution, an idea that appears to have been central, as Łukaszewicz's correspondence with Kampelík has shown, in the discussions at the conference in Brno.

Under Vrchovský's continuous prodding and Ludovít Štúr's prompt execution of his Viennese mentor's instructions, within a year Spoločnosť doubled its membership by opening its doors to Catholic students and establishing contact with alumni of the lyceum, most of them Lutheran pastors officiating in various regions of the northern part of the Kingdom of Hungary. The diligent and very conscientious Štúr saw to it that the reading materials in the library were replenished with donations from members of the Viennese Slavic circle as well as from other sources. In order to formalize its status, Spoločnosť even acquired an official seal.[66]

When Štúr assumed full leadership of the organization a year later, his inaugural speech mirrored the ideas he imbibed from the letters of his Viennese mentor, perhaps at times even surpassing Vrchovský in patriotic fervour. For example, in one of his speeches he reminded the students, "The spirit of their awakened nation was calling upon every educated Slovak to ... defend the national honour in face of those who were attempting to trample the nation's heritage and political existence," or when he spoke of the "unifying force of the voices of their forefathers, living brothers and of the generations yet to come" – voices that had the power to solidify them into a formidable rampart of their nation.[67] The content of this speech shows that Štúr was familiar with the revolutionary literature drawn from the book deposits of Young Europe. But for the emotional content of his awakened patriotism he was first of all indebted to his charismatic mentor from Vienna. Vrchovský, according to reminiscences of those who were acquainted with him, was an extraordinary individual, even if we take into account the fact that the following description by an admiring contemporary may have been written with some exaggeration. Jozef Miloslav Hurban, a young seminarian in Bratislava, remembered Vrchovský during those days as a "beautiful youth, rather short in stature, with bright azure eyes, brown curly hair, round countenance, immaculate complexion of milk and roses, spellbinding eloquence, and a personality full of inspirational thought. This fairy tale–like radiant figure entered the circle of young men in Bratislava in the second half of the 1830s, leaving an enduring imprint on the generations to come."[68] Štúr fell under Vrchovský's spell, as many of his contemporaries did, and continued to hold his mentor in high esteem, even when their paths parted on the question of tactics a few years later. Contrary to a widely held belief, Štúr's letters and speeches clearly testify that he became captivated by the spirit of Mazzinian nationalism before his departure to study at the University of Halle. The young leader of Spoločnosť expressed his admiration for his mentor, the Slovak pioneer in modern political thought in a touching, lyrical poem:

> Who is it praying under that splendid linden tree?
> Whose eagle eye is fixed on it so intensely?
> His gaze filled with longing, ruffles the leaves gently
> Their kisses carried by the wind are touching his heart.
> Oh wind, just keep on swaying that linden tree honoured by Slavín
> Look, there kneeling under it is our brother, Boleslavín.[69]

National consciousness among the Slovak students and political activists in Spoločnosť was augmented by readings from the works of Ján Hollý, a learned, multilingual Catholic priest and a brilliant writer from northern Slovakia. Especially influential were Hollý's poems "Svatopluk" (1833) and "Cyrilo-Metodiada" (1935), heroic national epics about the early Slavs and the medieval Slovak Kingdom of Moravia. These works were rapidly replacing Kollár's *Slávy dcera* as the most popular reading material among the politically awakened young men in Bratislava. It was under the influence of these works that in 1836 a group of students from that city made a pilgrimage to the ruins of the nearby fortress of Devín, the seat of the medieval Slavic Kingdom of Morava celebrated for its greatness and glory in Hollý's works. His patriotic verses declaring that it was "better to choose glorious death and heroic suffering ... Rather than bewail the lost freedom under the yoke of slavery"[70] were loaded with political meaning for the present. During this emotionally charged event, the younger members of Spoločnosť who had not yet adopted medieval Slavic names like Boleslavín, Svatopluk, Miloslav, or Cyril, ceremoniously accepted them as their middle names. This practice spread to other Slavic lands, acquiring great popularity, especially among Ukrainian national awakeners in Galicia.[71]

Jan Béder and Vladimír Matula, two historians who devoted the lion's share of their scholarly endeavours to the study of archival documents on the national awakening of the Slovak people, accentuate the central role of Vrchovský, stress the importance of Kampelík and Chalupka, and present the Brno meeting as the pivotal event in the national awakening of both the Czech and Slovak nations. Both authors emphasize the significance of the Polish connection: the heightened patriotism of young Poles generated by the events connected with the November uprising. Jan Béder sums it up with great precision in one of his essays:

The new era of Spoločnosť begins with the academic year 1834/35. Spoločnosť came under the reinvigorating influence of Boleslavín

Vrchovský [Boleslavín was Aleksander Vrchovský's adopted Slavic name], Samo Chalupka, and Cyril Kampelík, who were members of a larger group of motivated patriots tied to the Polish revolutionary movement. Spoločnosť in Bratislava became the object of their interest after the meeting in Brno in 1834. Under Kampelík's leadership and with the participation of a Polish delegate from a secret association in Cracow [Łukaszewicz] negotiations were conducted among Czech, Moravian, and Slovak patriots regarding cooperation and exchange of literature. Through Spoločnosť they wished to link Bratislava with the network of the already existing [underground] centres: Praha, Lvov, Pest, Brno.[72]

Béder's penetrating insight regarding the importance of the Brno meeting is truly remarkable, especially because it appears that he did not have at his disposal the correspondence between Łukaszewicz and Kampelík. Had he had a chance to examine the content of Łukaszewicz's letters, he would have put even greater emphasis on the political issues discussed at the meeting, in particular the different estimates regarding the time needed for the preparatory stage of the anticipated revolution. The Poles felt very strongly that the ten-year period suggested by their hosts was far too long. Jan Béder also does not seem to have been aware that the secret Polish organization that Łukaszewicz represented was tied directly to Young Poland. The author, however, knew that the relationship was close and that through this link both the Czech and Slovak patriotic groups that emerged in the mid-1830s were part of the Young European movement. It is for this reason that in his works on this subject he consistently refers to Spoločnosť and its subsequent conspiratorial offshoot, Vzájomnosť, as Mladé Slovensko (Young Slovakia). On the basis of his research, it was clear that the guiding ideas and the founding principles of both organizations were rooted in the program of Young Europe.

In his meticulously researched articles, Béder does not pretend to be original. He acknowledges that he is not the first to use the designation "Mladé Slovensko" (Young Slovakia) when referring to the generation of Slovak national awakeners of the 1830s and 1840s, pointing out that there have been references to "Young Slovaks" or representatives of "Young Slovakia" in works of literary scholars during the interwar period, adding that these references were made not only to designate a break between the older and the younger generation, but also to point out the ideological links between the Slavic peoples and the quest for freedom that exploded in Europe with the Revolution in Paris in July 1830. The Slovak historian cites the literary scholar Štefan Krčméry, who in 1936 wrote about the links between Young Europe and the Slovak,

Czech, Polish, and Ukrainian student groups in Bratislava, Prague, and Lviv and notes that Krčméry's contemporary, Milan Pišút, expressed a similar opinion.[73]

All sources are in full agreement that it was through the agents of Stowarzyszenie Ludu Polskiego, a front organization of Young Poland, that links were established with young Slovaks, Czechs, and Ukrainians in the lands under the Habsburg and Romanov control. Łukaszewicz's seemingly indefatigable energy and personal drive to establish these links proved to be remarkably successful. Both he and Vrchovský, like many other leading figures in the nineteenth century, bring to light the importance of charismatic, energetic, and highly imaginative individuals, especially in drives for national liberation.

Kampelík's Secret Journey to Cracow

When Kampelík arrived in Cracow at the beginning of June 1835 in accordance with very detailed travel and security instructions from Łukaszewicz, the Association of the Polish People was a fully established organization with a charter consonant with that of Young Poland and an Executive Council (Zbór Główny) led by Januszewicz, Goszczyński, and Łukaszewicz. The Czech guest was received with the most cordial hospitality and comradely welcome. During an induction ceremony taking place in Januszewicz's apartment in the presence of the three above-named Polish conspirators, Kampelík took a solemn oath to uphold the association's charter and professed Young Poland's declaration of faith. He assumed the role of an initiator, whose task, according to Young Europe's statute, was to promote the establishment of similar organizations among the Czechs in Bohemia and Moravia, as well as among the Slavic inhabitants in Silesia and in Hungary: the Sorbs, Slovaks, Serbs, and Croats. These future groups of nationally awakened patriots, tied loosely to Young Europe, would disseminate ideas of freedom and democracy among the intelligentsia and the common people. Kampelík was provided with copies of the organization's statutes for the Czechs and Slovaks, as well as for the leaders of the southern Slavs, whom he and Amerling were planning to visit in August of that year.[74]

Everything went smoothly in accordance with Łukaszewicz's prearranged, carefully thought out plan. In one sweep, not only was Łukaszewicz able to formally incorporate the Czechs into the operations of the international organization, but through them as intermediaries, prospects of ties with the southern Slavs would become possible as well. Like Mazzini and Konarski, Łukaszewicz possessed an extraordinary power of persuasion, together with an infectious youthful exuberance that made his appeals irresistible to people who were not necessarily ready to embark on the road of radical revolutionary action. The power of ideas passed on by such dynamic individuals could overcome personal predispositions and at times reached far beyond what to some appeared to be outside the realm of possibilities.

No detailed records have been preserved of the meetings in Cracow. The important matters that Łukaszewicz stressed with such urgency may never be known with certainty, but a laconic postscript in the letter of 8 May could provide a clue: "It would be proper for all of you to become acquainted with matters of importance that are taking place in Vienna."[75] This cryptic remark most likely referred to the death two months earlier (2 March 1835) of the Austrian Emperor Francis I and the accession to the throne of his feeble-minded son, Ferdinand I, a development that took place in the interval between the first and the second letter. This sudden change at the very top of the Austrian political pyramid must have sent a message of dread and fear to the liberal and radical circles of central Europe, because with a physically weak and mentally impaired monarch on the throne, the already powerful arch-conservative Austrian prime minister, Prince Clemens Metternich, would undoubtedly acquire unlimited powers. According to custom, the new ruler was to be crowned in Prague as King Ferdinand V of Bohemia in the near future. Could the preparatory work to assassinate the new emperor during the coronation ceremonies scheduled to take place in Prague for September 1836, in which Kampelík was deeply involved, have been that matter of utmost importance that could not be postponed according to the plans of radical revolutionaries in Cracow? According to Jakub Budislav Malý, Kampelík's friend and a member of the plot, the conspirators held their meetings on the second floor of the annexe in the courtyard of a building known as "U Ježků" on Konviktska Street in Prague, a house that, coincidentally, is located just around the corner from the Bethlehem Chapel, where 400 years earlier the Czech national hero Jan Hus used to preach. The house was obviously chosen as the headquarters of the conspiracy, not for sentimental reasons, but because it was situated near the strategically located Charles Bridge leading to the imperial castle. The planned assassination was averted just at the last minute through pressure applied by the moderate, more sober-minded Czech activists in Prague.[76] From the perspective of radical Young Europeans, if a regicide was carried out successfully, it could have provided the spark for the anticipated revolution and thus prevented the onset of severe police repressions that indeed were to follow at the end of the 1830s.[77]

After this astoundingly adventurous plan failed to be carried out, prudence and moderation were the guidelines in the life and work of the Czech participants in the Brno meeting. The former conspirators tended to limit their activities to the publication of works related to Czech culture, dissemination of materials with revolutionary content through trusted contacts, and discussions of political themes in small circles of trusted family members and friends. The former radical activists kept their spirit alive through trips to Bratislava and Vienna, as well as long hikes in the Carpathian Mountains. During one of these extended trips through the Slovak countryside, Kampelík's younger colleague František Rieger made a secret visit to Cracow, where he had a meeting with Łukaszewicz and during a solemn walk with his Polish friends to the Kosciuszko's mound took a vow of eternal friendship with the Poles.[78] One of Kampelík's closest associates, Jan Oheral, dedicated his life to editing a Czech journal *Morava*. His pro-Polish sympathies were well known, even to the authorities, for he too maintained contacts with the Polish underground. As a journalist, well-attuned to the repressive political atmosphere of the times, he was acutely aware that his and his colleagues' activities were closely watched by the police. Indeed, as it became known later, the correspondence of the Czech activists was under close scrutiny of the authorities, personal letters were as a rule intercepted, and any observation tied to politics even indirectly was subjected to scrupulous analysis by Metternich's agents. The idea of an all-embracing national movement in cooperation with their Slovak colleagues and other nationalities continued to be a theme in private discussions, but a cautious, well-thought-out path in the day-to-day life and work became the rule. It is because of this deliberate choice of vigilance and moderation that contacts with the southern Slavs flowed not through Prague or Brno – as one would have assumed, on the basis of Kampelík's and Amerling's plans for the summer of 1835 – but through Vienna and Budapest, with Vrchovský assuming the strategic role of coordination. After all, Vienna, Bratislava, and Budapest were centres in which educated individuals with different Slavic backgrounds traditionally met and socialized. Vrchovský – first through his studies in Vienna and later through professional contacts – had ties to all three centres.

With the completion of his legal studies in 1836, Vrchovský settled in Bratislava to oversee the work of Spoločnosť, yet he did not sever his ties with his Viennese acquaintances. It was on Vrchovský's initiative that in that year preparations were made for the publication of a collection of poems dedicated to illustrious personages of the Slavic world under the title: *City vděčnosti mladých synů Slovenska* (Sentiments of gratitude of young sons of Slovakia). The introductory note written by Vrchovský spoke of the close mutually beneficial ties that existed among the Slavic nations and ended with an emotional phrase: "Oh men of Slavdom, it is for you that our hearts are beating."[79]

While this publication of cultural content was under preparation, matters of political nature were also part of Vrchovský's concerns. A letter written by Vrchovský in the name Spoločnosť to a Croat student group in Zagreb was similar in content to his epistles two years earlier to Štúr. It was couched, however, in a language that made the national objectives more clearly defined. The letter spoke of "natural rights" of every nation to self-determination, in the sense that each nationality had the right to an independent existence with its own government and constitution, as well as the right to struggle to attain this objective. Even though cooperation among Slavic nationalities was the ultimate aim, it was stressed in the spirit of Young Europe that each national group ought to concentrate first on the attainment of national emancipation of its own people.[80] With prudence and calculated caution, ties with the southern Slavs, both cultural and political, continued under Vrchovský's and Kampelík's supervision, even after the onset of political repression in the following decade.[81]

Student stirrings and demonstrations in Bratislava at the end of 1836 and at beginning of 1837 under the slogan "Fairness, humanity and freedom" led to the dissolution on government orders of all student organizations, including Spoločnosť. This development did not create excessive anxiety within Vrchovský's circle, because by this time it was decided that after three years of intensive preparatory work, the time had arrived for the formation of a secret organization with national liberation of Slovak people as its principal aim. At the end of 1837, under Vrchovský's leadership, this organization became known as Vzájomnosť. This clandestine, tightly knit group consisted of the more radical, trusted members of Spoločnosť carefully selected by the founder. New members, whose background was to be meticulously screened, were required to take an oath of loyalty upon entry into the organization. Among Vrchovský's closest confidants who represented the core of the organization were Benjamin Pravoslav Červenák and P.V. Ollík. Both men assumed leadership in Vzájomnosť when Vrchovský directed the organization's affairs from Budapest, where he permanently settled after opening his private law practice in that city at the end of 1837.

With respect to the structure of Vzájomnosť, Vrchovský felt that the organization was ready to spread its wings into the outlying regions of the Slovak lands by forming underground cells led by trusted individuals whose identity would not be known to the rank and file. The task of the organizers was to spread ideas of national liberation among the people in the countryside, acquaint them with republican principles, and prepare the masses for the ultimate upheaval that would bring down the existing order of emperors, kings, and feudal lords. Coordination work among the underground units was entrusted to Červenák, who assumed the editorship of a bimonthly newsletter. In addition to the triumvirate of Vrchovský, Červenák, and Ollík, some of the young men destined to play an important role in Vzájomnosť and subsequently in the Slovak national movement during the 1840s were Michal Miloslav Hodža, Citobor Zoch, T. Hroš, Jozef Miloslav Hurban, Ladislav Paulini, A.H. Škultéty, Br. Vusín, and many other younger members of the Slovak intelligentsia brought up in the spirit of Vzájomnosť. Ivan· Holovatsky, a Ukrainian medical student in Vienna with close bonds of friendship with Kampelík and his circle of Czech and Slovak activists, wrote to his elder brother Yakiv in Lviv that the young Slovak enthusiasts, including some clergymen, were spreading revolutionary ideas during the summer months among the people in the countryside and that one could detect among them "the first signs [of the idea] of an independent existence."[82] He was happy to report that Kampelík had high regard for the Ukrainians, being convinced that they would play a major role in the fall of the Russian Empire. In addition, he reported that Kampelík's good friend Jozef Podlipský was promoting the idea of a federation of all Slavs inhabiting the Habsburg lands on the model of the United States.[83]

Ľudovít Štúr, though continuing to be faithful to the basic ideals instilled in him by Vrchovský during the year of their close collaboration, chose to follow a more moderate, guarded path after spending a year as a student at the University of Jena. After his return to Bratislava in 1837, his attention was focused not on political issues but on the development of Slovak language and literature. His cultural endeavours and the political underground activities of Vzájomnosť did not collide but represented complementary efforts aiming at the same objective through different paths.[84] Peter Brock, a British-Canadian scholar known for his well-documented, penetrating, and highly objective studies of the Slovak, Czech, and Ukrainian national awakening, highlights the importance of the work of these young men, especially that of Štúr, in the 1830s: "It was Štúr, along with Michal Hodža and Jozef Hurban, his fellow students in Bratislava, who in the next decade would take the final step in the creation of literary Slovak and in making the Slovaks a modern nation."[85] This accomplishment would not have been possible without the initial stimulus provided by Vrchovský and his group of enthusiasts gathered in Vienna, Bratislava, Brno, and Prague in the mid-1830s.

The activities of Vzájomnosť, though initially under tight supervision of Vrchovský, were influenced, to some degree at least, by Czech national awakeners who maintained contacts with their better-organized Slovak counterparts through frequent visits and correspondence. An example of their cooperative effort was a joint meeting held in Bratislava at the beginning of May 1839, during which members of Vzájomnosť, headed by Vrchovský, met with a delegation of Czech activists: Kampelík, Rieger, and Schneider. Among the more important matters discussed at this gathering was the question of intensified efforts by liberal Hungarian politicians to accelerate the assimilation of the Slavic peoples in the Kingdom of Hungary. In spite of their customary cordial discourse, on this occasion the Czech delegates bluntly reproached their hosts in Bratislava for what was viewed from Prague and Brno as an unwelcome sign of a pro-Russian course undertaken by certain Slovak cultural leaders, among them young men with ties to Vzájomnosť. Open demonstrations of pro-Russian sympathies, Kampelík charged, might have provided the Hungarian politicians with a convenient pretext to justify the intensification of assimilation. It was primarily the liberal wing of Hungarian political activists that was engaged in spreading rumours in Vienna that the Slovak cultural leaders professed a deep devotion towards an all-Slav entity commonly identified with Russia. What appeared most deplorable from this point of view was the fact that the tsarist empire had the most reactionary system of rule in Europe. "One heart ... one tongue ... and one fatherland" was believed to be the motto of the pan-Slavs led by Russian nationalist agents. The Czech delegates at the meeting advised their Slovak colleagues to be on guard, because the amiable scholars from Moscow and St Petersburg who had visited Bratislava were in reality tsarist agents with a mission to sow confusion and discord among the Slavs. To this accusation Vrchovský responded with a firm assertion that all members of Vzájomnosť were loyal to their republican principles and that they considered themselves Slovaks first, then Czecho-Slovaks, and only in the broad sense, also members of a larger all-Slavic community.[86] Vrchovský, by now permanently settled in Budapest, had been actively involved in coordinating relations with the southern Slavs and Ukrainians in East Galicia. Therefore the question of Slavdom was very close to his heart, yet at no time did this committed republican express any words of praise or admiration for Russia.

For Štúr, however, being a Slovak first did not preclude friendly contacts with visiting scholars in service of the Russian tsar. In 1842, for example, Štúr and his circle of cultural activists at the Slavic Institute in Bratislava arranged an especially warm reception for Izmail I.

Sreznevsky, a young historian soon to assume a teaching position at the University of Kharkiv. The budding scholar was elated to meet men with interests so close to his own. In a letter to his mother, Sreznevsky glowingly described the encounter: "We have spent the evening in the company of Ľudovít Štúr and Mikhail Hodža and [in the course of the evening] became brothers for life. One can be truly proud of such brothers."[87]

What made these close bonds of friendship possible during these visits was undoubtedly the fact that Sreznevsky, as well as another distinguished scholar from Moscow, Osyp Bodiansky, was an intellectual of the highest calibre with a genuine interest in the development and promotion of Slavic studies. True, they were obliged to pay homage to the government that made their extensive scholarly journeys possible, but the principal objective of their visits involved first and foremost intellectual pursuits, not politics. They were not members of conservative groups supporting the autocratic regime in St Petersburg, nor did they promote the dominant role of Russia in an idealized Slavic union, as did some well-known Russian intellectuals and writers. Bodiansky was a Ukrainian by both birth and conviction, while Sreznevsky, even though only partly Ukrainian, cultivated a genuine interest in Ukrainian studies, especially in the Cossack wars of independence. Future developments showed that it was not the visitors who influenced their Slovak hosts but rather it was the other way around. Both scholars, through their extensive travels and interaction with such luminaries in the world of Slavdom as Pavol Josef Šafařík in Prague, and the group of ardent Slovak patriots led by Štúr in Bratislava, appear to have been captivated by the western Slav idea of Slavic unity based on the principle of equality. Sreznevsky became a popular history professor at the University of Kharkiv, the seat of the Ukrainian cultural and scholarly renaissance in the first half of the nineteenth century. One of his star students there was Mykola Kostomarov, who in the mid-1840s became the founding member of the first modern Ukrainian political organization, the Cyril and Methodius Brotherhood, an association advocating national independence, republican government, and the idea of Slavic unity based on the principle of equality. Fresh from the visit to Bratislava, where he became acquainted with the writings of Slovak national awakeners, it was most likely Sreznevsky who instilled in his student an interest in Ján Hollý's *Cyrilo-Metodiada*, which was presented to him during the visit. Bodiansky, a professor in Moscow, would in the years to come captivate his listeners by inspirational lectures on Jan Hus and induce one of his students to write a dissertation on the life of the Czech national hero. Bodiansky would be also instrumental in inspiring his talented fellow countryman, the Ukrainian poet Taras Shevchenko, to write one of the finest literary works promoting the Slavic idea of equality and freedom in a poem depicting the trial and execution of Jan Hus. In the spirit of reciprocity, Shevchenko – also one of the leading members of the Cyril and Methodius Brotherhood – would dedicate the poem to the eminent Slovak and Czech scholar, Šafařík.[88]

On the whole, in spite of occasional disagreements on the question of a separate Slovak language, relations between the Czech and Slovak national awakeners remained cordial throughout the 1830s. In fact the Czech publication *Květy*, edited by Jaroslav Pospíšil in close cooperation with Kampelík, consistently devoted a great deal of attention to cultural life in Slovakia and provided generous space to works by Slovak authors. This was appreciated by members of Vzájomnosť as well as the Štúr group, because Slovak publications such as *Tatranka* and *Hronka* tended to appear at irregular intervals only, for lack of funds.[89]

Maintaining utmost secrecy within the tightly knit groups of trusted activists in Vzájomnosť, and the extraordinary caution and vigilance exercised by Czech national activists proved to be of great benefit as the decade was coming to a close. In the spring of 1838, after more than two years of intensive pursuit, the Russian police captured Szymon Konarski, the key figure in Young Poland's revolutionary underground operating in the western provinces of tsarist Russia. In the course of a protracted investigation and lengthy interrogations often accompanied by torture, the tsarist police was able to uncover the wide network of interlocking units operating under different names, with ties to Ukrainian, Czech, and Slovak groups. In many instances there were serious consequences for the key players in the revolutionary underground, but this development did not arrest the national awakening that now encompassed a wide range of educated young men and women in the cities and throughout the countryside. The Czech and Slovak contingents of Young Europe, as will be shown later, were least affected by the repressions that would follow Konarski's arrest and execution. Though many of the national awakeners were interrogated by the police in Prague, Brno, and Bratislava, only Kampelík was imprisoned and brought to trial in the Galician capital, where the underground organization had the largest number of committed followers of Young Europe's celebrated emissary to the Slavic lands.[90]

Chapter Four

East Galicia: The Testing Ground of Young Europe's Ideals

Some kind of great spirit of freedom has overwhelmed me.... I had a dream which caused a profound change within me; I dreamt that I had liberated the Ruthenians and given them independence. This has become such a mania with me that I can think of nothing else.... In my opinion, it would be best if Poland would rise; I have great plans.... The Ruthenians are most on my mind; let the Poles think about themselves, and I shall think about my own kind. No one will think worse of me for that.[1]

By the time Szymon Konarski arrived in Cracow in July 1835, the final draft of the association's charter, prepared by Łukaszewicz, Januszewicz, and Goszczyński, was ready for adoption. Besides minor changes considered expedient from the point of view of adjustments to local conditions, the constitution conformed fully to the principles of Mazzini's organization, and thus the emissary of Young Poland approved the document without reservations. The charter endorsed the republican form of government as well as ideals of brotherhood and solidarity among nations whose principal mission was to fight for their freedom and aid one another in the struggle against tyranny and despotism. In line with Lelewel's instructions and appeals, the document emphasized the need to draw people of all nationalities to the cause of national liberation.[2] The Executive Council headed by Goszczyński, Januszewicz, and Łukaszewicz was expanded to include Konarski and two of his colleague-conspirators.[3] A month after his arrival Konarski, elatedly reported to his émigré superiors that a spirit of harmony and concordance prevailed among the leaders of the organization representing Young Poland in the home territories.[4]

Meanwhile, a dramatic event in Cracow brought about a significant change in the composition of the council and the operation of the association. Łukaszewicz was not exaggerating when he reported in his letters to Kampelík that freedom in the "free city of Cracow" was illusory only. As the number of Polish fugitives continued to increase within the walls of the city – it was estimated that as many as 15,000 political activists from different provinces of Poland's partitioned lands resided there – persistent pressure from the political residents of the three partitioning powers led to the imposition of strict police surveillance in the city. The situation became critical for the Polish underground when in February 1836 two brothers, Adolf and Leon Zaleski, both members of the radical wing of the Polish democratic society, became implicated in the execution of a tsarist agent, Berens-Pavlovsky, who had skilfully infiltrated Polish organizations at home and in emigration.[5] The Zaleski brothers, though not officially members of Young Poland, had ties to Konarski as well as to some of his colleagues in the association's Executive Council. By this time Young Poland's emissary was no longer in Cracow, but other members of the Executive Council found themselves in a highly perilous situation when the three partitioning powers placed the city under military occupation. Januszewicz, being a native of Volynia, a province under the rule of Russia, immediately fled to France. Goszczyński, also from the territory under Russian suzerainty, opted to seek safety in East Galicia. Of the triumvirate heading the association, only Łukaszewicz, born in eastern Galicia and therefore an Austrian subject, felt safe to remain in Cracow. Some of the younger, recently recruited members left the city for the environs of Warsaw with the aim of planting branches of the organization in that region.[6]

The Galician Capital as the Hub of Conspiratorial Action

As the majority of the members of the Executive Council found themselves scattered in different parts of Europe, it was decided to move the organization's headquarters to the Galician capital and there elect a new Executive Council. The main responsibility for this undertaking fell to Goszczyński. The poet-conspirator was very well suited for this task. As a former participant in the November insurgency, he had first-rate connections with Polish émigrés associated with Young Poland, as well as with the remnants of the Carbonari groups that were still operating in Galicia. As a popular writer with marked Ukrainophile tendencies, he was in a favourable position to win the sympathy and trust of the Ukrainian intelligentsia concentrated mainly at the Lviv University and the Greek Catholic seminaries in the province. In his effort to unify the scattered groups of the Polish underground and bring them and their Ukrainian sympathizers closer to the bosom of Young Poland, Goszczyński was ably assisted by Lucjan Siemieński, like himself a Polish writer from territories ruled by Russia with a pronounced Ukrainophile bent.

Even though some influential members of the Carbonari cells in East Galicia continued to adhere to the rigid rationalism of the Enlightenment and resisted the merge with the association, after a period of tense negotiations, they agreed, nominally at least, to endorse the program of Young Poland. Soon after Goszczyński's arrival in East Galicia, numerous underground groups – now directly tied to Young Poland – sprang up in the cities and towns of that region. In accordance with Lelewel's directives – a point that Mazzini considered of great importance – women became active participants in the organization. They constituted autonomous units operating according to rules of a similar but separate charter. The principal task of these women's groups was dissemination of political ideas by educating the youth in the spirit of Young Poland. Among the members of the underground in the Galician capital who became directly involved in the project of organizing and educating women was Henryk Bogdański, a young lawyer with ties to both the District and the Supreme Council of the association, as well as to an influential faculty member in the Greek Catholic seminary, the Rev. Mykola Hordynsky.[7] Within a very short time, a Polish author observed, "Galicia was covered with a tightly knit network of local, district, and regional units of the Association of the Polish People,"[8] yet, for security reasons, as already noted, not all members were aware of the organization's international connection.[9]

The Galician capital became the hub of the conspiratorial network in the Austrian Empire with Goszczyński playing the pivotal role in the new Executive Council. In the absence of Januszewicz, who, as noted earlier, fled to France, and Łukaszewicz, who remained in Cracow, Goszczyński had to rely on local activists, all former members of the Carbonari underground, who found it difficult to follow the new organization's directives. Among them, the most resourceful and cooperative was Franciszek Smolka, while the most obstinate in his refusal to conform to the spirit of Young Poland proved to be Leon Korecki.[10]

As in Cracow, the recruitment to the organization in the Galician capital focused primarily on young people attending the university or other institutions of higher learning. Like in the Slovak and Czech lands, special attention was paid to the seminarians of both Roman Catholic and Greek Catholic denominations. This was in line with Mazzini's conviction that members of the clergy could be most useful during the preparatory stages of the revolution. It is quite certain the Italian conspirator did not consider the secular educators only when he wrote, "Priests of my fatherland, take your place at the head of the people and lead them on the road to progress."[11] Even though Mazzini's hostility towards Rome was widely known, as his biographer Roland Sarti points out, his criticism of the Church represented "a selective anticlericalism that spared the lower clergy and lashed out at the papacy. Recalling the Jansenist priests who had educated him, he would always regard the lower clergy as a potential source of support for the revolution."[12] Frequent references to Christian moral principles and humanistic ideals in the propaganda literature of Young Europe facilitated access to the minds and hearts of young men coming of age in Eastern Europe in the era of Romanticism.

In the eastern part of Galicia, the Greek Catholic seminary was of singular importance for recruitment, because of the stress in Young Poland's program on the inclusion of the common people in the forthcoming revolution, and it was known that the majority of the inhabitants of this part of the province were Ukrainians whose leadership consisted of clergy, as it did among the Slovaks.[13] Goszczyński cultivated an interest in Ukrainian history, culture, and customs long before he became involved in conspiratorial political work. In one of his compassionate, moving poems dedicated to Ukraine, while recognizing its right to an independent existence and while expressing admiration for the people's enduring faith in the possibility of this dream's realization, he foresaw only a slim chance for Ukraine's survival as a nation:[14]

> To you, oh Ukraine,
> My gratitude for your songs.
> Only in my final resting place
> Will I hear such familiar groans....
> For your song of pain
> Is a prisoner's moan.
> And so, my Ukraine
> I respond with a consoling song.
> How hard it is to wilt
> While forced into a throng of strangers,
> If from your heart has been torn away
> All that brings joy to others.
> Yet how sweet it is to have faith
> With so much nourishing water,
> That if imbibed from a shared cup
> It brings joy to a neighbouring brother.

An attitude that recognized Ukraine's separate identity and, by im-
plication, the right of its people to an independent existence, even without much confidence in the possibility of the right of that realization,
won the sympathy and confidence of the emerging Ukrainian intelligentsia in East Galicia.

The Polish poet-conspirator had been fully aware of the important
role that members of the clerical profession could play as disseminators of Young Poland's political ideas in the countryside. It is worth
noting that because of his keen understanding of the importance of the
religious factor in Eastern Europe, when he was drafting of the charter
of the association in Cracow, Goszczyński persuaded his colleagues to
include in the document a profession of faith found in Young Europe's
charter but omitted in Young Poland's analogous document. As noted
earlier, the preamble in the former began with the declaration that
there is "only One God; One Supreme Authority: His Law; One interpreter of the law: humanity." This spiritually inspired statement was
not acceptable to some émigré members of Young Poland, because the
condemnation of the Polish November insurrection by the Church of
Rome was still vivid in their minds. Thus the opening paragraph of
Young Poland's charter had a purely secular ring reminiscent of the
spirit of the Carbonari era. The charter simply began with a statement that the supreme authority resided in the people; that the only
ruler of the people was the law, and the only lawgiver was the will
of the people.[15] Even though at this stage of his life Goszczyński had
not been known for professing deep religious convictions, he was,
like Lelewel and Łukaszewicz, keenly attuned to the fact that religion
was of particular importance to the devout peoples of Eastern Europe.
Thus in his speeches and writings he often reminded his free-thinking
compatriots – the majority of whom had earned their revolutionary apprenticeship in the Carbonari underground – "If our nation is not all
Catholic, it is almost entirely Christian. An active political organization would act in a highly irresponsible manner if it looked down upon
Christianity or trivialized its significance. A charge of atheism brought
against the democrats could be a powerful weapon in the hands of enemies, for [religion] still carries a great weight among the people."[16] The
religiously inspired writings of Mickiewicz and Lamennais were well
suited to convey a spirit of republicanism build on religious foundations. The works of these writers became widely distributed among the
seminarians in East Galicia of both the Latin and Eastern Rites.

Considering their deep interests in Ukrainian ethnography and
folklore, both Goszczyński and Siemieński were familiar with the
well-known work of the Polish ethnographer Adam Czarnocki who,

during his travels just a few decades earlier, had been deeply moved when he observed the compassionate care and gentleness with which the Greek Catholic priests treated their parishioners.[17] Czarnocki's notes were corroborated by more recent traveller-observers. Iakiv Holovatsky, a priest's son and a student at the Greek Catholic seminary in Lviv, noted during his travels, "The Ruthenian clergyman, inseparable from his faithful, is with them in their every need with aid and advice. Whether it is a birth or a funeral, the priest is in their hut with his blessing. He does not spurn the meagre meal that the peasant provides. In a word, he lives with the people like the people."[18] The unique privilege granted by Rome to the Greek Catholic clergy – the right (if they so desired) to marry – placed this category of clerics in an especially favourable position in their relations with the rural people. As husbands and fathers, this priestly cast shared many problems and responsibilities with the secular members of the parish. In addition, according to a well-established custom, the priests' wives – in the majority of cases brought up in clerical families – became involved in charity work among the village poor. With the exception of Lutheran clergymen among the Slovaks, no other educated group in this part of Europe had such easy access to the hearts and minds of the village inhabitants as the Greek Catholic priests.

On the basis of these observations, both Goszczyński and Siemieński understood very well that if tactfully approached and properly instructed, a Ukrainian clergyman in Galicia could serve as an excellent conduit for the dissemination of revolutionary ideas. By the third decade of the nineteenth century, most Greek Catholic seminarians had excellent educational foundations. The Austrian school system provided them with knowledge of at least three foreign languages: Polish, German, and Latin. By the time of their third year in the seminary, students were well prepared to absorb and comprehend the political ideas found in the clandestine literature transmitted to them by the emissaries of Young Europe.

Revolutionary Currents in the Greek Catholic Seminary

Direct contacts between the Polish underground and the students of the Greek Catholic Seminary in Lviv existed even before it was decided to move the headquarters of the association to the Galician capital. Similar to the Slovak theology student Samo Chalupka, the Greek Catholic students in East Galicia shared vivid memories of the stirring events connected with the Polish November insurgency. Some, like Teofil Kulchytsky, were direct participants in the revolutionary war. Others expressed their eagerness to do so. Many became personally acquainted with Polish insurgents as they passed through Galicia on their way to Western Europe, or who, like Siemieński, Kulczyński, and Goszczyński chose to establish their residence in the eastern part of the province. Inspired by the bravery of the insurgents and fired by the high ideals for which the Polish patriots fought, many were eager to participate in the work of the Polish underground on behalf of what they considered a lofty cause. According to the memoirs of Henryk Bogdański, the Polish chronicler of the political underground during this eventful decade, among the first twelve recruits from the Greek Catholic seminary to a newly established Carbonari group, Związek Pryjaców Ludu, was Markian Shashkevych, soon to lead in the national awakening of Ukrainians in East Galicia. In addition to Markian Shashkevych, other members of the organization listed by Bogdański were: Ivan Seletsky (initially the main link between the underground and the seminary), Sylvester Mieisky, Mykhailo Gadzinsky, Teodor Kulchytsky, Mykhailo Mynchakevych, Osyp Okhrymovych, Ivan Pokinsky, Dmytro Mokhnatsky, Klement Mokhnatsky, Romuald Kryzhanovsky, Dezyderii Hrechansky, and the Rev. Mykola Hordynsky.[19] In subsequent years many more students were recruited from the Greek Catholic seminary, but Shashkevych's name disappears early from the list of active members. Most likely he decided to withdraw because of his involvement in literary projects, but he remained on good terms with many of his politically active friends. Another Greek Catholic seminarian, Hipolit Stanchak, fearing dire consequences if the secret organization was uncovered, also decided to sever his ties with the underground. It was on account of his defection, which constituted a breach of an oath each member of the organization was required to take during the induction ceremony, that some seminarian-conspirators felt duty-bound to execute Stanchak. There was also a plot to kill Shashkevych, but undoubtedly, thanks to the presence of a Greek Catholic cleric both in the seminary and the organization, neither of these plans was carried out.[20]

The program of the conspiratorial group called for the re-establishment of Poland in accordance with its pre-partitioned boundaries but with a federal structure and with a republican form of government. Membership was open to all, irrespective of religious denomination or social background.[21] It was during this early post-revolution period, referred to by a Polish historian as the era of crystallization of national consciousness for the Ukrainians, Lithuanians, and Belorussians,[22] that Shashkevych, together with his Greek Catholic colleagues, worked together with Siemieński and a group of young Polish poets on a Polish literary almanac, which would appear under the title of *Ziewonia* in 1834.[23]

The Greek Catholic seminarians who joined the Polish political underground were guided by principles of two ideological schools of thought and according to these principles were pursuing two related but distinct political goals. One group embraced the new Romantic ideal of national renaissance, with its stress on culture and the right of each nationality to an independent existence. For these young men, the question of attaining Ukraine's independence either as a separate state entity or as a constituent part of a democratic federal republic represented a noble aim.[24] This objective they hoped to accomplish by cooperating with Polish revolutionaries who, like Goszczyński or Siemńieski, were willing to acknowledge a separate Ukrainian identity and showed a genuine interest in Ukraine's history and culture. They were eager to participate in radical ventures designed to bring about an end to the existing unjust political, social, and economic system but at the same time were directly involved in Ukrainian cultural projects coordinated by Markian Shashkevych, even after the emerging leader of the Ukrainian national renaissance in Galicia withdrew from active participation in the Polish underground. In line with the ideals of Romanticism, they were interested in the recovery of their national roots, viewing cultivation and promotion of their nation's heritage as a task of importance for the educated members of the community. Among those actively engaged in the political underground, who also showed an interest in Ukrainian cultural development by helping to prepare an almanac edited by Shashkevych, were the following seminarians: Mykhailo Minchakevych, Ivan Vendzylovych, Ivan Pokinsky, Teodor Kulchytsky, Yosyf and Ivan Okhrymovych, Romuald Kryzhanovsky, and Kyrylo Slonevsky.[25] Some of them would suffer dearly for their involvement in radical politics, but those who, like the Rev. Theodor Kulchytsky, survived lengthy imprisonment and harsh realities in the life of a former political prisoner, would continue their involvement in cultural endeavours while keeping a watchful eye on the political interests of the Ukrainian people.[26]

The other, much smaller group of Greek Catholic seminarians consisted of students who, like a considerable number of their politically involved Polish colleagues, held on to the lingering rationalism of the Enlightenment, with its emphasis on the material rather than spiritual, the general rather than the particular, a mode of thought that had a somewhat longer lifespan in Galicia, mainly because of the strong Carbonari roots in this easternmost province of the Habsburgs. For these young men the question of political, economic, and social emancipation was of primary concern, while the idea of nationality, the unique qualities of national cultures, and especially the cultivation of dying languages was viewed not only as a wasteful diversion, but as a hindrance in constructing a society founded on principles of material well-being and social equality. Their convictions reflected rather closely the line of reasoning Mazzini encountered during his first years of exile among the older generation of Italian Carbonaris who showed no interest in the Risorgimento's call to free Italy from foreign domination.[27] The brothers Dmytro and Klyment Mokhnatsky, and their close colleague Ivan Seletsky, represented this group. Seletsky was a well-known figure among the politically involved seminarians because of his efforts to recruit Greek Catholic students to the Polish underground before he was forced to transfer to the faculty of law at the university and subsequently to flee abroad.[28]

Klyment Mokhnatsky's reminiscences *Pamiętnik spiskowca i nauczyciela 1811–1848* (Memoirs of a conspirator and a teacher) illustrate rather well this group's mode of thought. From the memoir the author emerges as an individual who has been untouched by the prevailing currents of Romantic nationalism, especially as it expressed itself among the young members of the intelligentsia in Eastern Europe. If, for example, the Mokhnatsky brothers ventured into the countryside, it was not because of an interest in the way of life of the common people, nor in order to study folk customs, proverbs, and songs, but rather to search for a terrain that would be best suited for military exercises or for similar needs of the underground. Usually accompanied on these exploratory ventures by Polish colleagues, the author was unpleasantly surprised by the cool and at times hostile reception his group encountered when visiting a Ukrainian village. It did not enter the author's mind that the group's indifference to the common folks' way of life as well as its use of the Polish language might have been the reason for expressions of hostility and mistrust, even after he observed that in rural regions inhabited by Polish speakers the reception was much warmer and friendlier.[29]

In their relations with other seminarians, the Mokhnatsky brothers were antagonistic to the Shashkevych circle, in particular because of its interest in the cultural accomplishments of Ukrainians under the rule of the Russia. They accused them of harbouring pro-Russian or "Muscophile" sympathies and derisively called Shashkevych and his group as "Mikolajci," that is, fans of Tsar Nicholas.[30] Such charges must have sounded malicious to those young men in the seminary who only a few years earlier, during the November insurgency of 1830, found it difficult to restrain Shashkevych from joining the Polish anti-Russian rebels.[31] There were frequent intellectual battles between these two ideologically divergent camps, but if no dire consequences resulted from these political clashes, it was largely thanks to the watchful eye and mediating influence of a "revolutionary in a cassock," Henryk Bogdański's good friend and confidant, the seminary's prefect and philosophy professor, Mykola Hordynsky.[32]

A Pedagogue, a Priest, and a Conspirator:
The Rev. Mykola Hordynsky

In the history of the Ukrainian national awakening, of special interest is the elusive and today almost forgotten figure of the Rev. Mykola Hordynsky, a scholar and educator whom Bogdański credits with the great success in the recruitment of Greek Catholic seminarians to the revolutionary cause[33] and who a decade later would impress Austrian prison authorities by his extraordinary intelligence with a mastery of six foreign languages.[34]

Born in 1802 in the village of Hordynia in the Sambir region to a family of petty gentry, which in his lifetime produced at least two Greek Catholic priests, young Mykola had the good fortune to receive an excellent secondary education, in the course of which he was introduced to German literary works, selections from classical philosophy, and writings involving liberal political thought. Early in life, as the priest-conspirator notes in an autobiographical sketch he wrote while awaiting a trial for his underground political involvement, he became captivated by the republican form of government through readings of classical writers of ancient Greece and Rome. After completing his secondary education, he proceeded to study philosophy at Lviv University and theology at the Greek Catholic seminary. Soon after his ordination as a celibate priest in 1830, he became a professor of philosophy and theology as well as a prefect at the seminary, positions he would hold until 1837. In his spare time during his tenure in the seminary and involvement in the underground organization, he translated Thomas Paine's *Rights of Man*.[35]

According to his sworn testimony made at a political trial of conspirators in 1842, it was in 1833 that through a colleague with whom he shared an interest in political thought,[36] he was introduced to Napoleon Nowicki, a well-known Polish Carbonari activist, who invited him to join the Carbonari cell, Związek Pryjaćol Ludu. In 1835, when under Goszczyński's leadership the Carbonari groups in East Galicia were merged with the Association of the Polish People, Hordynsky was asked at the recommendation of Lev Bilynsky and in the presence of Siemieński to join the organization's District Council.[37] Appointed to the post of the correspondent secretary, he was placed in a pivotal position, for it enabled him to be in direct contact with district units of what was at that time the Galician branch of Young Poland.[38] He also had the responsibility to oversee the receipt of books sent from Western Europe via Budapest to the Galician capital through an underground railroad supervised by the emissaries of Young Europe. In this task Hordynsky was assisted by Teofil Madejewski, who saw to it that the forbidden literature was delivered to trusted members of the organization, most often either to a centrally located apartment of Jan Marin or to a local pub owner, Jan Prochaska.[39]

Hordynsky's concurrent professional functions as a prefect and a professor at the Greek Catholic seminary made him an excellent guide for the recruiting agents in the underground, because the positions enabled him not only to assess the students' intellectual abilities but also provided him with an opportunity to observe at close range the young men's strong and weak personal qualities. It was largely because of the meticulous care with which he selected prospective candidates for the association that, in spite of repeated orders sent by the provincial chief of police, Leopold von Sacher-Masoch, to conduct thorough searches in the students' dormitories, no serious incriminating evidence was uncovered on the premises of the seminary, and no leaks to the police came from within the institution. In the spring of 1837 the pressure from the police headquarters became so strong, however, that a newly appointed rector of the seminary asked Hordynsky to look for another position. Until then, according to Bogdański, the success in the recruitment of Greek Catholic seminarians was beyond all expectations.[40]

It is remarkable that Hordynsky remained in his influential position for such a long time, because more than two years earlier, on 21 January 1835 the bishop of Przemyśl, Ivan Snihursky, wrote to the Greek Catholic metropolitan, Mykhailo Levytsky, that he had information according to which the priest-educator had ties to an underground group of which Ivan Siletsky, a seminarian already under police suspicion, was a member.[41] The good relationship Hordynsky cultivated with the brother of the metropolitan, the rector Venedykt Levitsky, and the excellent reputation he enjoyed in the seminary as a scholar and a pedagogue, must have been responsible for his longevity as a professor and prefect.

Reports regarding revolutionary currents circulating among the students of the Greek Catholic seminary were reaching the police headquarters even earlier than Bishop Snihursky's note. In 1832 and later in 1834, Symon Pidlashetsky, a Greek Catholic priest, informed the police authorities in Vienna and subsequently in Lviv as well that during the summer recess seminarians were discussing ideas derived from forbidden revolutionary literature.[42] Especially telling in this connection was a letter from a shocked Greek Catholic cleric, Mykhailo Gerovsky, to his brother, Yakiv, at the University of Lviv, complaining that Polish students from the Latin Catholic seminary as well as "some civilian scoundrels" were disseminating revolutionary books and brochures published in Paris among Greek Catholic clerics. In these books, the writer noted, the emperor was referred to by various derogatory epithets while the idea of the sovereignty of the people was elevated to the highest level. Among the revolutionary books Gerovsky mentioned was a work by Lamennais, as well as a history of the Polish people. "Woe to our land, especially to us, the Ruthenians," lamented the scandalized Greek Catholic priest.[43]

It is mainly from Bogdański's detailed reminiscences chronicling the web of intricate relationships in the political underground of the 1830s, as well as his record of the prison years in the 1840s, that there emerges a rather well-defined portrait of Mykola Hordynsky, the cleric-conspirator active within the walls of the Greek Catholic seminary during the pivotal years of Ukrainian cultural and political renaissance in East Galicia. Bogdański was in an excellent position to do so, because from the very beginning of Hordynsky's involvement in the underground both he and the Greek Catholic conspirator were members of a Carbonari cell before it blended with the Association of the Polish People, served together on the association's General Council, and worked side-by-side in the organization's Seminaries Committee. Subsequently, after the conspiracy was uncovered in 1841, they shared a cell in the notorious Špilberk prison,[44] to which many of the key figures of the underground were consigned after a lengthy trial, which began in Lviv in 1842.[45]

From Bogdański's reminiscences the priest-educator-conspirator emerges as a highly enlightened, sensitive, and gentle individual with a deep commitment to the national cause. Because of his erudition and good-natured qualities, Bogdański notes, "he was capable of earning respect, confidence, and affection among all who came to know him, especially among his subordinates."[46] His involvement in the revolutionary organization was carefully guarded, so that among the seminarians who were recruited to the political underground between 1834 and 1837, only two trusted students, Lev Bilynsky and Bazylii Hrab, knew about the prefect's ties to the underground, and it was through them that matters relating to conspiratorial work were communicated to a select group of seminarians. Hordynsky reported information to Bogdański pertaining to recruitment and other matters relating to the organization, and Bogdański passed this information to the Supreme Council of the association. For reasons of security, Hordynsky did not attend regular meetings of the underground cell to which he, Bogdański, and the seminarians belonged. Thus, with the exception of the two intermediaries noted above, no one within the seminary walls knew about the prefect's political involvement. It was for this reason that when in 1838 Dezyderi Hrechansky, a former seminarian-conspirator and in that year a newly ordained priest, suffered a mental breakdown and gave to the police the names of his former colleagues involved in the underground, the prefect Hordynsky does not appear on the list of the organization's members.[47]

Being an intelligent and experienced educator, the priest-conspirator was well aware that not every student in the seminary was suited for conspiratorial work. Thus, Bogdański notes, a select group of gifted young men with exceptional intellectual abilities were given special assignments that would enhance their general knowledge and increase their proficiency in languages, history, and culture. At the same time, these young men were inculcated with high moral values so that they could become exemplary priests dedicated to the well-being of the people they were obliged to serve.[48] Even though Bogdański does not mention specific names, it is logical to assume that Shashkevych and his group of highly skilled colleagues involved in works for the advancement of Ukrainian studies – such as the preparation of a dictionary, a reader for parish schools, or the translation of Thomas à Kempis's *The Imitation of Christ* from the Latin original – represented this select group of talented individuals. This could be one of the reasons why Shashkevych, who was a member of the Polish underground during the first year of recruitment, was no longer on the list of the organization's members in the years that followed.

It was primarily through these two channels – one linked to the preparation of a revolutionary upheaval deemed essential for the destruction of the existing oppressive political and economic system, and the other involving a constructive educational program designed to raise the moral and intellectual level of both the Ukrainian elite and the masses – that the priest-educator hoped to fulfil his chosen mission to serve the national cause. That for Hordynsky this mission involved the interests of the Ukrainian people would come to light when this mild-mannered, soft-spoken cleric known for the habit of addressing those close to him by tender terms of endearment,[49] fought with vigour and determination for the recognition of the Ukrainian members in the Association of the Polish People as a separate national unit by adding the word *Ruthenian* to the organization's official name.[50] When the majority of the Supreme Council rejected this request, Hordynsky's spirits were not overly dampened, for he promptly saw to it that a parallel organization called Kolo Rus'ke (The Ruthenian circle) was established for the Greek Catholic members of the underground. In the spirit of Young Europe, this group conducted its activities not in opposition to but rather parallel with the association. The program of Kolo Rus'ke called for a federal system of government based on the principle of equality in the future democratic republic of Poland.[51] The Kolo Rus'ke became, so to speak, the Ukrainian branch of Young Europe in Galicia.

A recent study in Ukraine[52] provides biographical sketches of more than fifty Greek Catholic priests educated at the Lviv seminary during the 1830s and 1840s who distinguished themselves as dedicated pastors as well as responsible cultural and political activists on behalf of Ukrainian causes in the second half of the nineteenth century. Swayed by ideological considerations, Soviet studies of this period, as well as Western authors who have been influenced by them, claim that better education introduced in the seminaries during the rule of the Habsburgs created a rift between the clergy and the peasant masses. These authors ignore the influence of Romanticism, with its idealization of the country folk, as well as the concerted effort by responsible educators to inculcate in seminarians a respect and compassion for the common people both for religious and political considerations. Of course, there were occasional clerics who did not follow the guidelines taught at the seminary, but the custom of relating humorous anecdotes about the country folk at celebratory feasts of the clergy that could have irritated the sensibilities a young, idealistic member of the intelligentsia influenced by socialist ideas, is not evidence of alienation between the clergy and the masses. It is an established fact in history that a more enlightened education, especially one with an emphasis on high moral values, tends to lead to better human relations rather than class antagonism.

Finding a Modus Vivendi with Conservative Officialdom

By the mid-1830s, the higher administrative bodies of the seminary, as well as the hierarchy of the Greek Catholic Church became seriously troubled by the frequent charges by the office of the chief of police regarding the students' involvement in radical political causes. These charges, if proven true, were potentially dangerous, because they could damage the excellent reputation the Greek Catholic Church enjoyed in the eyes of the ecclesiastical and secular authorities in Vienna, where for decades it had been viewed as a loyal institution profoundly grateful for the benefits the Greek Catholics had been receiving from the Habsburg rulers, especially in the sphere of education. Consequently, not only did Rector Levytsky issue strict orders to conduct periodic searches in the students' dormitories but also sternly forbade the students to frequent local bookstores from which, the police claimed, they were obtaining forbidden literature smuggled to Galicia from the West. In addition, the Rector's Office inaugurated formal commemorations of the emperor's birthday at which the most noteworthy seminarians delivered celebratory speeches in honour of the reigning monarch. Furthermore, purportedly with the intent to divert the interests of the youth from politics, the teaching staff was instructed to encourage students to deepen their knowledge of Ukrainian history and culture and to perfect their ability to speak Ukrainian, so that after their ordination they would be prepared better to perform the pastoral duties they were being trained for. The Rector's Office also provided financial support to those students who were interested in collecting materials for a Ukrainian (Ruthenian in the original) dictionary and in translating pedagogical works for primary schools. Special funds were apportioned for the enrichment of the library with books that would benefit the development of the Ukrainian language and culture.[53]

Even if the project for the enhancement of Ukrainian studies was not suggested to the rector by his good friend, the prefect-conspirator – Bogdański's memoirs suggest that Hordynsky shared with him precisely this idea[54] – it is certain that the plan had the prefect's enthusiastic support. The fact that Hordynsky had been on good terms with Rector Levytsky since the years the two educators spent together at Lviv University corroborates this assumption. Similarly, there is a strong indication that the proposal of formal eulogies in honour of the emperor introduced in the seminary in 1834 originated from the same source to shield the politically engaged students from suspicion. In fact, after the conspiracy was uncovered, it came to light that the most highly praised panegyrics delivered in honour of the emperor were presented by seminarians who were deeply involved in the political underground. A good example is one of the first speeches delivered on 4 October 1834 by Dezyderii Hrechansky, who, according to Bogdański, was considered the most promising youth in the political underground.[55] Only a very intelligent conspirator like Mykola Hordynsky, with direct access to the rector, could have been responsible for devising such a clever plan of protection for politically engaged students who in most instances had been recruited at his personal recommendation. On the basis of documentary evidence, it would be difficult not to agree with a Polish author who asserts without reservations that the panegyrics were indeed designed to serve as a cover for the politically involved seminarians.[56]

On the one hand, political literature arriving from the West through secret channels directed by Mazzini's emissaries in Marseilles familiarized the seminarians with republican principles and ideals. On the other, the effort made by the Rector's Office to enhance the students' proficiency in Ukrainian language, history, and culture created an ideal environment for the awakening and strengthening of national-cultural and political consciousness among members of the emerging Ukrainian intelligentsia. One pursuit complemented and reinforced the other. It corresponded perfectly with the plan of action envisioned by Mazzini for members of the semi-independent, loosely tied branches of Young Europe. And who could have been better acquainted with Young Europe's program than the person placed in charge of distributing the incoming forbidden books in the Galician capital – the seminary's prefect, the multilingual educator, Mykola Hordynsky. A copy of Thomas Paine's *Rights of Man* that Hordynsky translated while at the seminary[57] must have reached him through Young Europe's underground channel leading to Lviv.

It was this new approach to read and analyse documentary sources and literature that propelled the more inquisitive and intellectually gifted theology students, irrespective of whether or not they were in in the underground, in the direction of political thought and corresponding action. The first steps were timid and slow, as usually is the case at the opening of a new venture. A contemporary of the events described above reminisced about the dawn of the Ukrainian national political awakening in "Moloda Rus'" [Young Rus' or Young Ruthenia] published in a Ukrainian newspaper, *Zoria Halytska* in 1850:

> I still recall as though it were yesterday, because my young years saw those moments when my peers at Lviv University often spoke about the Ruthenian world, about the past, about our sacred homeland and tears streamed down many a pale face. They longed for something; they desired and expected something; they wanted to say something to the world, proclaim it to their neighbors, but words could not yet convey the feelings that were bursting from the depths of their hearts. Indeed, here and there a voice was raised; however, it was frightened, weak, like a child that begins to whimper. The bard had not yet appeared; the nightingale had not yet sung.[58]

In the course of just a few years the political atmosphere in the seminary experienced a profound transformation. Highlights from the life of Markian Shashkevych, as well as of his close associates Iakiv Holovatsky and Ivan Vahylevych, a trio of activists soon to become known as the "Ruthenian Triad," illustrate the process of this transformation.[59]

The "Ruthenian Triad" in the Context of Radical Political Thought

Similarly to the preponderant majority of the Greek Catholic semi-narians, Markian Shashkevych was born into a priestly family with a long lineage of clerics. After completing his secondary education at the Dominican Lyceum in the Galician capital in 1829, he continued his studies both at the university and the Greek Catholic Seminary in Lviv. Because his behaviour did not conform to the strict rules of conduct at the seminary (the details of this incident are still shrouded in mystery), young Markian was expelled from the institution just at the opening of the Polish uprising of 1830. According to his inti-mate friends, the high-spirited seminarian not only sympathized with the insurgents but expressed a passionate desire to join the revolt.[60] There is circumstantial evidence suggesting that he might have partic-ipated: the period of his absence from the seminary coincided rather neatly with the Polish war of independence, and during this time he, according to the official version, resided not at the vicarage of his conservative father but in the home of Tadeusz Wasilewski, the Polish vice-marshal of the Galician Estates Diet and the host in the years to come of well-known members in the underground, among them Seweryn Goszczyński and Lucjan Siemieński.[61]

Irrespective of whether Shashkevych took part in the actual fight-ing or stayed as a guest at the estate of a Polish patriot, the impact of the event on a passionate young man must have been profound. It was largely thanks to the influence exerted by Wasilewski as well as Markian's maternal uncle, Ivan Zakhar Avdykovsky – an official in the Austrian bureaucracy in Lviv who happened to be on excellent terms with the higher echelons of the Greek Catholic clergy – that it was possible for the expelled student to be readmitted to the seminary in the autumn of 1831. Tradition dictated that the young man study for the priesthood, and Markian dutifully followed in the footsteps of his ancestors, but his interests during the seven-year period spent at the seminary tended to gravitate, as already indicated, towards the study of history, political thought, literature, and the Ukrainian language.

A library-museum also known as the Ossolineum located in the neighbourhood of the seminary was the favourite place for the intel-lectually gifted and politically inquisitive student. The meticulously kept and carefully preserved records of the Ossolineum show that in 1834 Shashkevych was one of the most frequent visitors of this rich depository of scholarly studies and that the first book he requested was a work on history written by Lelewel. It was also in the Ossolineum that he and his close colleagues became acquainted with scholarly and

Figure 4.1. Seweryn Goszczyński. Portrait by Kajetan Wincenty Kielisiński, 1836. Courtesy of Europeana.

Figure 4.2. Markian Shashkevych. Portrait by Ivan Trush. Courtesy of Wikimedia.

Figure 4.3. Ivan Vahylevych. Courtesy of the Internet Encyclopedia of Ukraine.

Figure 4.4. Yakiv Holovatsky. Courtesy of the Internet Encyclopedia of
Ukraine.

Figure 4.5. Lucjan Siemieński. Portrait by Maksymilian Fajans. Courtesy of Polona.

literary publications written by members of Ukrainian intelligentsia in imperial Russia. The list included Ivan Kotliarevsky's *Eneida*, a collection of Ukrainian songs by Mykhailo Maksymovych, studies on the Cossack wars, and *Istoriia Rusov ili Maloi Rossii* (History of the Rus' people or Little Russia). The last work, of unknown authorship, was an important document of Ukrainian political thought from the end of the eighteenth or beginning of the nineteenth century. It vividly depicted the historical development of Ukraine, its people, and statehood, from the remote past to 1769, focusing mostly on the periods of the Cossacks, Bohdan Khmelnytsky, and the Hetman state. The underlying principle of *Istoriia Rusov* was that each nation had a natural, moral, and historical right to an independent political existence. Its main theme was the struggle of the Ukrainian nation against Russian or Polish domination.[62]

It was in the Ossolineum that Shashkevych had the opportunity to meet Lucjan Siemieński, as well as other members of the Polish underground. Because of his recurrent visits and lengthy hours spent in the reading room, the studious seminarian fell under suspicion of the police and was interrogated, after it was brought to the attention of the authorities that the library contained forbidden literature smuggled to the Galician capital from Western Europe. This time the theology student was spared a second expulsion, but the reading room was closed and its director, Konstanty Słotwiński, received a six-year sentence for distributing and printing illegal literature.[63]

In view of his sympathies with the democratic ideals of the Polish insurgents a few years earlier, his acquaintance with men involved in the Polish underground like Lucjan Siemieński, as well as his interest in Lelewel's works, it is likely that Shashkevych, while taking out non-censored books, had the opportunity to read clandestine literature reserved by the librarian-conspirator for trusted visitors. Even though Markian's circle of friends were fascinated with the glories of Ukrainian medieval statehood, the seminarian requested an eleventh-century legal code more than twenty times probably because it could have served as a convenient cover for reading illicit literature. At least it may have appeared to have been so to the police and thus caused the investigation. Documentary evidence does not provide an explanation for Shashkevych's interrogation by the police, but an authority on this period, Vasyl' Shchurat, suggests two probable reasons: first, the seminarian's entries in the library records may have provided a cause for suspicion; second, Shashkevych collaborated on an anthology he was preparing for publication with Ivan Vendzylovych, an artist he knew from the seminary who served as the illustrator for the illegal literature printed in the Ossolineum.[64]

In spite of the suspicion that fell upon him in connection with the Ossolineum, the young seminarian did not deem it necessary to suspend his avid interest in the poetry of Mickiewicz. He not only continued to read the Polish bard's works but also translated some of his verses into Ukrainian, including a part of the already mentioned "Ode to Youth." As noted earlier, this had been a highly popular poem among the Czech and Slovak national awakeners. And even though in his writings Shashkevych does not quoted Mickiewicz's celebrated phrase "Force is to be resisted by force," in one of his poems about the well-known Ukrainian Cossack leader, Nalyvajko, the young theology student expresses an idea that conveys a similar message: "Arise young men, [let's fight] for freedom!"[65] Documentary sources indicate that Mykhailo Kozlovsky, a relative of Shashkevych and one of his most frequent correspondents, had in his possession copies of *Pólnoc*, the Polish émigré journal edited by Konarski.[66] Being familiar with Markian's sympathies with the Polish national uprising, it would be difficult to believe that Kozlovsky did not share this literature with him.

During the years that the members of the triad spent at the seminary, they had the good fortune to hold lengthy, intimate discussions in the hospitable home of Markian's uncle, Zakhar Avdykovsky. Beside the members of the triad – Shashkevych, Holovatsky, and Vahylevych – among the regular attendees of these meetings were Mykola Ustyianovych, Mykhailo Kozlovsky, and Mykhailo Minchakevych. As already noted, the last of these, while collaborating with the triad on its literary projects, continued to be a highly active participant in the radical underground throughout the 1830s. All members of the group, including Minchakevych, would play an important role in the national awakening of Galician Ukrainians in the years to come. After the closing of the Ossolineum, unlike their less fortunate fellow students-seminarians, these young men did not need to seek a safe, secluded place on the seminary grounds or in the city's apartments and taverns to read and discuss subjects that would not be approved by the Rector's Office. Iakiv Holovatsky conveys vividly the ponderous, yet emotional atmosphere that generally prevailed during their meetings:

> Our joy knew no bounds. We discovered relics of the language of statecraft and governance from such distant times, and on the basis of these discoveries we determined that these documents were nothing less than the continuation of the political and material life of that Ruthenian nation that lived and flourished during the time of the independence of the Principality of Halych [a Ukrainian name for Galicia] under the rule of Volodar, Vasylko, Iaroslav, Roman, Danylo, and Lev. In our imagination we

saw a powerful state stretching along the whole of the Carpathian high-
lands, from the source of the Neman River to the mouth of the Dnieper
and the Black Sea.[67]

Even when linguistics, language, or literature was the subject of
debate, the emotional approach of the speakers testifies that cultural
issues were seldom divorced from political concerns. A good example is Shashkevych's discussion of the significance of the Ruthenian
language and literature, as related once again by Holovatsky: "When
he [Shashkevych] unwound about Ruthenianness, about nationality,
about the native language and the native literature, then the power of
his spirit became apparent.... His eyes glistened keenly, and with a kind
of holy inspiration his brow became wrinkled and his face took on a
kind of fierce seriousness. He spoke with sincerity; he was powerfully
persuasive because his thoughts flowed from his heart; all of him lived
and breathed this [Ruthenian] spirit."[68]

One did not need to be a direct participant in a clandestine organization in the city of Lviv in order to become a part of the national political
awakening, because the intellectual currents that pulsated within and
outside the walls of the seminary in the mid-1830s injected a powerful
dose of revolutionary energy into an atmosphere that, had it not been
for the concentration of the radical underground in the Galician capital,
would not have crossed the boundary of a purely cultural renaissance.
To be sure, this generation of Ukrainian national activists, just like their
Slovak and Czech counterparts, showed an interest in the writings of
Kollár, but in addition to their fascination with ethnography, culture,
and Slavic languages, their minds were turned to those periods during
which they saw their country as independent, prosperous, and strong.
Through their published works they wished to bring to the attention
of their contemporaries the greatness and glory of their nation. This
aspect of their endeavours, naturally, could not escape the watchful eye
of the government authorities.

The Tortuous History of Two Anthologies

A good example of the coexistence of the cultural and political in the
thought and work of the Ukrainian national awakeners in Galicia is an
anthology prepared by the triad for publication in 1834. Characteristically, the Romantically inspired title of the collection, "Zoria" (The star),
featured on its front page not an idyllic pastoral scene from the Ukrainian countryside but the seventeenth-century leader of Ukraine's struggle for independence, Bohdan Khmelnytsky. Articles on the Cossack

wars as well as selections illustrating the glory of the medieval Kyivan period indicate that political questions dominated the seminarians' interests and concerns. It is, therefore, not surprising that the first attempt to publish the anthology did not get the final approval of the authorities. Jerenej Kopitar, the Viennese censor of Slavic works, gave the manuscript a high rating, considering it an "exceptional phenomenon," the publication of which could not only significantly contribute to the awakening of national consciousness among Ukrainians in Galicia but also produce an impact on the Ukrainian elites in the Russian Empire. However, the cautious imperial censor left the final decision for the authorities in Lviv, where, permission was promptly denied by the newly appointed censor, Venedykt Levytsky because of the tense atmosphere resulting from charges of political involvement of the seminarians. It is worth noting that the majority of the contributors to the proposed publication were members of the secret Carbonari cell "Związek Pryjaćol Ludu." The censor's good friend, the prefect Mykola Hordynsky, was very aware of this fact. By stopping the publication, it can be argued, the censor prevented attracting attention of the police.

During the years that followed, Venedykt Levytsky was often scathingly criticized for forbidding the publication of the anthology and for stopping the distribution of another that would appear two years later. One of the severest critics of the higher ranks of the Greek Catholic clergy during the second half of the nineteenth century was Mykhailo Pavlyk. At the end of his life, however, even this radical political thinker softened his criticism of the censor, explaining that by forbidding the distribution of a subsequent publication, *Rusalka Dnistrovaia*, Levytsky saved the Ruthenian Triad from imprisonment.[69] While occupying the position of rector, Venedykt Levytsky, as noted earlier, contributed generously to the expansion of Ukrainian studies in the seminary. To what degree he was aware of the political involvement of the students might never be known, but one thing is certain: until he remained the rector, Hordynsky's position as a professor and prefect in the Greek Catholic institution remained secure.

When two years later a second, and this time successful effort was made to print the *Zoria* material outside of Galicia, it no longer contained selections that were considered highly sensitive, such as Shashkevych's article on Bohdan Khmelnytsky or literary works of the politically engaged seminarians. This second anthology, appearing under a politically most innocuous title *Rusalka Dnistrovaia* (The nymph of the Dniester) too did not remain unnoticed by the vigilant eye of the imperial officialdom. Soon after its application, the majority of the printed copies landed in the hands of the police.[70]

As one would expect, throughout the tortuous period connected with the publication of the two manuscripts, the members of the triad were subjected to the most gruelling police interrogations and nerve-wrecking searches. These intimidation tactics did not prevent the Rector's Office from selecting Shashkevych to deliver the solemn tribute to the Austrian monarch in 1835. In this case, too, the possibility that the speech was used as a shield of protection should not be excluded. It should be noted that in addition to his association with two banned publications, only a year earlier he was interrogated by the police. What caught the listeners' attention were not the grandiose phrases expressed in honour of the emperor but the fact that the speech was delivered not in the customary Latin, German, or Polish, but in Ukrainian. According to the reminiscences of Mykola Ustyianovych, the speaker's words had such a beautiful and powerful sound that they immediately "raised the Ruthenian spirit [among the seminarians] by one hundred per cent."[71] It is highly unlikely that the student-listeners in the auditorium paid much attention to the oration's content – praising the emperor was a formality that the politically sophisticated generation of the post–November Polish insurgency would have taken for granted. It was the Ukrainian language, eloquence, and the manner of delivery that, as the observer noted, enthralled all present.

The Polish historian Jan Kozik, most likely under the influence of Ukrainian authors during the interwar period as well as the Soviet era, interprets this speech as a step directed against the Polish dominance in eastern Galicia.[72] Considering the good relations that Shashkevych maintained with his Polish acquaintances such as Siemieński and Wasilewski, as well as with many of his Ukrainian colleagues who remained active in the Polish underground, it would be closer to the truth to view the first address in spoken Ukrainian as a step on the part of the speaker to assure the future unhindered development of Ukrainian studies.

Young Poland under Goszczyński's Leadership

After asserting his position of leadership in the association, the Polish poet-conspirator Goszczyński took a closer look at the Ukrainian political activists, almost exclusively Greek Catholic seminarians who joined the Polish political underground after the November insurrection. His observations reinforced his assumption that the Ukrainian theology students would not only be well prepared to grasp the meaning and spirit of Young Europe but were even better suited for underground activities than the recruits from the Roman Catholic institution.[73] As developments in the late 1830s and early 1840s would reveal, a large number of theology and philosophy students exhibited an inordinate interest in the revolutionary literature and activities tied to the underground. It must have been the protective role of the prefect Hordynsky that shielded the seminarians from expulsion or imprisonment, for the periodic searches conducted in the 1830s failed to reveal any trace of serious seditious material on the premises of the seminary. The only "incriminating" item most often found in students' possession would be a pipe or pack of tobacco. Thus, whenever a group of young men congregated in isolated areas on or close to the seminary grounds, the usual explanation for these get-togethers was "smoking." Since this type of "recreation" was forbidden, the students were appropriately reprimanded and occasionally punished. This and similar transgressions entailed minor yet meticulously documented penalties, as the minutes of the meetings of the seminary's administration testify. One wonders whether the smoking "clubs" or some drinking revelries in local taverns where the students were apprehended on occasion served as a cover-up, a camouflage for meetings during which political questions were discussed. Punishment for smoking or drinking was relatively mild, while political affiliation with the revolutionary underground could result in an immediate expulsion or imprisonment, as developments would show.

The periodic meetings held by the administration on the question of how to deal with the repeated charges by the police regarding the seminarians' involvement in the radical underground – meetings during which Hordynsky had been present, as his signature on the minutes testifies[74] – enabled the prefect-conspirator to warn the politically involved students of an impending interrogation or search. The fact that the members of the administration could demonstrate their vigilance by reprimanding or punishing frequent transgressors for smoking or drinking appeared sufficient for being absolved from charges of neglect of disciplinary measures. The expressions of loyalty to the emperor in speeches delivered routinely by the seminarians – some of whom figured prominently on the police list of suspects – served as evidence that the administration took steps to inculcate sentiments of loyalty and devotion to the imperial authorities within the walls of the Greek Catholic institution. At times when police officials presented the administration with explicit orders to deny ordination to theology students who were on the list of suspects, the Rector's Office responded with a strong defence, arguing that the listed individuals were exemplary young men, highly regarded both for their academic excellence and sterling moral characters. In one instance, two senior seminarians by the name of

Kurylovych and Zahaikevych who appeared on the police list were praised by the rector, not only for their diligence, but also for their readiness to offer tutorial assistance to younger classmates. In addition, Kurylovych was lauded for delivering a splendid eulogy in honour of the emperor.[75]

These assurances notwithstanding, Masoch's deputy, Lorensi, retorted with a stern warning that the seminarians' impending ordination would provide the new clergymen with opportunities to maintain contact with younger students in the seminary, as well as to spread dangerous ideas among the people in the countryside. It is quite astounding that the police official did not consider it prudent to alert the rector of the dangers that might result from the "willingness" of an "exemplary" but politically suspect seminarian to provide tutorial lessons to younger colleagues! Pressure continued for the administration to tighten the disciplinary control, even though repeated searches failed to produce evidence of seditious materials. Not infrequently the rectory succeeded in rescuing a student from incarceration by providing the suspect with excellent recommendations and assuring the police that he would be kept under close supervision.[76]

In 1837 the inordinate pressure exerted on the Greek Catholic seminary not only by the Police Department but also by the Governor's Office prompted the Metropolitan Mykhailo Levytsky to order even stricter vigilance over the habits and activities of the seminarians. In March of that year the metropolitan requested the Rector's Office to provide information regarding the books the seminarians were reading. After a thorough search, the Rectory replied that aside from the newspaper *Allgemeine Zeitung* and *Novalia Polonica* [*Novela Polifonica*?] and some books the students purchased at the local bookstore, nothing was found in the students' possessions. The metropolitan's office responded with instructions to forbid the students to purchase any printed materials at the local bookstore.[77] The seminary issued regulations to this effect on 10 March 1837, but this order appears to have been ineffective, for it had to be repeated again on 8 February 1838. Similar orders continued to be issued well into the 1840s.[78]

Even though no concrete evidence was uncovered against Hordynsky's involvement in conspiratorial activities, at least not until 1841, enough police pressure was applied to induce a newly appointed rector, Hryhorii Yakhymovych, to ask the prefect and philosophy professor to look for a position at another institution. Because Hordynsky's attempt to obtain a teaching appointment at the Greek Catholic Seminary in Przemyśl – another active centre of political conspiracies – proved unsuccessful, the former professor and prefect had no choice but to assume the duties of a parish priest in the village of Batiachyn, from where, though far removed from the epicentre of underground politics, he continued to maintain ties with his colleague-conspirators. Soon after his arrival he joined a secret group called Nowa Sarmacja (New Sarmatia), an organization ideologically linked to the association. The full extent of his and the Greek Catholic seminarians' participation in the political underground would surface only later at a protracted trial in Lviv in the early 1840s, at which Hordynsky, together with other former conspirator-seminarians was formally charged with treason and received a death sentence. The death sentences were subsequently commuted either to life imprisonment or to incarcerations ranging between twelve to fifteen years in Austria's notorious prison-fortress Spilberk in Brno.[79]

During the 1830s, however, the most common punishment for suspicion of involvement in underground politics was transfer, as in the case of Hordynsky, or denial of ordination for seminarians under police observation. This was partly the reason why two members of the Ukrainian Triad, Holovatsky and Vahylevych, were not able to be ordained for a long time, even though clear evidence of their political involvement was not established.[80] The fact that the third and leading member of the triad, Markian Shashkevych, was ordained in 1837 may have been due once again to the influence of his uncle among the members of the Greek Catholic hierarchy and the extreme caution with which the talented seminarian learnt to tread after his expulsion at the beginning of the 1830s.

Occasional interrogations, arrests, and trials of theology students attending the seminary had been taking place since the mid-1830s, but the outcomes of the prosecutions tended to be relatively mild, rarely exceeding two or three years of imprisonment. On one occasion, two seminarians, Yosyf Konstantynovych and Venedykt Kushchykevych, were tried for being part of an underground cell led by the former seminarian Ivan Seletsky, but charges against them were dropped in 1838 on account of insufficient evidence. Both seminarians continued their clandestine political involvement after ordination. In the same year that charges against the conspirators were dropped, Kushchykevych, together with Vasyl Podolynsky and Marian Lapchynsky, organized an underground group with a radical political program under the name of Vilni Halychany (Free Galicians).[81] When the full extent of their involvement in the underground was uncovered at the trial of 1842, both Konstantynovych and Kushchykevych, together with a number of seminarian-conspirators, were charged with treason and sentenced to death.[82]

Throughout the 1830s, the Austrian police encountered enormous difficulties in extracting information from the young political activists, partly because of the firm commitment to secrecy among the young conspirators, and partly because of the incompetence of the search squads sent to inspect homes or institutions under suspicion. A telling incident involved a police search of the family residence of two brothers, Anton and Maksym Lubovych, both philosophy students in the town of Ternopil. They were suspected by Masoch's office of being involved in copying and disseminating revolutionary works secretly transmitted to Galicia from Paris, as well as of passing these materials through underground channels to territories under Russian control. A thorough inspection of the family home was ordered, but to the great disappointment of the police chief, no incriminating documents were found. According to family reminiscences related years later, the young men escaped arrest because the police investigators failed to check the drawer of a large dining room table, most likely the very table at which the suspects were interrogated![83]

Among the works occasionally found in the students' possession were copies of Lamennais's *Paroles d'un croyant*, a work promoting respect for democracy and republicanism (available in Polish translation under the title *Słowa Wieszcze*), Constanin Volney's *Les Ruines, ou meditation sur les revolutions des empires*, Heinrich Laube's *Das Junge Europa*, works of German philosophers, Mickiewicz's *Księgi narodu polskego, Do Matki Polki, Dziady*, and poems by Romantic writers and poets such as Krasiński, Scott, Byron, and Goethe, among others.[84] In other words, works that generally enjoyed great popularity among members and sympathizers of Young Europe in the West. A good part of this literature had its origin in the collection of forbidden books, Bibliothèque du Proscrit, a library that Mazzini founded in 1836 specifically to spread democratic ideas throughout Europe. In a letter to his close friend Luigi Amedeo Melegari, entrusted with the actual organization and management of the library, Mazzini explained that this collection of printed materials ought to include "all banned works of exiles worthy of note that, in accordance with the ideas of *Young Europe*, deal with history, literature, etc."[85] Some of these books were delivered to a popular bookstore in Lviv owned by Jan Milikowski through a secret well-guarded route passing either through Prague and Budapest or through the port of Odessa.[86] Milikowski's bookstore was frequented by students of both Greek Catholic and Roman Catholic seminaries. The Czech political activists Kampelík and František Ladislav Rieger, as well as the indefatigable Polish revolutionary Leslaw Łukaszewicz in Cracow, were instrumental in making sure that the delivery of revolutionary literature flowed unhindered through Prague, Budapest, and Cracow to the Galician capital.[87]

With the exception of older former Carbonari members of local origin in the association's Supreme Council like Leon Korecki, the top leadership of the Polish underground conducted its relations with the Ukrainians in a spirit of collegiality exemplified by the conduct of Goszczyński, Kulczyński, Siemieński, and Bogdański. Especially telling in this connection are the reminiscences of Bogdański:

> We did not distinguish between Ruthenians and Poles in our activities.... We infused the Ruthenian priests and seminarians with our spirit, so that through selfless actions to gain completely the confidence of the peasants they would establish schools; so that as intermediaries between the peasants and the *szlachta* they would draw these two strata closer to each other and [thereby] obliterate the hatred and suspicion of the peasant for his lords, and through this rectify his perception of the *Liakhy*; and so that by preserving his nationality they would facilitate a close union of the two in the fraternal oneness that the pride of the *szlachta* and the fanaticism of the Jesuits had weakened. And we presented to the *szlachta* in Rus' the advantage and the necessity of aiding the Ruthenian priests in these undertakings, of drawing closer to them and the peasant, and of enlightening him and preparing him for self-reliance.[88]

Bogdański also notes that efforts were made by the members of the organization to maintain the purity of both the Polish and the Ruthenian languages by preventing the incursion of German words and phrases, a trend especially noticeable among recruits of both nationalities.

Another prominent Polish activist concerned with the task of reaching out to the Ukrainians, both the rural masses and the intelligentsia, was Ignacy Zegota Kulczyński, as already noted, an influential member of the association's Executive Council and a confidant of Konarski. A landowner from the province of Volynia and a veteran of the November uprising, the mature, reflective conspirator was well aware of the shortcomings of the Polish insurgency in territories in which the majority of the people were Ukrainians. Kulczyński made it his special mission to find young Poles in Galicia who spoke or were willing to learn the local language and who were familiar with the customs and traditions of the Ukrainian masses. Julian Horoszkiewicz, a rank-and-file member of the association who became closely attached to Kulczyński during the latter's activities in the countryside, wrote about the Polish soldier-patriot with admiration:

> His strategy was to bring all social strata closer together, to convince the landowner of the need, absolute necessity and obligation to abolish serfdom. He called upon them to do this in the name of love for the fatherland,

which could not be freed without these conditions; without them it was "not worth its freedom." On the other hand, he stressed the need to work on behalf of the people, to enlighten the people, to elevate the people morally, to unite the people with the enlightened strata, to awaken in them the desire for and faith in freedom ... and to prepare them gradually for the coming necessary general struggle for common liberties through the political freedom of the fatherland.[89]

One of Kulczyński's recruits for the designated task was an idealistic young lawyer with a literary bent by the name of Kasper Cięglewicz. Born in the deep Ukrainian countryside of the Pokuttia region and schooled in revolutionary thought, first during his gymnasium years in the town of Sambir, and later during his law studies in Lviv, fluent in both Ukrainian and Polish, young Cięglewicz was a perfect candidate for the role that Kulczyński had in store for him. It was mainly through Kulczyński's encouragement that Cięglewicz switched from Polish to Ukrainian in his literary pursuits. According to the young man's reminiscences, Kulczyński urged him to write in the language the common people could understand: "Why don't you create songs for the people? The people here are Ruthenians and, therefore, they need Ruthenian poetry – simple, easily comprehended in the village." He counselled him to "be like a ploughman sowing seeds. In some places it will fail to grow, in others it will sprout."[90] These words of an older, experienced revolutionary struck a responsive chord in Cięglewicz's mind. It all appeared to him logical and simple, as he notes in his reminiscences: "I have grown up in Ruthenia [na Rusi] and therefore I knew the language of the Ruthenian people. With eagerness I took upon myself the task of writing Ruthenian songs."[91]

The young man undertook his mission in earnest. With enthusiasm and ingenuity, he began to set his verses to popular folk melodies so that they could be easily learnt and disseminated in the countryside. These verses often described the hardships and wrongs endured by the common men under the feudal conditions, blaming the Austrian authorities for the impoverishment of the countryside and calling upon the masses to stand firmly together in the forthcoming struggle against the kings and emperors. The songs were copied and distributed by patriotic women's groups associated with Young Poland. Cięglewicz 's revolutionary calls to arms were often interspersed with moving expressions of compassion for the common men and women whom he befriended and obviously learnt to commiserate with and love:

If only I could be your shadow, I would carry behind you
And everywhere in front of you, the image of your wretchedness;

That image covered with blood like that of the crucified Christ
Who on the cross died in agony on behalf of humanity.[92]

Because of his involvement in the underground, Cięglewicz was arrested in 1835 but two years later was able to escape from prison with the aid of two women conspirators, who supplied him with a wig and other accessories so that he could elude the guards. It would have been in his interest to flee abroad, but he chose to stay close to his roots because, as he wrote in his reminiscences, it was precisely at that time, that "Szymek [Szymon Konarski] was passing through Galicia." After giving some thought to follow the revolutionary leader to Lithuania, Cięglewicz decided that it was his duty to remain in Galicia to continue his mission as a Ruthenian (*czerwono-ruski*) songwriter.[93]

Cięglewicz's songs were widely circulated in Galicia. Some of them found their way even to the neighbouring territories inhabited by the Slovaks. There they were exceptionally well suited for stirring the masses to action, because the social and economic conditions in the land inhabited by Slovaks were almost identical to those in Galicia. It is for this reason that the words of these songs were copied and meticulously preserved by Aleksander Vrchovský, whose contacts, as already noted, extended not only to the Poles and southern Slavs, but to the Ukrainians in Galicia as well.[94]

Cięglewicz and his mentor Kulczyński were well aware that spreading revolutionary ideas among the masses could be best promoted not only through enlightened clergy but also through educated Ukrainians, young men and women whose number was rapidly increasing with the spread of education. In most cases these were village school teachers and minor provincial bureaucrats. It was for this group that the Polish conspirator prepared *Instructions for the Teacher of the Ruthenian People*. It was widely distributed through underground channels throughout Galicia. The highly incendiary nature of this guide, written in spirit similar to the verses, can be gleaned from its concluding statement: "We will shout 'Down with the bondage of the emperor and lords,' and we will follow the common men who are showing us the path to happiness and freedom."[95] Through his enthusiasm and creative imagination, Cięglewicz found eager followers in the towns and villages of the province. One of his most active and successful disciples was Mykhailo Popel, a Ukrainian student from the town of Sambir, attending the same gymnasium in which Cięglewicz began his revolutionary apprenticeship. Young Popel was encouraged by his mentor to pursue his studies with utmost diligence, concentrating on Latin and German, but at the same time, not neglecting "the languages of the fatherland: Polish and

Ruthenian."[96] For Cięglewicz, these two languages represented "one and indivisible tongue" of the Polish Commonwealth. Cięglewicz obviously assumed that the two languages could or would be used interchangeably or, perhaps, one of them would remain the language of the common people, while the other that of the educated elite. To him both linguistic groups represented one nation, a nation that constituted a single component in the family of the Slavic brotherhood. Cięglewicz's views closely followed a mode of thought made popular by a well-known Polish poet in Galicia, Wacław Zaleski, who claimed that the population of the region was inhabited by two branches of a single nation who spoke different but mutually intelligible dialects. He predicted a merger between Ukrainian and Polish, just as he assumed there would be a fusion between the Czech and Slovak tongues.[97]

For Popel, who, unlike Cięglewicz and Wacław Zaleski, came from a Ukrainian background, the distinction between the two languages was real, just like the differences between the two nationalities. There was a common bond between them, but it was based on the principle of equality within the family of a wider Slavic brotherhood. Popel expressed this idea in one of his poems: "Slavdom is our mother and our heavenly father; all Slavs are our brothers." Popel's works indicate his familiarity with the ideas of the Czech Slavophiles, the Kolo Ruske, the Ukrainian Triad, and the Polish Romantic writers. He exhorted all people inhabiting the regions of the Dnieper, Dniester, and Buh Rivers, irrespective of their religion or national descent, to live in harmony and peace: "We shall extend our hands to the just *Liakhs* proclaiming: 'Long live freedom! We are with you, you are with us; down with the tsars and landlords, down with the institution of bondage in our lands.'"[98] Popel was convinced that the Poles had a better understanding of the idea of freedom than the Russians, because they already fought for liberty, and therefore he asked rhetorically as a Ukrainian familiar with the ideals of Young Europe, "Is it better to join with those who are so far removed from freedom, that is, with the Muscovites, or with the Poles? Is it better to join with those who in their blindness fight against freedom, because such are the Muscovites, or to fraternize with those who fight for freedom, that is, with the Poles? To disperse the kings and the emperors, let us not only fraternize with the Poles but with all the nations that struggle for freedom, and we shall become stronger."[99]

The revolution of 1830–1, as well as the ideas to which it gave birth, left an indelible mark on the minds of educated youth in Galicia. According to Andrzej Józefczyk, a Polish political activist in the 1830s, "In Galicia, life in the Polish sense began from the [November] uprising. It was during the uprising that youth here began to feel Polish."[100]

At this very time, for a very similar reason, the Greek Catholic seminarians began to feel Ukrainian, colourfully presented in the recollections of Iakiv Holovatsky, as he reminisced some years later: "Not long ago, about a decade or so ago, a new spirit – a Ruthenian spirit – began to appear. Neither a genius awakened [our] somnolent nationality, nor any [internal] event that shook the nation; perhaps it was the neighboring thunder that sounded or the example of the other Slavic nations that roused us."[101] One of his colleagues from the Greek Catholic seminary in Przemyśl, Mykola Kmytsykevych, seemed no less bemused by the transformation he experienced during that pivotal year. This he expressed vividly to a Polish friend, Kazimierz Turowski: "Some kind of great spirit of freedom has overwhelmed me.... I had a dream that caused a profound change within me; I dreamt that I had liberated the Ruthenians and given them independence. This has become such a mania with me that I can think of nothing else.... In my opinion, it would be best if Poland would rise; I have great plans.... The Ruthenians are most on my mind; let the Poles think about themselves, and I shall think about my own kind. No one will think worse of me for that."[102] It was precisely this life-sustaining desire to fight for freedom on behalf of one's nation that the founder of Young Italy and Young Europe was aiming to rekindle among the peoples of Eastern Europe through his emissaries and the revolutionary literature of his underground library.

The Polish historian Adam Kozik sums up the relationship between Poles and Ukrainians during the 1830s succinctly: "Polish influences penetrated the Galician Ukrainian community in various ways. Polish belles-lettres played one role as the model for literary efforts by the younger generation of Ukrainians, whereas revolutionary agitation after 1831 constituted a quite different influence. Literature brought the two peoples closer, but the political activities achieved an end that the Poles had not intended. By seeking to subordinate the Ukrainian movement to their own revolutionary aspirations for national liberation, the Poles awakened and strengthened the Ukrainians' feeling of national separateness."[103]

A somewhat deeper analysis of the era also showed that the political ideals of Young Europe facilitated the formation of at least some deeper bonds of friendship between the revolutionaries of the two nations. Popel's readiness to extend a helping hand to a "just" Pole is an example. The Kolo Ruske, working not in opposition but side-by-side with the Association of the Polish People is another. Ideologically both organizations were closely related to each other but formed two distinct national groups. Hordynsky and the cohort of Greek Catholic co-conspirators looked forward to the establishment of a federal democratic republic in which both constituent parts would enjoy full equality. Working along with fellow Polish conspirators like Bogdański, Goszczyński, and Siemieński, these hopes appeared to rest on solid ground.

The attitudes of the Poles differed considerably. The sensitive poet-revolutionary Goszczyński, who was well acquainted with Ukrainian history and culture, recognized a distinct Ukrainian identity and commiserated with Ukraine's continuing struggle for independence but had little faith that this objective would be realized. Siemieński and Bogdański seemed to share a somewhat similar sentiment. Conspirators like Kulczyński and Cięglewicz skilfully utilized Ukrainian language and songs as instruments for spreading revolutionary ideas among the common people but were convinced that the superiority of Polish political leadership as well as the attractiveness of Polish culture would overwhelm the frail beginnings of Ukrainian national awakening, once Polish independence was regained. This attitude reflected the views of a large segment of the Polish revolutionary underground.

Goszczyński's Departure and the Eclipse of the Association

By the end of 1837, because of the precariousness of his status as an illegal resident in Galicia, Goszczyński's influence in the Executive Council of the Association steadily declined. Forced to go into hiding, he seldom could attend the meetings.[104] The political situation in Galicia became even tenser when in the spring of 1838 the tsarist police captured Konarski, with whom both Goszczyński's and Kulczyński had been closely interacting.[105] Goszczyński fled abroad while, as already noted, Kulczyński when faced with the inevitability of arrest, committed suicide. In the absence leaders who exercised a moderating influence on the Polish members of the Council from the beginning, quarrels among factions steadily increased. As Bogdański described the situation, "Until Goszczyński's vigilant eye saw to it that the conspirators adhered closely to the important principle of tolerance and circumspection based on experience, the association was able to surmount the oncoming dangers. The time was approaching, however, when this would come to an end and the organization would fall apart into feuding, irreconcilable groups of which it was composed."[106] Among these new formations, the most active were the Nowa Sarmacia (New Sarmacia) and Vilni Halychany (Free Galicians).[107]

Before suspension of the activities of the association, with the exception of a bitter quarrel between Korecki and Hordynsky, in general, throughout the mid-1830s and the following decade relations between Ukrainians and the Poles tended to be civil and at times even cordial, until the events of 1848 brought to the fore issues that caught both sides, especially the Poles, by surprise. While everyone took for granted the influence of the November uprising on the resurgence of Polish nationalism, few activists in the Polish underground anticipated the impact that this event, combined with the new ideas coming from Western Europe, would have on the awakening of national self-awareness among the Ukrainians. Nevertheless, the quarrels that ensued between Ukrainians and Poles at this later stage did not result in violence. In fact, even during the heady days of the Spring of Nations, the ties of friendship based on ideological principles emanating from a common source, though often strained, were not completely severed. Irreconcilable differences between the Poles and the Ukrainians emerged only after Mazzini's "nationalism with a human face" was overshadowed in the first half of the twentieth century by a new version of the national idea: nationalism marked by Social Darwinist ideology, according to which the principle of the natural right of the strong to dominate the weak became the norm in determining relations within society and among nations.

Chapter Five

Young Poland's Revolutionary Underground in Russian-Ruled Lands

Who among us is not a prophet? Each one of us who has by word, pen, great deed or act served the sacred cause has been a prophet, has been a civil servant of the national call to action, has had a premonition of that what ought to happen.[1]

Szymon Konarski's visit to Galicia in the summer of 1835 was only a brief stopover intended to provide moral support and advice to the Association of the Polish People, the new branch of Young Poland in this strategically located Austrian province. From the start of his mission, Konarski's attention was focused on the western provinces of the Russian Empire, where intensive preparatory work for an all-encompassing popular upheaval was considered of vital importance for the realization of a successful revolution in Eastern Europe. As soon as he took care of the association's formal administrative matters in Cracow and Lviv, Young Poland's emissary crossed the Austro-Russian border at the northeastern Galician town of Brody with the assistance of the experienced conspirator from Volynia residing illegally in East Galicia, Ignacy Kulczyński. The passage proved to be smooth and uneventful, in spite of the fact that the tsarist authorities were warned by the French police to be on guard because a dangerous agent of the Polish underground under the assumed name of Hajpelman was expected to be on his way to Russia. The Russian consul in Brody was known for keeping a close watch on all suspicious persons requesting entry to Russian-controlled territories, but at the very time of Konarski's crossing in September 1835, the Russian official found no newsworthy item to pass to the police headquarters in Kyiv other than information about a trial and imprisonment of conspirators belonging to Young Italy in faraway Milan.[2]

Appropriately disguised by dyeing his reddish-blond hair jet-black and sporting a matching moustache, equipped with a set of pseudonyms and a

number of addresses, Konarski immediately plunged into the whirlwind
of conspiratorial action as soon as he reached his first contact in Volynia. As
in Galicia, his first undertaking involved the unification of the still existing
Polish Carbonari cells and other clandestine groups under the umbrella
of Young Poland. This assignment was complicated by the organization's
goal to win the loyalty of all people living in the territories of Belarus,
Lithuania, and Ukraine – the vast majority of whom were of non-Polish
background – while the nationally conscious, patriotic element on whose
support the organization could rely for military leadership and material
backing belonged in most instances to the Polish gentry and titled nobility.
    Konarski was fully aware of the problems he would be faced with,
even before he embarked on his dangerous mission. He knew that he
had to put aside his utopian beliefs on issues of economic and social
justice and closely follow Young Poland's cautious, moderate program.
He became even more convinced of the necessity to make this ideological shift once he came face-to-face with the actual state of affairs
in the field of operation. In spite of his readiness to mend his convictions for the good of the cause, his former opinions voiced only a year
or so earlier through his fiery editorials on the pages of *Północ* were
not easily overlooked by the politically astute members of the Polish
elite. Furthermore, his hidden radical convictions did occasionally surface while he was campaigning on behalf of Young Poland's program,
since he was known to be a passionate speaker. From the beginning of
his arrival, Konarski encountered criticism, especially from the aristocratic circles, very few of whose members were willing to support his
organization's program, even in the more liberal political milieu of the
emigration. Not infrequently, Young Poland's emissary was accused of
spreading fanciful foreign ideas that were alien to the traditions and interests of the Polish people.[3] In his correspondence with Lelewel, Konarski confided that even within the groups of trusted conspirators whose
addresses he received before his departure, there were men who were
driving him up the wall "by their gentry-mindedness and lethargy."[4]
He urged that more revolutionary literature be sent from abroad and
that a better communication system be established between his headquarters and the organization's centre in emigration. With a heavy heart
he informed Lelewel that in the territories in which he was operating,
each class needed to be politically re-educated starting at the elementary level, or as he put it, "from the ABC of our new world." Therefore,
he urged that separate appeals be prepared for every group in a spirit
that spoke to the heart and not, as was still the custom, to reason. He
suggested themes that would focus on the misery and worthlessness of
life in the present and show the way to happiness of the human existence in the days to come. Such appeals were important, he explained,

because the people he came in contact with tended to be decent individuals in the majority of cases who just needed to be enlightened, so that they could become conscious of the power that resides within them and be able to distinguish men who were considered good just because they "do not bite" from those who are willing to sacrifice their lives for the welfare of humanity. Those in the first category were to be shunned, while those in the second were to be emulated. In other words, what was needed, reported Konarski in an elated spirit of youthful idealism, was a concerted effort by all involved to awaken among the people the ability to look deeper into their souls, because most of them were not even aware of the soul's existence and therefore did not have faith in the power that resided within them. This task could be best accomplished through the dissemination of underground literature and by appeals coming from highly respected authorities, first of all from the organization's leader and Konarski's superior, Lelewel himself.[5] These carefully delineated guidelines coming from a student to his mentor on the content and form of the appeals contain a good dose of material that Konarski learned a few years earlier, during the time he spent in Switzerland in the company of Young Europe's ideological master, Giuseppe Mazzini. For Lelewel's generation, still on the subconscious level at least, tied to the rationalistic thought of the Enlightenment, it was not always easy to comprehend and fully understand the power of the new Romantic spirit pulsating in the veins of the young.

With the passage of time, Konarski's assessment of the people he had to work with was not all negative. In his letters that followed he had nothing but high praise for the hardworking, dedicated members in the women's organizations, especially the principal coordinator, Felicia Felińska. Among the young people too he found many enthusiasts capable of grasping new ideas and showing talent for conspiratorial work. What was needed, he stressed again firmly, was a larger supply of revolutionary literature and better lines of communication with the émigré centre.[6]

Szymon Konarski: A Mazzinian in Action

It had been Konarski's singular achievement that in the course of only one year under his leadership, he was able not only to unify the remnants of the widely scattered but still functioning Carbonari cells and various grievance committees that sprang up spontaneously after 1831, but planted new tightly organized conspiratorial groups at the University of Kyiv, the University of Dorpat (Tartu), a medical college in Vilnius,[7] as well as in a few other strategically located educational or cultural centres. By the end of his two-and-a-half-year period of indefatigable toil, he even made two daring trips to St Petersburg in order to establish contacts with Polish students and with trusted military personnel in the Russian capital.[8] In the spring of 1836 and again a year later he visited Odesa to meet with an agent of Young Poland, Ignacy Mołodecki, a local businessman involved in the export of grain to a number of West European ports, including Marseilles. It was with Mołodecki's aid that Young Europe's literature flowed through Konarski's underground channels to Kyiv and to other parts of Ukraine.[9]

Konarski's ability to recruit a considerable number of idealistic people of both Polish and non-Polish background into the ranks of Young Poland was facilitated by the fact that the repressive measures under Tsar Nicholas I left little room for any form of legal means to voice even the most innocent complaints. These tsarist policies forced even the more moderate segments of society to move underground. The need for clandestine operations registered itself with stark clarity when the police authorities responded to petitions in defence of Polish culture with open persecution of the signatories.

But it was also Konarski's charismatic personality, his unswerving dedication to the mission of Young Europe that drew both men and women of all backgrounds and ages to follow his call. He has been described by both young and old who had the opportunity to meet him during the two-and-a-half years of his underground operations as a highly intelligent, attractive young man with impeccable manners, fluency in several foreign languages. and a special gift in the art of persuasion through his logical, concentrated manner of thinking and speaking. He attracted both men and women of all classes and national backgrounds. This youthful soldier-political activist with a highly sensitive nature, even during the tense years of underground toil, found time to play the flute and even to fall in love with an idealistic young woman, Emilia Michalska. who, like him, belonged to the Calvinist denomination, a small religious minority among the predominantly Catholic Poles.[10] Emilia inevitably was drawn into the work of the underground by quietly spreading Young Poland's ideas in a private *pension* (boarding school) she was attending in the town of Vinnytsia. The fact that the *pension* was headed by F. Girardot, a French educator favourably disposed towards the republican cause, contributed to the success of the young woman's endeavour.[11]

Konarski's continuing appeals to the young led to the transformation of a Polish student group into a secret revolutionary cell at the University of Kyiv in December 1835. This he accomplished with the aid of Piotr Borkowski, a headmaster of a local private pension for gymnasium and university students in the provincial capital. The secret group was skilfully led by Wladyslaw Gordon, a highly popular student in

Figure 5.1. Szymon Konarski. From *Szymon Konarski: w 60-tą rocznicę stracenia*, 1902. Biblioteka Narodowa, 215.711. Courtesy of Polona.

Figure 5.2. Ewa Felińska. From August Sokołowski, *Dzieje porozbiorowe narodu polskiego ilustrowane*, 1904. T. 2, cz. 1. Courtesy of Wikimedia.

the mathematics and physics department at the university. Being a devout admirer of Konarski, Gordon followed the instructions of his master with filial devotion, especially with respect to the recruitment of not only Polish but also Ukrainian students attending this institution of higher learning. That the participation of non-Poles in the secret organization was not of marginal nature was evident from the fact that among the top leaders holding the important rank of *soltys* (or leader), there were two Ukrainians: Arystarch Sosnovsky and Aleksander Chornyi.[12]

Entry into the secret organization involved a solemn ceremony during which the candidate took an oath of loyalty and imparted a kiss on the crucifix while holding a handful of soil in his hand. Such ceremonies were usually arranged during evening strolls on the banks of Dnieper River [Dnipro River] or walks in the environs of the medieval Golden Gates in Kyiv, a place of inspiration especially to the Ukrainian recruits.[13] Considering the social background from which most members of the secret cell originated – the majority came from the ranks of Polish gentry – it is not surprising that among them revolutionary traditions of the not too distant past, such as practices of Polish student circles, the *Filareci* and the *Filomaci*, as well as the ideals of the November uprising were a dominant presence. "The slogans of the *Filareci* injected the new generations of educated youth with sentiments of love of their land and their nation, with readiness for action, for struggle and for sacrifice,"[14] with reverential admiration, wrote Wacław Łasocki, one of the students attending the university a few years later.[15] The underground circle's chosen motto – "Faith, Hope, and Charity" – echoed the pre-November 1830 revolutionary ideals of patriotic Polish youth. But while the traditions tied with love of one's homeland represented vestiges of the past, the recruitment of non-Poles and women into the organization, as well as stress on the dissemination of revolutionary propaganda among the masses represented a new approach springing from the ideological foundations of Young Europe. The old and the new currents reinforced one another, creating a powerful bastion of energy for what was hoped to be the forthcoming all-encompassing upheaval.

The main duties of the inducted members of the secret cell in Kyiv involved dissemination of the organization's political objectives among students at the university and in secondary schools, spreading enlightenment among the people and collecting statistical data in the countryside. The last-named task was in conformity with Young Poland's instructions concerning the need to assess the value of landed estates and other properties for the purpose of apportioning contributions for the needs of the planned revolution. In case the presence of these "assessors" aroused suspicion, the conspirators were instructed to respond that they were engaged in the sale of tobacco. The secret organization was divided into several sections, each headed by a *soltys,* a trusted individual who alone could communicate with the central leadership. For reasons of security, pseudonyms were given to each recruited member, and no general meetings of the entire group were ever held.[16]

Clandestine literature for the members of the organization was delivered first through Galicia with the help of the indefatigable, ubiquitous Kulczyński, who used the services of two bookstores in Kyiv owned by foreign residents Mielville and Lauron. Revolutionary literature was also delivered directly to these bookstores from Odesa. According to police records based on subsequent interrogations following Konarski's arrest in 1838, a large part of the seized literature in this important port city on the Black Sea was designated for university students in Kyiv.[17] Well-known works of Mickiewicz, such as *Księgi* and *Dziady,* Lamennais's *Paroles d'un croyant,* and of other authors, among them Mauricy Mochnacki's *Historia powstania polskiego 1830–1831 r.* (History of the Polish uprising of 1830–1831) were read and discussed by groups of students at homes of members, among them Pawel Bogdanowicz and Jan Lubowicki. This intensive underground indoctrination effort was camouflaged by a light-hearted, jovial spirit exhibited by the organization's members in their day-to-day interaction with the politically non-involved young men at the university.[18]

A secret society tied to the association/Young Poland was also established at the University of Dorpat, where both Polish and Ukrainian young men were pursuing their studies in the 1830s and 1840s. As a port near the Baltic, Dorpat served as a convenient conduit for the delivery of revolutionary literature designated not only for the students at the university but also for the organization's branches in Lithuania, Belarus, and the Russian capital. The founder of this group was Karol Hildebrandt, who formerly studied in Berlin, where he first became acquainted with ideas of Young Europe. In addition to Hildebrand, among the more active members of the secret group were Bronisław Zaleski and Edward Żeligowski, who, together with some other fifteen to twenty student-members, disseminated democratic ideas among the gentry and the youth.[19]

One of the most active secret cells that proved especially useful for the maintenance of contacts among the association's members in Lithuania was organized by two Belarusian poets, Frantiszek Sawicz and Jan Zahorski, both pursuing their studies at a medical school in Vilnius. In addition to recruitment among the students, the organizers also succeeded in drawing into their ranks professors and even a few local artisans. Sawicz proved especially successful in his effort to establish bonds of friendship between Belarusians and Poles. He was a frequent visitor at Konarski's secret residence in Lisova in Volynia, and, being an advanced student in medicine, proved invaluable in providing medical treatment whenever the indefatigable revolutionary leader, frequently exhausted by travels and work, succumbed to illness. Inspired by the events of 1830–1, Sawicz composed fiery poems in his native language that circulated in manuscript form among Belarusians, Poles, and Ukrainians.[20]

By the end of the first year, through the mediation of one of his most dedicated woman co-conspirators, Felicia Felińska, as well as with the help of sympathetic local clergymen, Konarski succeeded in gaining the support of influential Polish magnates in Lithuania, who, as noted earlier, initially stood aloof from his cause. The emissary's ability to successfully execute practically every task assigned to him by the émigré leaders of Young Poland was bound not only to bolster his spirits but also propel him to look with optimism towards the future.

It was barely a year after he embarked on his mission that Konarski thought it timely to counsel Lelewel that "a prolonged conspiracy has a tendency to break," suggesting to his inordinately cautious superior that the preparatory stage of the revolution ought not to last much longer. In September 1836 he reported with enthusiasm that if he proved successful in bringing together a group of dedicated and talented men, it was not improbable that within the next six to nine months, the hour for the uprising would be at hand.[21] The establishment of an organization under local leadership, in fact, became a reality in the spring of 1837, when a branch of the association came into being during an annual fair in Berdychiv, a town not far from Kyiv. The energies exerted to assemble armaments and prepare for the establishment of a local printing press in the months that followed were indications that Konarski would soon announce that the time of the impending uprising had arrived.

But the news of Konarski's success reached the ears not only of trusted émigré activists but also some important individuals in diplomatic circles, including the Russian ambassador to France. This development was not entirely unexpected, for already in the autumn of 1836 Tsar Nicholas received information from Paris about Konarski's underground operations. Very soon thereafter, the most sophisticated secret agencies were set into motion to track down the centre of the conspiracy and capture the master conspirator.[22] It was partly the ineptitude of the tsarist police in the provinces – whose headquarters had been informed of Konarski's intended mission already a year earlier – and partly the

long years of experience in conspiratorial work among Polish revolutionaries, that made it possible for Young Poland's emissary to continue
working on preparations for military action until the spring of 1838.

Arrest and Execution of a Young European

A number of incidents involving the tsarist police and members of the
underground did occur after the intensification of vigilance initiated by
St Petersburg at the end of 1836. During a routine search in Kyiv, for
example, the police uncovered forbidden books and manuscripts in a
student's apartment. The incendiary nature of these materials alarmed
the entire provincial police apparatus and prompted its chief to send a
report to the headquarters of the Third Section of His Majesty's Chan-
cery in St Petersburg.[23] The imperial authorities responded promptly:
the minister of education, Sergey Uvarov himself, came to oversee the
investigation of the apparent conspiracy in Kyiv. The first person to be
interrogated was Stanisław Strojanowski, whose handwriting on one of
the confiscated manuscripts was incontrovertible proof of his ties to the
illicit material. The investigators were able to extract from the fright-
ened young man the names of three of his co-conspirators, but the punishment that followed was relatively mild. Because of his willingness to
cooperate, Strojanowski suffered no punitive consequences. Two of his
co-conspirators, Julian Bujalski and Pawel Bogdanowicz, however, did
not fare so well. They were despatched to serve in the army. Stanisław
Rutkowski, also tied to the group, was sent to faraway Kazan to teach
at a local school. Of the four students under investigation, only Bujalski
and Bogdanowicz belonged to the upper rungs of the organization. The
fact that they proved strong enough not to divulge any incriminating information about the underground cell at the university made it possible
for the branch of the organization in Kyiv to function for another year.[24]

Of course not every tsarist police department was as unskilled as it
appears to have been under the lethargic governor general Guriev in
Kyiv. In April 1838 its contingent in Lithuania apprehended Konarski
while the conspirator was in the process of purchasing a printing press,
one of his final steps in the preparatory work for the planned uprising.
The lengthy interrogations that followed were accompanied by physi-
cal and mental tortures. In a note bearing Konarski's signature, the
large, distorted letters in the handwriting of the captured prisoner indicate that the interrogators attempted to force their prized captive to
admit that seven women, whose names were brought to the attention
of the police by an informer, were actively involved in his organization.
Konarski stood firm in protecting the women, denying to the end that

they were in any way connected with his cause. He sealed the statement of denial with a signature in large, bold letters.[25]

After a year-long imprisonment and a lengthy trial, the legendary Polish revolutionary, together with four of his top co-conspirators, was publicly executed in Vilnius. The capture of the leader and the intense interrogations that followed triggered a wave of arrests, especially in Kyiv, Dorpat, and Vilnius. Konarski's devoted Belarusian follower, the medical student Frantiszek Sawicz, was sent to the Caucasus to serve in the army as a private. He was more fortunate than most of his apprehended comrades, because he had the good fortune to escape and through the organization's underground network was able to settle in a Volynian village where, under an assumed name, he provided medical care to the rural people while in his spare time teaching the village children to read and write. While caring for the sick during a cholera epidemic, Sawicz caught the disease and died in 1848.[26] That he and many of his co-conspirators who were able to evade arrests and police surveillance would continue to disseminate revolutionary ideas among the intelligentsia in the years to come is evident from the appearance of a new cohort of young men with similar political ideas, especially among the Poles and the Ukrainians already in the first half of the 1840s.

In the course of the investigation in Lithuania, a minor government official who formerly belonged to the student underground at the University of Kyiv broke down under police interrogations and spilled information about the main conspiratorial group in Ukraine.[27] This time the central police authorities responded promptly and efficiently. On the orders of St Petersburg, the inept, lethargic governor of the Kyiv province was dismissed, and the new appointee, Dmitri G. Bibikov, made sure that the investigation of all conspiracies in Kyiv and its environs were efficient and thorough. On 6 March 1839 the military court in the provincial capital handed down sentences of capital punishment to eleven student-conspirators.[28] All eleven belonged to the leadership of the organization holding the rank of soltys. The principal task of the soltys involved recruiting, educating, and guiding new members. The other sentences among the thirty-four students who were brought to trial were somewhat milder but not without serious consequences for the health and future careers of the conspirators. Some were sent as common soldiers into the dangerous regions of the Caucasus, while others were transferred to the University of Kazan or to educational institutions in other distant regions. After their military service or completion of studies, they were required to spend ten years in the outlying parts of the empire on government assignments. Altogether eighth of the student body at the university went through interrogation and trial, while about two-thirds of the entire enrolment fell under a cloud of suspicion. Consequently the university was closed for a year, all students were temporarily expelled, and most professors with Polish background or those who fell under suspicion were dismissed. The number of civilians arrested and tried in Kyiv was even higher than at the university. Among these, the founder and promoter of the secret student group at the university in Kyiv, the headmaster of the private pension, Piotr Borkowski, received a death sentence.[29] All members of the Michalski family, including Konarski's fiancée, Emilia, were tried and imprisoned.[30]

What disturbed the tsarist authorities in particular was the fact that not only Polish but Ukrainian students were deeply involved in the conspiracy. The two Ukrainians belonging to the top leadership, Arystarkh Sosnovsky and Aleksander Chornyi, received death sentences, which later, thanks to the "magnanimity" of the tsar, were reduced to long years of army service as privates in the Caucasus.[31] The police records, while referring to the Ukrainian membership, specifically singled out the dangers emanating from the organization's international affiliation.[32] It became evident that not only educated Poles but also Ukrainians became linked to revolutionary causes with ties to Western Europe. The fact that Chornyi knew a number of foreign languages, among them French, German, English, Italian, and Latin, indicated that he could easily read books sent from Young Europe's library in Marseilles, literature that reached Kyiv via Odesa and Galicia. Furthermore, since it was expected that members in the Konarski's organization would spread political ideas among the masses, peasant names appear on the list of the arrested conspirators, in addition to those of students.[33]

What undoubtedly helped the process of drawing members of the non-Polish intelligentsia as well as other social groups into the Konarski movement was the spirit of Young Europe that served as the foundation of the organization. According to the association's charter, the central aim of the movement was the attainment of national, social, and political freedoms within a democratic Europe. Article 28 of the association expressed Mazzini's central idea very well: "All peoples have, besides their own [national] obligations, an important duty towards humanity. Therefore, they should comply with the requirements of humanity. Men of all nations are brothers. Therefore, all men and all peoples, like a family and a single brotherhood, should respect each other and help each other to re-establish and defend freedom."[34] Furthermore, the charter warned, "Men, families, classes, and nations who wish to dominate others are the enemies of the nations, i.e., of the human community, and the alliance of peoples should struggle against them."[35] In article 58 of Young Poland's charter, this idea was expressed with even stronger emphasis. It stated that not only individuals but also nations ought to be punished for oppressing other nationalities. "Whoever wishes to oppress any nation becomes the enemy of others, i.e., the entire human community, and as such ought to be declared guilty by the alliance of peoples."[36]

It should be noted that this important principle, the cornerstone on which Young Europe was founded, constitutes the first instance according to which not only rulers or classes were held accountable for oppression, but also entire nations. Other international revolutionary movements of the day were preoccupied with social and economic issues, and the liberals in Western Europe focused almost exclusively on the rights of an individual. Both had neglected the nationality factor in the struggle for equality and freedom. Among the Polish intellectuals before the founding of Young Poland it was routinely accepted, even by such broadminded luminaries as Mickiewicz, that aside from the nation with which he identified, the other nationalities of pre-partitioned Poland were either too small to be viable as independent entities (the Lithuanians) or too weak after centuries of foreign domination (the Ukrainians) to assert their separate existence. It was Mazzini's deep concern with the rights of all nationalities, no matter how small or politically impotent they might have appeared, that strengthened the position on this question of Polish intellectuals like Józef and Bohdan Zaleski, among the émigrés, and Łukaszewicz and Goszczyński, on the home front. It was also partly on account of this attitude towards the local population that Konarski's reception by some Polish members of the provincial gentry in Volynia and Lithuania was often unfriendly and even hostile. As already noted, at the beginning of his mission he was accused of being out of touch with the socio-political realities at home as a result of his infatuation with foreign ideas.[37] It was Konarski's ability to subdue this opposition that permitted his organization to reach out successfully to the non-Poles in the territories in which he operated. On the other hand, it should be noted that even though the idea of autonomy or independence for the non-Poles of the former commonwealth was implied in the charter, it was not openly propagated by members or supporters of Young Poland both at home and in emigration.

After Konarski's capture, arrests and interrogations followed in Kyiv, Dorpat, St Petersburg, Kremenets, and Odesa. Hundreds of books were seized in the two main bookstores in the southern port. The police official responsible for the confiscation of literature and the arrests turned to the administrator of the Odesa school district with a request to despatch translators skilled in Western European languages, stressing in particular the need for those with knowledge of Italian.[38] Judging by these police reports, as well as the fact that Konarski's principal contact for underground literature in Odesa, Mlodecki, was conducting business with Marseilles, the source of the major part of these books must have been Mazzini's Bibliothèque du Proscrit centred in that city.[39]

The Impact of Konarski's Arrest in Galicia and in the Neighbouring Slavic Lands

Even though they treated the revolutionary work of Mazzini's organization with utmost seriousness when the leader resided on the Continent, the Austrian police adopted a somewhat more relaxed attitude towards branches of Young Europe once Mazzini was forced to move to England in 1836. Even though the indefatigable Italian revolutionary continued to pursue his revolutionary work from London with equal determination, his activities appeared less dangerous to the autocrats and their trusted officials in Europe. The authorities in Vienna became seriously shaken only after the tsarist police uncovered the full scope of the Konarski conspiracy in the spring of 1838. As the extent of the more than two years of intensive underground work directed by Konarski in the western provinces of Russia began to unravel during the interrogations and trial, the Austrian police acted speedily to check the operations of the organization's affiliates in its own territories. In October 1839, while conversing with the Prussian ambassador to Austria, Chancellor Metternich appeared disturbed by what he saw as the "Slavic intrusion" into the complicated political situation in Austria, especially since it appeared more and more likely to some observers that the future belonged to the Slavs. Therefore he issued immediate orders to counteract this potential threat.[40]

As noted earlier, Kampelík became the first Czech target of the police investigations. The Czech activist was subjected to a process of prolonged interrogations while being kept under guard in Vienna. Subsequently he, together with other suspects, mainly Poles and Ukrainians, had to stand a prolonged trial that took place in 1842 in the Galician capital. One of the incriminating documents held against Kampelík was a note he had written to his friend Jan Oheral regarding the capture and execution of Konarski. Even though Oheral was known for his pronounced pro-Polish sympathies and obviously must have followed the developments in the Polish underground with deep interest, his position as an editor of the journal *Morava* permitted Kampelík to claim that he was simply passing information about an event in Russia that could be of interest to his colleague's publication.[41] No significant evidence of any direct ties with the Konarski conspiracy was uncovered by the Viennese authorities, against Kampelík or his Czech or Slovak colleagues, even though the police chief in the Galician capital, Leopold von Sacher-Masoch, urged that a more thorough investigation of all Czech activists be conducted, because he had a written proof that one of Kampelík's close associates, Rieger, "was totally committed to the Slavic cause in the democratic sense of the word and that the young man and his friends are most likely members of a larger association."[42] The police chief was not far from the truth, because František Ladislav Rieger, like Kampelík, had ties to the Polish underground, communicated with conspirators in Cracow, and even made a pilgrimage to the shrine of a Polish national hero, Tadeusz Kościuszko, during a visit to the city.[43] It was either under the influence of his Polish hosts during the visit or the impressions he gathered in the course of his subsequent travels through the eastern part of Galicia that Rieger became convinced that the Ukrainians represented the "quintessence" of the Slavic world, that they together with the Poles were destined to bring down the tsarist empire and in this manner free all Slavic peoples from imperial oppression.[44]

After a five-month imprisonment during the investigation and the lengthy trial in Lviv, Kampelík was set free.[45] His colleagues in Vienna, Bratislava, Brno, and Prague were also interrogated but cleared of any direct ties with the underground, even though they, like Kampelík, would remain under intense police surveillance. The authorities kept a close watch on the Czech and Slovak activists by intercepting their correspondence and closely monitoring their whereabouts. Among the young men and women under observation, in addition to Kampelík and Rieger, were Juraj Brauner and his wife, Josef Slavomír Jelínek, Aloise Vojtech Šembera, Oheral, Amerling, Štulc, and many others who were referred to in the police records as "Slovany," men and women involved in the Slavic cause, which, the authorities were well aware, was not just a cultural venture of Romantically inspired youth. Even a friendly greeting containing the phrase "in our general sense" did not escape the interceptor's notice, especially if Czech activists tied to Young Europe in the West, such as František Zach were subjects of the correspondence.[46] The intense vigilance by the provincial police would continue. But at the central headquarters in Vienna it was decided that in the case of the Czechs and Slovaks it was sufficient to use intimidation through persistent surveillance, periodic interrogations, or brief imprisonments, rather than provoke anger by applying harsher measures against political activists of the two numerically small nations.

Furthermore, the draconian punishments that were meted out to the Polish and Ukrainian members of the underground at the trial in Galicia were viewed as powerful enough warnings to the intelligentsia in other Slavic lands.[47]

Suppression of the Political Underground in Galicia

Because of the prominent role he played in the association and at the same time his insecure political status as a Russian subject, Goszczyński, as noted earlier, had to flee to France in 1838. Kulczyński, also originally from a Russian-held territory, in view of his close ties with Konarski and the Polish underground network in Kyiv, committed suicide when his arrest was imminent. Łukaszewicz and his Polish and Ukrainian co-conspirators, including the former prefect of the Greek Catholic seminary, Mykola Hordynsky, were all tried and imprisoned. They conducted themselves stoically during the investigation and trial in Lviv, making sure not to implicate their Czech and Slovak colleagues in any way. Fifty-one members of the underground, among them a number of Greek Catholic priests – the former student-conspirators in the Greek Catholic seminaries – received capital punishment, a sentence that was later commuted by the emperor to lengthy imprisonment in the notorious Špilberk fortress at Brno.[48] Some, like the former seminarian Iosyf Okhrymovych, were not strong enough to survive the harsh prison ordeal, but for many with sturdier constitutions, freedom arrived as an unexpected gift from above, with the revolution of 1848. When the Spring of Nations, as the revolution is known in Central and Eastern Europe, swept Metternich from power and forced the Austrian authorities to grant amnesty to political prisoners, all surviving conspirators involved in the revolutionary underground of the previous decade were set free. By that time Mykola Hordynsky's health was seriously impaired, because of the punitive treatments he and his colleagues were subjected to by the prison guards. Upon his release, after being nursed back to health in the vicarage of his brother, the theologian-conspirator continued his scholarly endeavours in the private library of the Czartoryski family without making any attempt, openly at least, to return to his former pastoral, pedagogical, or political work.[49] Others, on the other hand, like the Rev. Teofil Ruchka Kulchytsky – who in his youth manifested his devotion to democratic ideals by joining the Polish uprising in 1831, was actively involved as a seminarian during the 1830s in underground work – survived the hardships of Špilberk and, in spite of his markedly weakened health, resumed his pastoral duties after the arrival of the constitutional era in the Habsburg lands.

in the second half of the nineteenth century. He continued to spread democratic ideas among his parishioners, often giving them political advice on issues of local importance, and during elections he did not refrain from campaigning openly on behalf of Ukrainian candidates. He provided an excellent education to his surviving sons (two of his children died during his incarceration at Špilberk) and remained in high demand as a father-confessor, especially for the young. According to an obituary appearing at the time of his death in 1882, Kulchytsky's sons represented "the flower of the Ukrainian intelligentsia."[50]

Leslaw Łukaszewicz, like other key figures tied to Young Poland, was sentenced to death, a verdict that was commuted to twelve years in Špilberk. The prison years proved to be especially agonizing for this energetic conspirator, who always brimmed with action. From the memoirs of Bogdański we learn that Łukaszewicz grew highly irritable and often annoyingly confrontational in day-to-day discussions with his fellow prisoners. The only cellmate who could calm his nerves and gain his confidence was the Ukrainian priest-conspirator Mykola Hordynsky, who induced Łukaszewicz to devote his monotonous daily existence in captivity to the study of classical Greek.[51] In 1848 Łukaszewicz must have left the prison walls in fairly good health, because shortly after freedom arrived he plunged once again into the whirlwind of revolutionary action. The second imprisonment that followed brought about his untimely death in the Terezín prison in 1855.[52]

Kampelík's clandestine involvement was masterfully concealed during the interrogations, not only by Łukaszewicz, but also by his Czech and Ukrainian colleagues. His key role in the conspiratorial plot of the mid-1830s surfaced only decades later in the memoirs of his close co-conspirator Jakub Malý.[53] After 1848 the untiring Czech activist continued to pursue the objectives of his youth by means of what became known in the second half of the nineteenth century as "organic work." His profession as a medical doctor provided him with ample opportunities to be in close contact with the Czech people in the countryside. Nevertheless, even during these years of small deeds of practical nature, he was undoubtedly aware that the patriotic fervour of his youth bore fruit. One of his classmates from his student days at the seminary in Brno, J. Grus, summed up the role of Kampelík and his associates at the dawn of the Czech political awakening very well: "It was through his [Kampelík's] efforts that national consciousness was awakened at the faculty of philosophy and at the theological seminary in Brno, from where it would spread through the land of Moravia. After being ordained as priests, we were sent to various corners of the diocese.... This was the mustard seed planted among the graduates that later grew, as you can see, into a mighty tree."[54] Among the Slovak intelligentsia to whom Kampelík felt close affinity, especially in his early years,[55] the number of national awakeners with a clerical background of both Catholic and Lutheran denomination was even larger than in the Czech lands. Similarly, as in the case of the Ukrainians in East Galicia, their work in raising the national consciousness among the people proved invaluable during the constitutional era in the Austro-Hungarian realm. As noted earlier, Samo Chalupka, even fifty years after the Polish insurgency of 1830–1, was fond of reminiscing about his partaking in that patriotic event during occasional discussions with members of the younger generation of Slovak awakeners.[56]

Chapter Six

Sprouts of Young Europe in Ukraine: The Cyril and Methodius Brotherhood[1]

Taras's muse has broken some underground dam, closed by many locks for centuries, buried in the soil, deliberately ploughed and cultivated, so that the very memory of the place where this underground stream flows is hidden from young generations. Taras's muse daringly entered this cleft with an inextinguishable torch and opened up the way for sunlight, fresh air, and human curiosity.... And no historical or moral carbonic acid will extinguish this torch, since this torch is aflame with immortal fire – the fire of Prometheus.[2]

The draconian measures introduced by the tsarist police in Ukraine, Belarus, and Lithuania after Konarski's arrest and execution produced a powerful impact on the politically attuned inhabitants in these provinces of imperial Russia. In Kyiv, a city with one of the largest concentration of conspirators tied to Young Poland's underground, some rank-and-file members and sympathizers had the good fortune of escaping arrests and subsequently passing the scrutiny of the screening process when the university was reopened in 1840. Their success is attested by the fact that very soon after the reopening of the university, both Polish and Ukrainian clandestine groups began to emerge. According to the observations of Hryhorii L. Andruzsky, who attended Kyiv University in that period, the Polish students were known for immersing themselves in books and secretly dreaming about the restoration of their lost statehood. The Ukrainians were engaged in lengthy discussions of the Cossack past and in the study of works on Ukrainian culture. Only the Russians, besides getting ready for their regular class assignments, did not appear to have any other interest except billiards, a favourite student pastime of the day.[3]

Panteleimon Kulish, one of the first Ukrainian students to pass the rigorous screening process at the reopening of the university, became a member of one of the secret groups. He notes in his reminiscences that because of the extreme caution required, his small circle of intimate friends had neither an official statute nor a written plan of action for the "salvation work" they wished to perform among the people. He and his colleagues to whom, incidentally, he gives a familiar appellation found in Mazzini's writings, "the apostles of people's freedom," were obliged to adhere strictly to the unwritten rule: "Let us be as elusive as air."[4] One can catch a glimpse of the nature of the unwritten program of this youth circle, known as Kyivskaia Molod' (Kyivan youth, or young Kyivans) from his reminiscences:

> [At that time] Ukrainian songs and literature of the Ukrainian people in-
> spired youthful minds in Kyiv with the salutary thought: to raise their na-
> tion out of the darkness that was destroying its well-being and making it
> impossible for spiritual forces to prevent the [nation's moral] decline. The
> Kyivan youth we are talking about was deeply inspired by Holy Scripture;
> it was a youth of great spiritual purity and was enthusiastic about spread-
> ing the gospel of neighborly love.... The teacher of the Kyivan group ...
> was He Himself [i.e., Christ]. They were all equal, and he was the first
> among them, who was their servant.[5]

These lines, though penned with great caution, betray the group's familiarity with the ideals of Polska Khrystusova, a religious, mystical group founded by Polish émigrés in which Józef Bohdan Zaleski (the soldier) played an important role; also with Lamennais's *Paroles d'un croyant* and with Mazzini's *Fede e avvenire,* the last two representing popular works in the political underground circulating through Young Europe's secret channels. Only a few years earlier, similar ideas mirror-ing Mazzini's thoughts were expressed by Szymon Konarski, the em-issary of both Young Europe and Young Poland, during his two-year underground political work in Ukraine.[6] The Italian leader's firm belief that every nation that had struggled for freedom or had shown a desire to do so ought to be independent was based on his deep conviction that foreign domination inevitably leads to moral degradation of the sub-jugated nation, because of the decline of the nation's spiritual values secreted in its traditions. Therefore it was the responsibility of nation-ally conscious members of that nation, in Mazzini's words, "the apostles of the people," to prevent their countrymen's continuing cultural and moral decline by recovering the treasures of the people's past. Through this effort, national consciousness would be reawakened, providing the spiritual nourishment needed for an all-encompassing national upheaval. In modern terminology it would mean a nation-building process, but not one that would involve a deliberate attempt to "create a tradition" but rather a conscientious effort to recover the nation's hidden spiritual treasures.[7]

The Kyivan Youth's political interests and aspirations can be detected not only from reminiscences of individuals who consciously strove to be "as elusive as air" but also from the fact that in 1846 its members became the founders of the first modern Ukrainian political organization, the Cyril and Methodius Brotherhood, with a program of Slavic unity loosely related to East European traditions, but with ideological links to the political ideals of Young Europe transmitted to Ukraine through the numerous channels tied to the Konarski underground.[8]

The legal expert in the group, Mykola Hulak, who joined the Kyivan Youth circle in 1845 soon after completing his studies at the University of Dorpat, was by no means a novice to secret political organizations and thought. Reports of a police informer as well as reminiscences and testimonies of the society's members are in agreement that Hulak arrived in Kyiv well prepared to reshape the still somewhat amorphous Kyivan Youth circle into a well-defined political organization.[9] There is no documentary evidence that Hulak was a member of the Association of the Polish People while attending the University of Dorpat, but his familiarity with the structure and traditions associated with clandestine organizations, his "preoccupation with corporations and secret societies," according to the testimony of a police informer, all point to the fact that this leading member of the Brotherhood had been acquainted with the political program of Young Poland / Young Europe.[10] It is also of interest to note that Hulak's younger cousin, who remained in Dorpat longer to complete his studies, was arrested on account of having ties with a clandestine student group.[11] But what is most significant in this connection are the details of conversations provided by the police informer, Aleksei M. Petrov, who, under police guidance, successfully infiltrated the brotherhood. During his meetings with the authorities, the secret agent reported that in the course of his initial discussions with Hulak the Ukrainian conspirator spoke about people who wished to bring about the transformation of the existing political and social system; that these people were not isolated individuals but constituted a large number of men not only in imperial Russia but also among other Slavic nations; that members of this society had a secret symbol representing their unity, which was a ring with an engraved motto "In the Name of Cyril and Methodius"; and that the Polish students at the University of Kyiv could be of assistance in the dissemination of the organization's ideas among the youth.[12] On the basis of these reports, it must have been clear to the authorities that Hulak played a central role in the society and that ties may have been already established between the politically involved Ukrainians and Poles.

Vasyl Bilozersky, a key figure in the Brotherhood, also displayed familiarity with Young Europe's program when he wrote in a note that it was "important to concentrate on influencing young people and women and try by all means possible to be of assistance to those among them who could be useful in preparing the people for the new order that might come about."[13]

Another important activist who was highly influential in formulating the program and charting the direction of the organization was Mykola Kostomarov, a recent graduate of the University of Kharkiv and a promising historian. He too arrived in Kyiv well prepared to join the secret conclave of young men immersed in the study of Ukraine's culture and history. During his student years, the University of Kharkiv was the centre of Ukrainian cultural renaissance, where ideas of Johann Herder and other Romantic philosophers and writers enjoyed enormous popularity, especially among the younger members of the faculty.[14] It was there that Kostomarov became familiar with the poetry of Adam Mickiewicz and other Polish writers, as well as with the scholarly works of Czech and Slovak Slavists. His deep interest in the study of Ukraine's past and Slavdom was awakened by a newly appointed professor at the university, the aforementioned Izmail Sreznevsky, who a few years earlier accompanied Osyp Bodiansky on his scholarly visits to Western Slavs. The young scholar's impressions gathered during his visits to Czech and Slovak cultural centres, his reminiscences about the warmth with which he was greeted by the national awakeners in Bratislava, and about the Western Slavs' fascination with the early history of the Slavic people, especially with Ján Hollý's *Cyrilo-Metodiada*,[15] must have captured the interest and imagination of his students. In fact, the name of the future Ukrainian organization may have had its origins in Kostomarov's familiarity with Ján Hollý's work on Cyril and Methodius, a copy of which Sreznevsky received from his Slovak acquaintances during the visit a few years earlier.[16] Also highly influential on the formation of the young historian's world outlook was Mikhail Lunin, who, like Hulak, was educated at the University of Dorpat. The fact that during his student days Kostomarov managed to master French, Italian, and Polish, in addition to classical languages,[17] would be of great assistance to him in his future political pursuits.

A year before Kostomarov's arrival in Kyiv to assume a teaching post at the university, the young scholar taught history at a secondary school in the Volynian town of Rivne, situated in a region where Konarski's conspiratorial activities had enjoyed great success. The majority of his students with whom he interacted in and out of the lecture halls were of Polish origin and of gentry background, children reared in families many of which had supported Konarski's cause in the preceding decade.[18] In his free time the young history instructor travelled widely throughout the province, visiting places of historical importance – as he carefully notes in his reminiscences – but at the same time these were places in which Konarski's underground work had been most pronounced. Among the places he visited was the town of Kremenets, in which some of Konarski's most devoted supporters had their family roots. During these travels the young history instructor had a number of friendly encounters and long discussions with local members of the Polish intelligentsia. It is not surprising, therefore, that the constitution of the Cyril and Methodius Brotherhood, an organization of which he was a co-founder, would be built on the ideals of Young Europe / Young Poland and that the *Knyhy buttia ukrainskoho narodu* (The books of genesis of the Ukrainian people)[19] also known as *Zakon Bozhyi* (God's law) would show an affinity to Mickiewicz's aforementioned *Księgi,* as well as to Bohdan Zaleski's and Seweryn Goszczyński's idealized depictions of Ukraine's Cossack past.[20] In fact, during the police interrogations that followed the society's unmasking in the spring of 1846, in order to distance himself from the *Knyhy* – one of the incriminating documents in Kostomarov's handwriting found among the society's papers – the historian claimed that he copied the material from a manuscript that had been most likely authored by a Pole because, as he explained to the interrogators, many of the ideas contained in it paralleled those of Mickiewicz and Lelewel and that furthermore, both Zaleski and Czajkowski had expressed dreams of resurrecting Ukraine and the country's former glories.[21]

The constitution of the Cyril and Methodius Brotherhood, was built on principles strikingly similar to those contained in Young Europe's Pact of Brotherhood but with a focus on the Slavic nations, rather than all nations of Europe. It proclaimed that the ultimate destiny of the Slavs was their spiritual and political union, but each constituent nationality to be represented in the future Slavic General Council was to be fully independent. The constitution stressed equality of all citizens as well as the principle of people's sovereignty. The legislation of the future republic was to be drawn up by representatives of the people in conformity with Christian moral principles. Education and moral purity were prerequisites for a person's participation in the government.[22] The constitution was supplemented by a set of rules to guide the conduct of the organization's members. In this section it was explained that the society was founded with the aim of spreading the ideas set forth in the constitution by means of educating the youth, publication of literary works, and recruitment of new members. It was further stated that the society was named after its patrons Saints Cyril and Methodius and that it chose as its symbol a ring or an icon with the names or portraits of the two medieval saints.[23] Membership was open to all Slavs, irrespective of an individual's social background. Each member was expected to take a solemn oath to work to the best of his abilities for the attainment of the society's goals, promising to keep strict secrecy in case of falling into the hands of police. Care was to be provided for families of activists who were imprisoned. All existing religious and national animosities were to be ended, and serfdom as well as any form of discrimination was to be eliminated. Both the society and each of its members were expected to conduct their activities in accordance with the principle of love, while the formerly accepted rule of underground organizations that "the end justifies the means" was declared inadmissible because it was atheistic.

These documents were supplemented by two appeals somewhat reminiscent of Lelewel's calls for unity and cooperation in the previous decade. The first was addressed to "Brothers Ukrainians" and the other to "Brothers Great Russians and Poles." The first enumerated the principles and objectives contained in the society's constitution. The second was a highly emotional call written with the intention of bringing about reconciliation between Ukraine and her two Slavic neighbours:

> This is what Ukraine, your impoverished sister, has to say to you who have crucified her and cut her to pieces, but she does not remember the harm that has been done to her and sympathizes with your misfortunes and is ready to sacrifice the blood of her children for your liberty. Read through this fraternal message; study this important work of your common salvation; awaken from your slumber and your lethargy; drive from your heart the irrational hatred for one another planted by the tsars and the landlords for the common destruction of your common liberty; feel shame for the yoke that weighs upon your shoulders and for your own corruption; condemn the sacrilegious name of the worldly tsar and the worldly lord; expunge from your minds the lack of faith brought by the Germans and the Romans and the harshness instilled in you by the Tatars; cover yourself with the cloth of the Slavic love of humanity; also remember your brothers who suffer both in the silken chains of the Germans and in the clutches of the Turks, and let the goal of life and activity of each of you be the common Slavic union, general equality of rights, brotherhood, and the peace and love of our Lord Jesus Christ. Amen.[24]

Both appeals, as well as other documents tied to the brotherhood, focused on the Slavic nations. The second appeal placed the blame for the negative traits acquired by the Slavs on the influence of conquerors,

Figure 6.1. Mykola Hulak. Courtesy of the Internet Encyclopedia of Ukraine.

Figure 6.2. Mykola Kostomarov. Courtesy of the Internet Encyclopedia of Ukraine.

83. ПОРТРЕТ П. О. КУЛІША.
Олія. [V 1843—1 1847].

Figure 6.3. Panteleimon Kulish. Portrait by Taras Shevchenko. Courtesy of Wikimedia.

Figure 6.4. Taras Shevchenko, a self-portrait. Courtesy of the Internet Encyclopedia of Ukraine.

the Germans and the Turks in particular.[25] It is here that the ideology of the Cyril and Methodius Brotherhood diverges from the program of Young Europe, which, in theory at least, embraced all nations as brothers. In Mazzini's writings the blame for the former and existing wrongs in history was placed on the imperial rulers and their underlings. Yet Mazzini too on occasions had been critical of the French for their tendencies to dominate, and not just the ruling elite but also the leaders of the revolutionary movements. He placed the blame for the French radicals' arrogant behaviour in the centuries-old hegemony that the French nation exercised in Europe in the preceding centuries. It was mainly on the basis of this that the founder of Young Europe conceived the idea that the best-suited nations to lead the future democratic revolution in Europe would be those nationalities whose history was not tainted by domination over others.[26] This novel concept, naturally, had a special appeal to the intelligentsia of the subjugated nationalities of Eastern Europe, including, of course, the founders of the Cyril and Methodius Brotherhood.

The Role of a Poet as a Disseminator of Young Europe's Ideas

As in the case of Mickiewicz, Krasinski, and Zaleski among the Poles, and Hollý, Chalupka, and Štúr among the Slovaks, the role of the poet is central in the Ukrainian national awakening. In Galicia, Shashkevych and a number of his close associates were poets. Kulish and Kostomarov, as well as some of the younger members of the Cyril and Methodius Brotherhood, attempted to write poetry, but the greatest living inspiration, the long-awaited bard yearned for in the 1830s by young men associated with the Ukrainian Triad in Galicia was to be a recently emancipated serf from eastern Ukraine, Taras Shevchenko.

From the time he arrived in Kyiv and joined the brotherhood, the poet was treated with awe and esteem by his Ukrainian colleagues and admirers. The powerful message of his poems calling for Ukraine's national awakening and struggle for freedom of all people under foreign rule became highly regarded by the leading figures of the Ukrainian, Polish, and Czech intelligentsia. Shevchenko, like Hulak and Kostomarov, was a newcomer in Kyiv, having spent most of his youth and early adulthood outside of Ukraine. Yet members of the brotherhood were all in agreement that the poet, like Hulak and Kostomarov, arrived ideologically fully prepared to join the secret society emerging from the circle of highly idealistic young men described by Kulish.

How did a recently emancipated serf, even though a highly talented artist and a graduate of the prestigious Academy of Arts in St Petersburg, manage to have access to political ideas disseminated by the revolutionary underground in Western and Eastern Europe? The conduits through which they passed are not too difficult to trace, if one considers the wide network of clandestine underground groups planted by Konarski, not only in Ukraine and Lithuania, but also in the north-western part of imperial Russia. As has been noted earlier, the resourceful emissary of Young Europe / Young Poland twice journeyed to St Petersburg in order to establish contact with Polish students and trusted men in the military.[27] Among Shevchenko's numerous friends in the Russian capital were Polish artists and writers whose language the poet spoke and with whom he felt a close affinity, having spent part of his early youth in Vilnius and Warsaw. We know that among Shevchenko's St Petersburg acquaintances were two Polish journalists by the name of Romuald Podbereski and Jan Barszczewski, both associated with *Rocznik Literacki*, a Polish publication known for its liberal views.[28]

There was also a Polish art student by the name of Leonard Demski immortalized in the poet's autobiographical sketch *Khudozhnyk* (The artist).[29] In this connection it is of special interest to note that the time and theme of the narrative suggest strongly that the author's encounter with the Polish artist took place precisely during the arrests and intensive police searches that swept through the Russian capital in the aftermath of the Konarski interrogations and public executions. The fact that Demski's idol – in fact the man he wished to emulate – was Joachim Lelewel reveals that Shevchenko's friend was familiar with the ideals of the pre-eminent figure in Polish émigré politics, at that time the leader of Young Poland. We learn from the narrative that the guest-lodger did have his own living quarters in St Petersburg to which he would return after his temporary stay with Shevchenko. Characteristically, during one of Shevchenko's subsequent visits to Demski's lodgings, the poet found among the artist's predominantly French books only two works by Polish authors: Mickiewicz and Lelewel. During the tense, politically charged atmosphere in St Petersburg, Demski must have been one of the many admirers of Lelewel and Mickiewicz who had to seek a safe haven from interrogations and arrests by the tsarist police.

Whether Demski's portrait drawn in the narrative reflected the real person or was a composite sketch based on the poet's Polish acquaintances in St Petersburg is not of great significance. What really matters in this context is the fact that in the Russian capital Shevchenko did have contacts with Polish patriots who were inspired by ideas expressed through the poetry of Mickiewicz and the works of Lelewel. The warm, intimate bonds of friendship with members of Polish intelligentsia during the tense period of Konarski's arrest and executions provide a clue for understanding why Shevchenko would have arrived in Kyiv ideologically fully prepared to join the Cyril and Methodius Brotherhood.

Furthermore, it is of interest to note that among Shevchenko's closest friends during his ten-year exile in Siberia were two Polish conspirators, Bronisław Zaleski and Edward Żeligowski. Both were members of the Association of the Polish People at the University of Dorpat, and both were arrested in connection with the Konarski conspiracy.[30] The friendship that developed between the Ukrainian bard and the two former members of Young Poland – to each of them Shevchenko dedicated a poem – were based not just on purely literary or artistic grounds.

Remembering with fondness his warm relations with Polish patriots in St Petersburg, Shevchenko was eager to establish contacts with likeminded members of Polish intelligentsia in Kyiv. As noted above, a Polish student circle emerged in the city at the same time as the core group of the future Cyril and Methodius Brotherhood, in other words, shortly after the university was reopened in 1840. As in the case of the Ukrainian students, the Polish youth group concentrated, on the surface at least, on cultural and literary pursuits as well as discussions of Polish scholarly works. A year or two later, when the group was augmented by a wave of patriotically inspired members, among them Izydor Kopernicki, Zygmunt Milkowski, Alexander Szumowski, Julian Bielina-Kędrzycki, Antoni Piętkiewicz, and Alexander Jabłonowski, it began to acquire the shape and the spirit reminiscent of the Polish underground in the past decade. The group's relations with individual members of the Ukrainian secret society were cordial but for reasons of safety, remained guarded. In spite of Shevchenko's eagerness to bring the two groups closer together, the more cautious members of the brotherhood, Kostomarov in particular, wisely advised that it would be politically risky to do so. Friendly encounters were not uncommon on an individual basis. This was especially true of Shevchenko and Julian Bielina-Kędrzycki, also a poet.[31] Contact through correspondence was maintained with Jerzy Wróblewski, a member of the Association of the Lithuanian People – an organization dating back to Konarski – while he studied at the University of Kharkiv.[32]

A lifelong relationship developed between Kulish and a Polish novelist and literary critic Michal Grabowski, at whose estate the aspiring Ukrainian writer was an occasional guest in the early 1840s and who, according to Kulish's reminiscences, became not only his friend but also his mentor and benefactor. The Ukrainian youth was amazed how tolerant and patient his host had been when, because of his youthful impulsiveness and hotheadedness, he made an excessively critical remark regarding some aspects of Polish history.[33] Young Kulish, of course, was not aware that in the previous decade Grabowski had ties with the Association of the Polish People, an organization that, as noted earlier, had on its agenda the recruitment of young members of the Ukrainian intelligentsia.[34] The top activists of the Konarski conspiracy may have been executed, but the ideals of Young Poland were not extinguished with the demise of its leaders. The "apostles of the people" the organization had left behind continued to perform their "missionary" work in a quiet, patient way once the storm of arrests and executions subsided. If one wishes to find a connecting link between the Ukrainian political awakening in Kyiv in the early 1840s and the Konarski conspiracy of the previous decade, the mentor–student relationship between the Polish writer and one of the central figures in the emerging Ukrainian political group would be a prime example.

A number of other politically and culturally active members of the Polish intellectual elite with ties through various channels to émigré groups close to Young Poland showed a keen interest in the developments of the young Ukrainian intelligentsia in Kyiv. Periodically they supplied their Ukrainian acquaintances with information, scholarly manuscripts, and, in some instances, as in the case of Grabowski, financial support. A Polish student by the name of Ludwik Jankowski, while writing a letter to his celebrated godfather, the poet Bohdan Zaleski, painted in glowing colours the great achievements in Ukrainian culture during the time when the Cyril and Methodius Brotherhood was in the process of formation. He described the growing interest of Ukrainian students in their history and culture with great enthusiasm, as well as the accomplishments of Taras Shevchenko both as a poet and as an artist. While concentrating mostly on Shevchenko, his art and travels through Ukraine, it is clear from the content that Jankowski had in mind the poet's circle of friends. In response from Paris, the young correspondent received an elated, emotional letter. Zaleski was especially pleased to learn about Shevchenko's travels and literary success and made an ardent plea that the Polish youth in Ukraine learn to love the local people and treat them with utmost deference. For this, the poet assured his godson, he and his friends would reap rich rewards in the "future Slavic union."[35]

Among other members of the Polish intelligentsia who had regular contacts with the Ukrainian activists, of special interest is Count Konstanty Świdzindński, who not only encouraged both Kostomarov and Kulish to follow their muse and scholarly pursuits, but also contributed to a fund for the publication of Shevchenko's poetry. The close relationship established between Kulish and Świdziński is attested by the fact that the Ukrainian aspiring writer had access to the count's rich collection of manuscripts, even when the master of the house was not present on the premises of his estate in Khodorkovo, near Kyiv.[36] That Świdziński was also a scholarly advisor to Countess Dionizja Ponia-towska, herself an aspiring historian and frequent traveller to France and Italy for reasons that, as has been already noted, were not entirely connected to her health, indicates that through Count Świdziński there existed a direct channel of communications between members of the Cyril and Methodius Brotherhood and Józef and Bohdan Zaleski, both prominent figures among the Polish émigrés with ties to Young Poland. Contacts between members of families torn apart by the November revolution was considered essential for most Polish émigrés, not only for emotional but also for financial and political reasons. This was true of both Zaleskis. Countess Poniatowska, as noted earlier, was the niece of the older Józef Bohdan Zaleski (a confidant of Lelewel in Brussels) as well as the "Ukrainian muse" of Józef Bohdan Zaleski the poet.[37]

Another line of contact between members of the brotherhood and the Polish émigrés could have been the headmistress of a boarding school for women in Kyiv at which Kostomarov taught briefly after his arrival from his teaching assignment in Volynia. This position may have been suggested to him by one of the many Polish acquaintances he had made while teaching and travelling through the province. In his autobiogra-phy Kostomarov identifies the headmistress as the "widow" of the poet Bohdan Zaleski [sic!],[38] but it is quite certain that the woman in question was the wife of the poet's older colleague and namesake, Jósef Bohdan Zaleski. The older Zaleski was still very much alive in 1845, but for reasons of political expediency it would have been prudent to consider him deceased. Bohdan Zaleski the poet, about twenty years younger than the "widow" Zaleska, married Zofia Rosengardt, one of Frederick Chopin's students in Paris in 1846 at the time of Kostomarov's acquaint-ance with the poet's purported "widow."[39] As noted earlier, the older Zaleski kept in close touch with his family in Ukraine through the fre-quent visits to Paris of his sister, Felicia Iwańska, who, together with her daughter Dionizja Poniatowska, was an important courier for trans-mitting information, literature, and funds to and from Young Poland's émigré centre to which both Zaleskis were tied. Considering the older Zaleski's participation in three campaigns against Russia (the Napo-leonic wars, the November insurgency, and the Zaliwski campaign), as well as his political connections with a revolutionary organization abroad, it would have been politically most expedient for the head-mistress of a *pension* to assume the role of the "widow" Zaleska, and if someone identified her "late" husband as the poet, for political reasons it would have been prudent not to correct this misconception. Even though in the second edition of his autobiography Kostomarov does not repeat this erroneous assumption, to this day the myth of the *pension*'s headmistress as the widow of the poet persists in all publications on the Cyril and Methodius Brotherhood, both in Ukraine and abroad!

Considering Zaleska's ties with the Polish political émigré group, that her boarding school might have served as a depository of Polish underground literature tied to Young Poland as well as for religiously inspired works of Polska Khrystusowa (Christ's Poland) – an émigré mystical society in which both Zaleskis, especially Zaleska's husband, were actively involved – is more than certain. It is of interest to note that on the day of Kostomarov's arrest in the spring of 1847, after the historian had had no professional ties to the Polish boarding school for more than a year, it was Zaleska who would make two unsuccessful attempts to warn her former employee of his impending arrest.[40] This suggests that "widow" Zaleska's ties to the Ukrainian historian during this time were of political rather than professional nature.

With all the information accessible to researchers in our day, it is astounding that the members of the editorial staff of the three-volume, meticulously annotated collection of documents on the Cyril and Methodius Brotherhood published in Kyiv in 1990 were bewildered by the identity of the "Zaleski" in Kostomarov's testimony, when the arrested historian attempted to distance himself from the manuscript, *Knyha butiia*. "It appears to me," explained Kostomarov during the interrogations, "that it [the manuscript] was authored by a Pole, because in the text all concepts of authority, truth, and servitude are interpreted in the same manner as in [the works] of Mickiewicz, Lelewel.... In addition many Poles from Southwest Rus', for example men like Czajkowski, Zaleski, and others, have been dreaming of the resurrection and glory of Ukraine to the point of losing [the support of] their compatriots."[41] The baffled editors suggest that the Zaleski mentioned in Kostomarov's testimony might have been Bronisław Zaleski, who befriended Shevchenko during the poet's exile in the 1850s.[42] This erroneous assumption is the result of the fact that in Soviet scholarship Bronisław Zaleski is consistently tied with the November revolution of 1830, even though in that year the future conspirator was only a boy of ten! We do know that Bronisław Zaleski was arrested a decade later during the Konarski interrogations on account of his membership in the Association of the Polish People / Young Poland at the University of Dorpat.[43] This and the "widow" Zaleska misconceptions may appear as minor errors, but they are indicative of the superficial treatment by Soviet historians of the Konarski conspiracy in general, but especially with respect to its connection to the Ukrainian political awakening in Kyiv. It is also indicative of the Soviet historians' lack of knowledge as well as interest in ties involving Ukrainian political developments with those of Western Europe resulting from their effort to stress the pre-eminence of Russia's role in the history of Ukraine.[44]

In spite of these weak spots in scholarship, the question of Polish influence on the Cyril and Methodius Brotherhood has not been a matter of dispute among serious historians. Most scholarly works would be in agreement with the conclusion reached by one of Kostomarov's biographers, Dmytro Doroshenko: "There can be no doubt that Kostomarov, Hulak, Shevchenko, Bilozersky, Savych, and other members of the [Cyryl and Methodius] group experienced the strong impact of Polish political thought, Polish underground organizations, and the writings of Polish poets and publicists."[45]

What has been overlooked in scholarly works on this subject is the search for documentary evidence regarding ties between the first modern Ukrainian political organization and Young Europe. A telling example is a work on the Cyril and Methodius Brotherhood published in Poland in 1990 by a historian who dismisses the connection with Mazzini's organization, by arguing that, though reflecting Mazzini's political ideas, the political program of the brotherhood had been influenced by the Konarski movement (Konarszczyzna) rather than by Mazzini's Young Europe![46] The historian, while recognizing the impact of the Konarski conspiracy on the Cyril and Methodius Brotherhood, is completely oblivious to the fact that the Konarski conspiracy and the organization known as the Association of the Polish People (as already noted, this was the cover name for Young Poland in Galicia and in the western provinces of imperial Russia – an organization over which, incidentally, the Polish revolutionary officially presided) had been a constituent part of Mazzini's Young Europe![47] In the introduction of the aforementioned three-volume collection of documents on the Cyril and Methodius Brotherhood published shortly before the dissolution of the Soviet Union, reference is made to parallel political developments in Western Europe, including the founding of Young Poland and Young Europe. But with respect to the question of influence on the Cyril and Methodius Brotherhood, only Russian clandestine groups and the Association of the Polish People are mentioned. As in the Polish study, the association is presented as an organization separate from Young Poland and Mazzini's Young Europe.[48]

In addition to Mickiewicz's celebrated work *Księgi*, ideological parallels have also been drawn between the brotherhood's *Knyhy buttia* and Hipolit Terlecki's *Słowo Rusina*, which appeared in Paris in 1849.[49]

It is probable that a copy of Terlecki's still unpublished manuscript had reached members of the brotherhood in Kyiv. In fact, Terlecki's text is considered to have been the mysterious document referred to as "Podnistrianka" during the police interrogation of Kostomarov. Considering the ties of friendship between Terlecki and Bohdan Zaleski in Paris and the latter's participation in the preparation of Mickiewicz's *Księgi*,[50] it is not surprising that similar ideas were present in these texts.[51]

The Legacy of the Cyril and Methodius Brotherhood

The life of the brotherhood was brief. The tsarist police liquidated the secret society in the early spring of 1847 with the arrests of its leading members. The society's significance for the Ukrainian national renaissance, most scholars agree, was of enormous importance, for it was instrumental in transforming what had been primarily a cultural national awakening in previous decades into a full-fledged political organization with a clearly defined ideology and a well-formulated political program.

The poet Shevchenko received the harshest sentence of all the members, primarily because of the political content of his literary works. The poet's writings, including the not-yet-published manuscript about the early fifteenth-century Czech national hero Jan Hus, were confiscated and remained under police lock until 1906! Fortunately for posterity, copies of large sections of the poem, including the dedication to the Czech scholar Šafařík, were safely hidden in homes of the poet's many admirers and friends. Upon his release in 1857, the first task that the poet set before himself was to recover the full text of "Jan Hus."[52] Both the author and his closest colleagues considered the work one of his finest creations. Vasyl' Bilozersky, a member of the Cyril and Methodius Brotherhood, wrote down his thoughts upon hearing a rapturous report about Shevchenko's reading of his work at a meeting he was not able to attend: "In an instant, a salutary thought flashed through my mind – what a genius we possess in the person of Taras Hr. [Hryhorovych Shevchenko], because only a genius through a deep emotional insight is capable to grasp the needs of the people and of the entire era."[53]

In the poem Shevchenko portrays Jan Hus as first and foremost a national hero, a patriot defending the rights of the Czech nation against the creeping advances of the aggressive Germans into his homeland. It was not too difficult for the police investigators in St Petersburg to figure out that in the loathsome portrait of Pope John XXIII painted by the poet, Shevchenko had in mind the Russian tsar, and that in his depiction of the prelate's contemptible German underlings he was describing Russian imperial bureaucrats attempting to strengthen their grip on Ukraine.

In Shevchenko's poem one would search in vain for even a hint of Russophile pro-tsarist leanings found in the aforementioned writings of Ján Kollár, and especially in the works of the Russian Slavophiles, in spite of the poet's friendly personal relations with a number of Russian intellectuals in St Petersburg and Moscow who shared their views. Neither does Shevchenko's slavophilism – an idea that runs like a red thread through the poem, in particular in the aforementioned dedication to Šafařík – have anything in common with Alexander Pushkin's notion of Slavic unity – a union that from the perspective of the celebrated Russian poet was to be forged by the hand of a powerful tsar personified by Peter the Great.

Elevating Jan Hus as a model for all Slavs to follow, Shevchenko formulates his Slavophile idea strictly on the basis of a free association of equal nations bonded together by the Christian idea of brotherly love. This concept, as noted earlier, represented the cornerstone of Young Europe's ideology embodied in the organization's charter, known as the Pact of Brotherhood.[54] This idea also was the founding bloc on which the statutes of the late offspring of Young Europe, the Cyril and Methodius Brotherhood, were based.

In the dedication of the poem Shevchenko eulogizes Šafařík as a Slavic philosopher who, following in the footsteps of Jan Hus, rescued Slavdom from being drowned in the German quagmire. At the end of the dedication, the poet expresses an ardent wish that all Slavs become brothers bonded together on the principle of equality in the struggle for justice and truth, treading in the footsteps of the Czech martyr, even at the price of being branded as heretics by the corrupt ruling elites:

Shchob usi Slaviany staly	So that all Slavs would become
Dobrymy bratamy	Good brothers
I synamy sontsia pravdy	True sons of the sun of truth
I Yeretykamy	And heretics as
Ottakymy jak Konstantskyi	Great as the one
Yeretyk velykyi	In Constance
Myr myrovi podarujut	They will bring peace to the world
I slavu voviky!	And glory for all times to come!

Even though the last stanza of the poem contains a vivid description of the Czech martyr's execution by fire – in line with the ideological principles enunciated in the Romantically inspired ideas found in the literature of Young Europe – the author does not conclude his work in a minor key. On the contrary, the last stanza resonates with ominous warnings to the pompous prelates of the papal curia – an obvious allusion to the tsarist officialdom of Shevchenko's day – that while those in power are celebrating victory, above their heads soars a menacing spectre, the mace of the old Hussite soldier, Jan Žižka:

Postryvajte!	Beware!
On nad holovoju	There, right over your heads
Staryj Zhizhka z Taborova	The old man Žižka from Tábor
Makhnuv bulavoju.	Has just brandished his mace.

Because of the thoroughness with which the tsarist police attempted to wipe out all traces of the Cyril and Methodius Brotherhood, most of the documentation connected with the program of the society, as well as the works of its members, remained hidden, either under the police lock in St Petersburg or in the homes of intimate friends and many sympathizers. Therefore it would be primarily through poems such as "Jan Hus" or "Kavkaz," as well as a number of other works written by the poet in a similar anti-imperialist, national liberation spirit, the spirit of Young Europe, that the ideas of the Cyril and Methodius Brotherhood would become known to the wider public in the years to come. The police informer, O.M. Petrov, made a valid observation in his report that the political ideas discussed at the meetings were creatively transposed into poems by Shevchenko.

It was not just by a sheer coincidence that half a century after the sweeping arrests of the Cyril and Methodius Brotherhood and the attempts by the tsarist police to wipe out the organization's traces in Ukraine, that Mykola Mikhnovsky, the author of a political pamphlet called *Independent Ukraine*, modelled the program of the future Ukrainian sovereign state on the ideals of the Cyril and Methodius Brotherhood. For this work Mikhnovsky was well prepared, because from his early youth he had direct access to the rich library of his godfather, Mykola Markevych, a noted Ukrainian historian and a good friend of Shevchenko. In the spirit of Slavic brotherhood as well as that of Young Europe, the program was based on the principles equality, sovereignty, and republican ideals. In preparation for the realization of this objective, Mikhnovsky sought contacts with Ukrainian national leaders in Galicia as well as with Czech political activists. He even made a special trip to Prague to participate in a congress convened by a patriotic Czech youth organization in 1909.[55]

Shevchenko's enormous popularity, especially after his untimely death in 1861, contributed to the dissemination of the society's ideas,

not only among members of the Ukrainian intelligentsia in the territories ruled by the two imperial powers, but among other Slavic peoples as well. According to witnesses, Šafařík was moved to tears when
the first part of the poem was delivered to him in Prague.[56] Interest-
ingly, the first copy of the dedication to Šafařík reached Ukrainians in
Galicia through their Czech contacts. Today there are at least five translations of "Jan Hus" in the Czech language alone.[57] The first translation
of the dedication to Šafařík was made by the Czech poet and prominent émigré political activist of Young Europe, Josef Václav Frič, who
not only saw to it that the translation appeared in print but promptly
began to work on a drama in verse on the subject of Ivan Mazepa, the
eighteen-century Ukrainian Cossack leader fighting for Ukraine's independence. The play, *Ivan Mazepa: Tragedie v 5 Dějstvích* (Ivan Mazepa:
A tragedy in five acts) appeared in Prague in 1865.[58]

Jan Hus was held in high esteem by members of Kampelík's circle as
well. In his memoirs Jakub Malý notes that the Czech martyr's image
remained unblemished, not only in the memory of the national awakeners, but among the common people as well, in spite of the strenu-
ous efforts made by religious fanatics to smear the martyr's name. One
of Kampelík's contemporaries, Jan Vlastimil Plánek, praised Hus for
"purifying his people as well as the Czech Church."[59] Martyrdom of
Jan Hus and the consequent upheaval of patriotic Czechs led by Jan
Žižka carried a message that would fit perfectly into Young Europe's
Romantically inspired political lore. It is worth remembering that for
Giuseppe Mazzini, the organization's founder, there was no defeat or
death if the memory of the struggle was kept alive in the hearts of the
people. The prompt "arrest" of Shevchenko's poem by the tsarist police
indicated that the imperial authorities were well aware of the dangers
emanating from the political and literary works of Shevchenko and
his co-conspirators. Both literature and political ideals in the writings
of this group were closely intertwined. The tsar was not far from the
truth when, during the lengthy police investigations of the first modern Ukrainian political party – proceedings that Nicholas followed with
undivided attention – he observed, "It is clear that this is the work of
propaganda from Paris."[60]

Young Europe: The Ideological Roots of "The Spring of Nations" in the Slavic World

The Poles should take the path of justice and opportunity! Recognizing the separateness of Rus' is just, because it signifies the recognition of the dignity in man. Separateness is possible, because fourteen million people desire it and demand it from mankind.... Call forth Rus' in the interests of Rus', Poland in the interests of Poland, and both in their common interest. Then the colossus of the north [Russia] will collapse.... From this vantage point, it does not seem strange that the Poles will act in the interest of Rus'.[1]

When Aleksander Vrchovský confided to Ľudovit Štúr that the Slovaks were not ready yet even to begin dreaming about their national liberation, he had in mind not only the uneducated people of the countryside but also the small enclaves of intelligentsia gathered at institutions of higher learning in the cities and towns spread throughout what was known at that time as northern Hungary.[2] When the situation changed radically in the course of only a few years, so that even such decisions as the codification of the Slovak language were determined by political considerations tied to the idea of national liberation, it was mainly due to the determined effort of a tightly knit group of highly motivated activists ideologically linked either through Cracow or Vienna to Young Europe. In this connection the Polish conspiratorial groups guided by the program of the Association of the Polish People served as a powerful catalyst. Had young Czechs and Slovaks like František Kampelík, František Rieger, or Aleksander Vrchovský missed the opportunity to befriend patriotically motivated members of the Polish underground with direct links to Young Europe, it is more than likely that many of them would have taken either the path advocated by Kollár – exploring the wonders of Slavdom while steering away from politics – or a lucrative road in pursuit of their careers, without taking a second glance at their Slavic roots. Once they became aware of the meaning and significance of national identity through contacts with politically charged young men like the "Viennese Slavans," acquiring in the process what Vrchovský referred to as "a sense of human dignity," they embraced passionately what they felt was their filial duty to the common people from whom they sprang. Their approach to the attainment of national emancipation may have varied, but in all instances – and this applies not only to the Czechs and the Slovaks – the question of raising the tongue spoken in the countryside to the level of a literary language figured prominently in the list of tasks to be accomplished in the immediate future.

Political Awakening among the Slovaks and the Czechs

For the legalistically trained, pragmatic Vrchovský, language was primarily a means to an end rather than an end in itself. He approached it as a tool by means of which one could communicate with the masses, gain their confidence, awaken their national consciousness, and in this manner prepare the people for a revolutionary upheaval destined to bring about both their social and national emancipation. Before this all-encompassing mission could be set in motion, it was necessary to train cadres of educated youth dedicated to the idea of national liberation, young men and women referred to by Mazzini as the "apostles of the people." The biblical Moravian Czech of Kralice then in use by educated Lutheran Slovaks, though useful as a medium of communication to bring the Czechs and Slovaks closer together, was too distant from the dialects spoken in the Slovak countryside. Vrchovský, though of Lutheran background, opted for the language of the common folk for political reasons noted above, as well as because he knew that it could serve as an important unifying link between the two main religious denominations among the Slovaks. Both advantages were carefully measured by the organizational strategist of the future Vzájomnosť. It was already in one of his first letters of instructions to Ľudovít Štúr that Vrchovský emphasized both the significance of language as an important instrument of indoctrination as well as a force capable of drawing into the ranks of the Lutheran-dominated Spoločnosť Slovak students of Catholic background.

The task of bringing about both social and denominational consolidation to a subjugated nation was one of the main responsibilities placed upon the shoulders of activists recruited to the ranks of Young Europe. The program of this organization was spread among educated Czechs and Slovaks primarily by Kampelík, whose mission, after being formally inducted as a full-fledged member of the Association of the

Figure 7.1. Slovak political leaders in 1849. First row from left to right: M. Rarus, J. Holček, A. Radlinský, K. Kuzmány. Second row: A. Kardaš, S. Chalupka, D. Lichard, M.M. Hodža, L. Štúr, J.M. Hurban, D.D. Bařík. *Slovensko v obrazkoch: Historia.* Juliana Krebesová, ed. (Martin: Vydavateľstvo Osveta, 1990).

František Cyrill Kampelík.

Figure 7.2. František Cyrill Kampelík. From František Komárek, *František Cyrill Kampelík: obraz životopisný*, 1895.

Figure 7.3. František Ladislav Rieger. From Jiljí V. Jahn, *František Ladislav Rieger: obraz životopisný*, 1861.

Polish People, involved the establishment of affiliated units of Young Europe among young men and women of these two closely related nations. Both Kampelík and Vrchovský became deeply committed to this undertaking. Unlike in the case of Kampelík, there is no documentary evidence that Vrchovský was formally initiated into Young Europe, but his familiarity with the organization's program and guiding ideals, as well as with the organization's method of action and his association with the Viennese Poles and some German activists with ties to Young Europe, indicate that he had been. In these matters utmost secrecy was the rule. Vrchovský's ultimate decision to establish his law practice in Budapest was influenced partly by the fact that from this strategically located city he would be in a better position to coordinate relations between the Slovak Vzájomnosť and both the Southern Slavs and Galician Ukrainians.

In Bratislava it would be Ludovit Štúr who would become responsible for the program's implementation; to this task, the young poet devoted his energies with unswerving zeal during his tenure as secretary of the formerly politically passive student association Spoločnosť. However, Štúr, unlike Vrchovský, was a man of letters very much under the spell of the Romantic ideals of his day. For him, therefore, language was much more than just a tool to be utilized for political objectives. Yet, at the same time, the practical aspects of the language tended to be present in his undertakings, irrespective of whether he was working on his literary projects or launching the first Slovak newspaper, *Slovenskje narodňje novini* (The Slovak national newspaper), in later years. During the revolutionary year of 1848, in the paper's literary supplement "Orol tatranský," Štúr publicized a poem written by a Lutheran minister, Karol Kuzmány: "Sláva šľachetným" (Glory to the noble breed). Considering Štúr's ideological background, it was to be expected that during the year of the peoples' revolutions he would be promoting Mazzini's ideals of national liberation. A free summary of the poem would read as follows: "Let my song resonate with glory for those who in the name of truth are being immolated in the sacred sacrificial pyre; for those who sacrifice their lives for the rights of humanity; for those who commiserate with the unjust treatment of the poor; ... for those who, for the sake of freedom, are willing to shed their blood; ... for those who will protect their homeland from the raging dragon; for those who value dignity and honesty;... for those who respect God's truth and God's law."[3] The poem, set to music, became an unofficial Slovak anthem for generations to come.[4]

That the national awakeners of Štúr's generation, deeply immersed in and captivated by the prevailing Romantic spirit of the day, found their endeavours in linguistic and literary studies both spiritually fulfilling and politically stimulating, accounts for the success that was achieved within a relatively brief time both in the cultural and political spheres. Unlike Kollár's cohort of Romantically inspired followers, Štúr's generation of national awakeners, trained according to Vrchovský's school of thought, was fully cognizant of the fact that, without political backing and without the government's encouragement and financial support, the language and culture of stateless people would be consigned to oblivion, and that only a government fully responsive to the interests and needs of the people would feel obliged to provide the necessary life-sustaining support for the culture's unhindered development. It should be noted that Mazzini became conscious of the urgent need for his nation's independence when, during his early years of immersion in literature, he realized that Italy's culture, particularly the refinement and complexity of its language, was deteriorating as a consequence of foreign domination over the Italian lands.[5]

In the course of the revolution of 1848 the Slovak political leadership sprang directly from the ranks of the national political awakeners of the previous decade: Štúr, Hurban, and Hodža, with Vrchovský and his protégé, Štefan Marko Daxner, providing guidance from Budapest. Štúr played a prominent role during the June days of 1848 at the Slavic Congress in Prague and, at the close of the revolution, the poet, editor, and political activist became involved even in an armed clash with Hungarian insurgents when the cultural and political interests of the Slovaks were threatened. Continuing to face opposition to the revival of the Slovak cultural and political development from Hungarian liberals, it was inevitable that Štúr and his group of Slovak leaders sought accommodation with the Austrian government in the years to come. In the second half of the nineteenth century, similar steps directed towards finding a modus vivendi with the imperial authorities in Vienna were sought by the Czechs in their struggle with the more powerful Germans in Bohemia and by the Ukrainians in Galicia when faced with Polish opposition to their nation's cultural and political interests.

In retrospect, it is interesting to note that the Czech and Slovak political awakeners were not too far off the mark when at the Brno conclave in 1834 they predicted that at least a ten-year period would be needed to prepare their people for a national upheaval. Certainly, by the mid-1840s the local intelligentsia in Bohemia, Moravia, and in the Slovak lands was not only fully conscious of its national identity but was ideologically committed to defending the people's cultural and political interests. Kollár's words of wisdom to avoid politics had little appeal for the new generation of educated youth. It would take at least another half-century to cultivate the seeds of national consciousness among the masses, but this was the case even among the more politically advanced European nationalities, such as the Poles and the Italians, as the abortive 1846 uprising in West Galicia and the revolution of 1848 in Italy would prove.

Among the Czechs, serious scholarly interest in the roots of Slavic cultures began earlier than among any other Slavic nationality. Following in the footsteps of the eighteenth-century Czech pioneers in Slavic studies like Josef Jungmann and Josef Dobrovský, their Slovak counterparts, Kollár and Šafařík, also chose to distance themselves from involvement in political and social issues, and, because of their scholarly isolation, they envisioned an eventual fusion between the Czech and Slovak languages and cultures. Their own as well as their predecessors' linguistic and literary studies had a strong impact on the small clusters of Slavic educated communities, but before the 1830s their influence on the newly emerging cadres of the intelligentsia was of little practical importance. When Kampelík entered the theological seminary in Brno at the end of the 1820s, not one of his classmates seemed to show an awareness of or interest in Slavdom. Yet the very presence of serious works on the subject of Slavic languages, history, and cultures did have an effect on the more intellectually inquisitive and politically alert individuals who, like the young activists at the Brno conclave, were one day inevitably be faced with a question: If a culture worthy of admiration exists, it ought to be protected and, in the world of competing cultures, this protection has to be placed in trustworthy hands, that is, in a government responsible to the people who are the carriers of this culture. This was one of the central ideas in the ideology of Young Europe. Neither Kollár nor the older luminaries of the academic communities were willing to embrace this idea or even capable of fully comprehending it. Kampelík and Vrchovský had no difficulty in understanding the significance of this fact once they became acquainted with the ideas of Young Europe.

In Prague, during the revolutionary days of 1848, it was the combined effort of the younger men from the scholarly sphere, like the historian František Palacký and the youthful political activists of Kampelík's milieu, like František Rieger, who dominated the political scene. But in the heady days of the Spring of Nations, political and cultural activists of Kampelík's generation, too, came to the surface from their enforced isolation of the early 1840s. As a member of the Svatováclavské Committee, in 1848 Kampelík began publishing pamphlets and leaflets calling for a liberal constitution. In June of that eventful year the seasoned Czech conspirator organized and brought a contingent of armed men to Prague from the neighbouring town of Příbram, and even though his seventy volunteers arrived too late to participate in the defence of the uprising – the city had just surrendered to the imperial forces when the enthusiastic insurgents arrived – Kampelík was forced to spend some time abroad during the post-revolutionary year in order to avoid arrest. The young Czech activist of the Brno-Bratislava-Vienna years remained very much a passionate revolutionary, even though he acknowledged in later years the value of organic work when constitutional government became a reality in the lands ruled by the Habsburgs. In spite of a series of disappointments in the second half of the century, he and his intimate colleagues were undoubtedly aware that the efforts of their earlier years had borne fruit, a feat of no mean importance. The impressive scholarly accomplishments of intellectuals like Šafařík and Palacký may have pushed the work of lesser known writers and political activists into the background, but it was precisely the "small deeds" of these men working assiduously with a missionary zeal among the educated men and the masses that would be responsible for awakening in the countryside an awareness of national identity both through personal contacts and publications designed explicitly for popular consumption.[6] Because the literary achievements of these politically inspired men tended to be relatively modest, and because their activities were intentionally kept under cover, their efforts were eclipsed by the accomplishments of the eminent scholars of the preceding decades. Thus there has been an erroneous perception regarding the fundamental nature of the years preceding the revolution of 1848. What has been overlooked in the assessment of that crucial and highly volatile period is the fact that a good part of what has been considered as principally a cultural endeavour of Romantically inspired but politically passive national awakeners had been, in fact, an effort driven by men with a political outlook and clearly defined political aims. Writing from the perspective of almost fifty years, J. Grus, one of Kampelík's classmates at the seminary in Brno, captured the significance of these early deeds of young men of the 1830s, which have been hidden from history: "It was through his [Kampelík's] efforts that national consciousness was awakened at the faculty of philosophy and in the theological seminary at Brno, from where it would spread throughout [the province of] Moravia. After being ordained as priests, we were sent to various corners of the diocese.... This was the mustard seed planted among the graduates, which later grew, as you can see, into a mighty tree."[7]

Beginning with the Brno conclave in 1834, political objectives figured prominently on the agenda of the national awakeners. Among the Slovaks, the role of the seminarians influenced by the ideology of Young Europe through the activities spread by members of Vzájomnosť was even more pronounced. Thus, it would be safe to say that the Spring of Nations in the lands of the Czechs and Slovaks had its beginning in the mid-1830s, both in the cultural and political sense. The two-pronged endeavour, especially its political component, had to be toned down considerably during the decade of police repressions, only to burst out with full force when the first opportunity for action arose in the spring of 1848.

The National Awakening of the Ukrainian Intelligentsia in Galicia

The national awakening within the ranks of the Ukrainian intelligentsia in Galicia in the 1830s was just as sudden and perhaps even less anticipated than among the Czechs and the Slovaks. As noted above, memoirs and letters of the period are filled with reminiscences about the "somnolent, lethargic atmosphere" enveloping the province at the opening of the decade, and the abrupt burgeoning of a "new spirit – a Ruthenian spirit" or "a great spirit of freedom" as the 1830s progressed.[8]

This unexpected awakening among young men tied almost exclusively to the Greek Catholic seminaries of Lviv and Przemyśl had been brought to life by the thunder of the Polish November uprising. The spirit of freedom embodied in the broadly publicized slogan "Za naszą i waszą wolność" (For your and our freedom) was nurtured in the years that followed by the underground currents of thought disseminated throughout the province by fleeing Polish revolutionaries, especially those who managed – in many instances with the aid of Greek Catholic clergy – to remain in Galicia. This development, together with the appearance of historical and ethnographic studies published by Ukrainian authors in the Russian Empire, provides an explanation for the dynamism and radicalism of the Ukrainian national renaissance in Galicia from its very inception. The almost overnight transformation of the dreamy provincial capital – according to contemporary memoir literature, this designation applied to both Ukrainian and Polish communities in the pre-November days – into a bustling arena of ideologies and radical conspiracies caused many a headache within the administrative offices of institutions of higher learning, as well as considerable frustration in the chambers of the Austrian provincial police supervised by its commander-in-chief, Sacher-Masoch.

Throughout the decade the conservative prelates of the Greek Catholic hierarchy were baffled by these unexpected developments, unable to grasp fully the potential danger that this sudden outburst of political radicalism among the seminarians could pose to the carefully cultivated and piously guarded idea of the Ruthenians' unwavering loyalty to the Austrian Crown. The administrative personnel of the rectory of the Greek Catholic seminary in L'viv attempted to apply punitive measures as well as cleverly conceived tasks and assignments to divert students' attention from politics. Few members of the seminary's administrative apparatus could have known that the decision of the Rector's Office to redirect student interests from radical politics to the study of Ukrainian language and culture could work hand-in-hand with the strategy of a revolutionary organization, but those who did, like the prefect-conspirator Mykola Hordynsky, obviously greeted this new direction with enthusiasm. If some seminarians camouflaged their political involvement in the underground by openly paying homage to the emperor in formal speeches that the rectory required them to make, this too was met with approval by the politically savvy members of the secret organizations both within and outside the walls of religious institutions of learning. After all, from the perspective of the revolutionary underground, it was advantageous if the Ukrainians in Galicia continued to be perceived as devout and loyal subjects of their royal benefactor in Vienna.

The political sophistication of the youth of the 1830s in Galicia has been consistently underestimated both by the higher ranks of the Greek Catholic clergy and, in later years, by Ukrainian historians who, with a few notable exceptions (Studynsky, Shcherbak) tended to play down the impact of Polish radicalism on the emerging Greek Catholic intelligentsia. The reason for this shortcoming in scholarship is not too difficult to fathom: at the turn of the nineteenth century Polish nationalism, by then fully entrenched within the ideological framework of social Darwinism, no longer espoused the humanistic ideals of brotherly love, cooperation, and tolerance promoted by the founders of Young Poland, even for the sake of appearances. Thus it was difficult for even the more discerning students of history to grasp that the relationship between political activists of the two nationalities in the previous era was significantly different. Even if instances of friction on the Polish-Ukrainian political front did emerge in the second half of the 1830s – as they did, for example, between Leon Korecki and Mykola Hordynsky within the leadership of the association – these differences were resolved by means of a compromise through the mediation of such farsighted Polish political strategists as Seweryn Goszczyński. In Galicia the leading members of the association and the Kolo Rus'ke, both guided by the principles of Young Europe, worked side-by-side, rather than against one another within their respective spheres of action. At no time did conflicting viewpoints lead to serious breaches of solidarity in the revolutionary underground, which was fraught with danger. At the trial of conspirators in the early 1840s, death sentences were meted out to Polish laymen, like Henryk Bogdański and Lesław Łukaszewicz, and to Greek Catholic clergymen, like Iosyf Okhrymovych and Mykola Hordynsky. It was not just a coincidence that the trial of political activists of Polish, Ukrainian, and Czech background took place in the Galician capital. The mass arrests of conspirators in the early 1840s – the fifty-one death sentences passed by the provincial court were not a common occurrence, even in Metternich's Austria – were partly responsible for the fact that most of the top-ranking Polish and Ukrainian members of the underground of the 1830s were not involved in the abortive Polish uprising that took place in West Galicia in 1846.[9]

Partly because of their direct exposure to the ideological principles of Young Europe and partly because of their literary interests and fascination with the Romantic ideas pervading the literary world of their day, for the Ukrainian national awakeners, as for their Slovak and Czech counterparts, it was of foremost importance that the question of raising the vernacular spoken in the countryside be raised to the level of a literary language. In this endeavour they had the good fortune of receiving generous financial backing from the conservative Greek Catholic hierarchy, as well as discreet encouragement from prominent members of the Polish underground (Goszczyński and Siemieński). A number of talented seminarians, both those who were directly involved in secret organizations or who only sympathized with the underground's democratic ideals but concentrated primarily on the development of language and culture, took advantage of this two-pronged support. In the forefront – on the surface cultural endeavour only – were the members of the Ruthenian Triad.

Ukrainian historiography – as in the case of the influence of Polish radicalism – tends to play down the political undertones that were present in the multifaceted activities of the young men who were connected, directly or indirectly, with the triad. Even serious scholars generally view the members of this group mainly as dreamy, Romantically inspired ethnographers, philologists, and poets, overlooking the fact that in the politically charged atmosphere of the 1830s, with the frequent police searches and interrogations to which the seminarians were periodically subjected – not to mention the perennial difficulties with censorship – this is exactly how the members of the triad wished to be perceived. Yet the subjects that captivated their imagination and the steps they undertook to achieve their objectives indicate that they had very little in common with groups similar to the apolitical Čecho-Slovanská Spoločnosť of Bratislava of the early 1830s. As their Slovak counterparts among the national awakeners, they were by no means willing to tread the safe path advocated by Kollár, for in their first attempt to publish an anthology of historical and ethnographic materials under the title of *Zoria* (The star), they intended to place on the cover of the publication a portrait of the seventeenth-century Ukrainian Cossack leader known for his resolute stand on Ukraine's independence. In their second – and this time successful – effort to see the collection in print, they chose an innocuous, Romantically inspired title without even a hint of political symbolism. They also decided prudently to set aside both the politically charged portrait of Bohdan Khmenytsky and Shashkevych's article about the Cossack leader's feats. In this instance, their political acumen appears to have been just as sophisticated as that of their colleagues involved directly in the political underground. Like their contemporaries among the western Slavs, the members of the triad admired Kollár's achievements in the field of Slavic cultures, yet they chose as the motto for their publication not a passage from the bard's Romantically inspired apolitical verses – a move that could have smoothed the path towards publication – but rather his Protestant-sounding message emphasizing the importance of clarity of vision and hard toil: "It is not when the eye is dim, but when the hands are busy that hope begins to grow."[10] In Buda, where the anthology would be published, the triad's emissary, Yakiv Holovatsky, sought help not from the influential yet politically conservative Kollár, but rather from Georgij Petrović, a Serb whose sympathy for the ideas promoted by the new generation of politically inspired national awakeners was well known.[11]

The ideological convictions of the triad could best be gauged by the political stand its surviving members adopted in the revolutionary days of 1848. During the early months of the upheaval, Holovatsky and Vahylevych, as well as Shashkevych's closest colleague, Mykola Ustianovych,[12] chose to support not the members of the Holovna Rada Rus'ka (The supreme Ruthenian council), backed by the conservative members of the Greek Catholic hierarchy, but rather the liberal, pro-Polish Sobor Rus'ki (Ruthenian council) in the conviction that, in the struggle for constitutional rights in Galicia, a cooperative effort with Polish democrats would be the best path to follow.[13] This pro-liberal, pro-Polish choice was taken in spite of the fact that the Supreme Ruthenian Council defended Ukrainian cultural and political rights in Galicia rather skilfully and in its program and proclamations approached the nationality question from a broad all-Ukrainian perspective, articulating ideas and often utilizing expressions found in the early works of the triad. The council's first proclamation, for example, proudly announced, "We Galician Ruthenians belong to the great Ruthenian nation that speaks one language and counts fifteen million people, two and a half million of whom inhabit the Galician land. It had its own perfected language, its own laws and princes, in a word, it was flourishing, prosperous, and powerful."[14] Furthermore, at the very beginning of the Spring of Nations, the Supreme Ruthenian Council spoke in the spirit of conciliation towards the Poles, at times sounding as if it were quoting directly not only from the works of the triad but also from the Statutes of Young Europe: "God and the law of humanity demand that we harbour no hatred in our hearts against those who, side by side with us, are working for the benefit of their nationality but as sincere neighbours of one land live in harmony and union."[15]

What the surviving members of the triad and their colleagues in the Ruthenian Council objected to was not the unwillingness of the council to defend the rights of the Ukrainians in Galicia but the methods through which the council chose to attain these goals, that is, by cooperating closely with the authorities in Vienna. In 1848 what mattered most to the young men who were actively involved in the underground in the preceding decade was the question of constitutional reforms, which at that time appeared attainable only through a concerted effort of all democratically inspired forces in Galicia, and that involved, first of all, the formation of a united front with liberal Poles.

During the initial stages of the Spring of Nations, confidence in the possibility of close cooperation between the Poles and Ukrainians for the attainment of democratic objectives was indeed strong. Even those political activists who in the 1830s were suspected of harbouring pro-Russian and thus conservative sympathies now eagerly joined the jubilant Polish manifestations in the cities and towns of Galicia, demonstratively wore Polish national colours (white-and-red cockades), and greeted Ukrainian and Polish political prisoners amnestied by the Austrian authorities with jubilation. In his poem a former Greek Catholic seminarian, Kelestyn Skomorovsky, greeted the Polish prisoners as "angels of peace" and courageous fighters for justice and truth. In the city of Ternopil, the elated author of the poem, and a Greek Catholic priest by the named of Vasyl Fortuna, harnessed themselves to a carriage in which a patriotic Polish clergyman was returning home from prison.[16] In the Sambir region, as noted above, among the better-known Ukrainian political prisoners who survived the hardships of the Špilberk Fortress were the physically frail but spiritually strong figures of Rev. Teodor Kulchytsky and the former prefect of the Greek Catholic Seminary in Lviv, Mykola Hordynsky.

The initial enthusiasm for Polish-Ukrainian cooperation waned considerably when it became evident during the summer months of 1848 that the major part of the Polish liberal intelligentsia chose to support the non-committal attitude of the Polish Centralna Rada Narodowa (Central national council) on the nationality question: the council promised to protect every citizen's civic liberties but did not address the issue of the political status of the Ukrainians as a separate nationality in Galicia.[17] Even more damaging to the formation of a strong, united opposition to Austria's authoritarian rule were the blatantly anti-Ukrainian articles appearing in *Dziennik Narodowy*, an influential Polish paper in the Galician capital edited by Leon Korecki, the former adversary of Mykola Hordynsky in the Supreme Council of the association.[18] Korecki's articles flatly denied the existence of a separate Ukrainian nationality, as well as of a distinct Ukrainian language. The paper claimed, in effect, that every Ruthenian was essentially a Pole![19] This point of view was supported by Kasper Cięglewicz, who, upon his release from prison, claimed to be both a Ruthenian and a Pole.[20]

The influential mediators in the Ukrainian-Polish controversies, Seweryn Goszczyński and Ignacy Kulczyński, were no longer on the scene in Lviv during 1848,[21] but naturally they both had followers who neither shared the extreme opinions of *Dziennik Narodowy* nor unequivocally supported the position of the Polish National Council. Sympathetic for Ukrainian national demands were expressed by influential individuals within Polish conservative circles, but in the Polish democratic camp conciliators were also to be found. B.K. Morawski, for example, appealed to his fellow Poles to grant the same freedoms to other nationalities they wished to attain for themselves. Calling attention to Poland's age-old enemy, Russia, the writer advised, in the spirit of Young Europe, that the best way for the Poles to safeguard their constitutional liberties in the years to come would be to live "with free men among free brothers and free fraternal nations."[22]

Słowo przestrogi as a Reflection of Ideals and Aims of the 1830s

Among the Polish-Ukrainian polemical fireworks exchanged in the 1848, one of the most comprehensive and consistently reasoned arguments was presented in a pamphlet entitled *Słowo przestrogi* (A word of warning), written from the Ukrainian perspective but penned in the Polish language because many of the arguments it raised were directed at the political stand adopted by the Polish daily *Dziennik Narodowy*. The author whose name appears on the pamphlet, Vasyl Podolynsky, attended the Greek Catholic seminary in Lviv at the end of the 1830s and became deeply immersed in the work of the revolutionary under-ground. Yet, in spite of his radical affiliations, Podolynsky managed somehow to be ordained as a Greek Catholic priest and even received a parish in a remote village during the 1840s.[23]

A close analysis of the pamphlet's content as well as the manner in which the arguments are presented – for instance, the author's utili-zation of examples from pedagogy, illustrations from the republican periods of classical Greece and Rome, allusions to Plato's *Republic*, and especially the author's first-hand familiarity with the political climate in Galicia during the first years of recruitment of Ukrainian seminari-ans into the Polish underground – suggests strongly that the relatively young village priest must have composed this thirty-two-page treatise under the guidance of an older, highly intelligent, and experienced educator well versed in classical philosophy and familiar with a broad range of questions in European history. The most likely candidate for the role of an ideological guide, a co-author, or even *the* author would be the already-discussed philosophy professor and prefect in the Greek Catholic Seminary in the 1830s, the Rev. Mykola Hordynsky.[24] Not only did Podolynsky attend the Greek Catholic Seminary in the Galician capital but during the suspension of activities of the association at the end of the 1830s both Podolynsky and Hordynsky were members of two closely linked underground political organizations.[25] It is very likely that in the euphoric atmosphere of 1848 – when both Polish and Ukrainian political prisoners were greeted with such fanfare and festive jubilations by their former students, colleagues, and admirers – the still-youthful former conspirator filled with revolutionary fervour[26] paid a visit to the dean of the Ukrainian underground, when the phys-ically frail but mentally very alert Hordynsky was convalescing at the home of his relatives in the Sambir region not too far away from Po-dolynsky's family roots.[27]

The fact that Leon Korecki, Hordynsky's main antagonist in the as-sociation[28] during the revolutionary year of 1848, had been the editor of the *Dziennik Narodowy* and that the author of *Słowo* appears to have been provoked to write the pamphlet by the virulently anti-Ukrainian articles appearing in that paper, furthermore points convincingly to Hordynsky's authorship or at least co-authorship. Even more convinc-ing is the fact that it is clear from the content that its author is inti-mately familiar with Polish-Ukrainian relations during the early stage of recruitment of Ukrainians to the Polish underground. Podolynsky's involvement in the conspiracy comes somewhat later, and even though he was directly involved in subversive activities, he managed to escape imprisonment and, as already noted, had the good fortune to receive the sacrament of the Holy Orders. The prefect-conspirator, on the other hand, was not only sentenced to death but was also defrocked by the church authorities during the trial. This could be the reason why someone in Hordynsky's position would have preferred not to write under his own name, for *A Word of Warning* was addressed not only to the Poles but also to politically active Ukrainians whose membership consisted almost exclusively of men tied to the Greek Catholic Church.

The pamphlet is of singular importance for the study of Ukrainian political thought of the 1830s, because its author, while singling out the dangers posed to the formation of a solid democratic Polish-Ukrainian front by the uncompromising stand adopted towards the Ukrainians by *Dzennik Narodowy*, proceeds to build his counterarguments by bringing to light the ideological principles guiding the Polish-Ukrainian relations in the 1830s. In other words, while being written as a lesson for the events in 1848, the pamphlet goes back to the roots of the political awakening of the Ukrainian intelligentsia after the November revolution of 1830.

In his lengthy and multi-layered discourse, irrespective of whether he addresses the subject of nationalism or cosmopolitanism, whether he is focusing on global political developments or local Polish-Ukrainian problems, the author approaches all issues from a broad European perspective, strictly speaking from the standpoint of the programmatic ideals of Young Europe that he obviously assimilated during the years spent as an active member of the underground in the previous decade. Only someone familiar with the program and terminology of Mazzini's organization could have written the following:

> Nothing can restrain us from pursuits common to the whole of Europe, and we shall not be silent unless Europe becomes silent. We all want to be free together with other European nations and are patiently yearning to attain this goal. We want to be a nation and without doubt will become one, because the voice of the people is the voice of God.... We Ruthenians[29] fervently believe in the resurrection of a free, independent Ruthenia. Whether this will be realized in the near future or later is of no great significance. Distance in time does not trouble us, because what does a century represent from the perspective of a nation's existence?[30]

While attempting to analyse the national characteristics of his fellow Ukrainians from the historical, sociological, and psychological points of view, the author turns his attention to what he considers to be his countrymen's most conspicuous trait: an intense, highly emotional sense of yearning. He goes on to explain that because the Ruthenians in Galicia have been deprived of their national independence for many centuries, the object of their yearning had been perceived only dimly, from a distance only, and consequently, for many years it has not been formulated into a definite political goal. Just in the recent past, he notes, these political goals were reawakened among the Ruthenians by their neighbours, the Polish patriots, who, in their drive to regain their lost statehood, turned to their closest neighbours for support. The author has nothing but high praise for those Polish democrats who, in their search to find allies in the struggle for their independence, inspired their neighbours with sentiments of national patriotism because, as he explains, "the better among them understood very well that when a Ruthenian is free, then the Pole too will be free and happy."[31] In order to re-establish a strong Poland, these Polish political activists tried to res-urrect their neighbouring Ruthenian nation in the best way they could, that is, by providing instructions in the Polish tongue but, at the same time, instilling among the new recruits the spirit of Ruthenian nation-ality, together with the democratic ideals of Polish civic liberty. In 1848, the author points out, in order to attain the most important goal of the revolution – the destruction of absolutism and the creation of a demo-cratic republic – the constructive Polish nationality policy of the 1830s ought to be reactivated and not sabotaged by denying the Ruthenian people their nationality with preposterous claims that the Ruthenians are a branch of the Polish nation! The author considers the denials of both the existence of a separate Ukrainian identity and a distinct Ukrainian language as historically absurd and politically suicidal for all Poles who desired to resurrect their country's lost statehood.

The writer foresees Ukraine's independent existence in a broad European confederation and believes this can be attained only through a cooperative effort of all democratically inspired Slavic nations. This cooperative effort he considers indispensable for the attainment of the moment's most important objectives: political independence and a democratic republic. In this context, the writer does not exclude the possibility of Ukraine and Poland existing side-by-side and working together in accordance with the principle of full equality as closely tied constituent parts of a larger Slavic confederation. He pleads for moder-ation, prudence, and willingness on both sides to come to an agreement on questions of secondary importance for the sake of achieving a united front on an issue that for all democrats at that particular moment ought represent the highest priority: to forge a strong union of all democratic forces for the struggle against the principal impediment to progress, the authoritarian imperial regime in Vienna.

To strengthen his plea for moderation and compromise, the author uses a variety of supportive arguments, including examples from pedagogy. In order to achieve the desired objective, he instructs, it is imperative for an educator to make appropriate adjustments to the needs of his students, for whenever only the students are required to adjust, the result is either obstinate resistance or abject sycophancy, neither outcome conducive to the realization of the desired goal. Mykola Hordynsky has been singled out by the leading figures of the Polish political underground in Galicia as the most distinguished intellectual, as well as a consummate pedagogue, both in terms of knowledge and experience. It is precisely the pedagogical method described above that the Greek Catholic cleric would apply in discussions during the long years of imprisonment with his somewhat younger co-conspirators, who were more prone to heated arguments.[32] It was precisely because of this approach that he earned affection and esteem, even from those political prisoners who, like Leslaw Łukaszewicz, grew despondent, irritable, and even belligerent during the lengthy prison ordeal. In due course the priest-educator was able to gain sympathy and goodwill of the prison chaplain who generously supplied him with books on ancient languages like Chaldean and Syrian, as well as with works of Greek philosophers. After refreshing his knowledge of the early Middle Eastern languages and perfecting his classical Greek and Latin, the scholar-conspirator spent the grim days of imprisonment with translations of Plato's works, to the delight and entertainment of his fellow co-conspirators with whom he had the good fortune to share a cell.[33] The reference in *Słowo przestrogi* to Plato's *Republic*,[34] as well as inclusion in the essay of verses with personages from classical mythology provides an additional supportive argument that Hordynsky indeed was the author of the pamphlet. Incidentally, in the Polish original of *Słowo przestrogi* it is clear that the author refers to the concept of the "philosopher king" found in the "Allegory of the Cave" in the *Republic*. This concept is lost in the Ukrainian translation made in 1962, a time when not too many Soviet scholars were well acquainted with the subtleties of Plato's political thought.[35]

In his evaluation of the positive and negative traits of the two nationalities, the author of the pamphlet idealizes neither the Ukrainians nor the Poles. The former, he believes, could still learn a great deal from their better-educated neighbours. He feels that the age-old injustices committed by the Poles in the Ukrainian lands ought to be set aside, for it is not right to blame the children for the sins of their fathers. On the other hand, he is deeply troubled by the fanaticism and excessive conceit displayed by some Polish activists, traits that he considers to be the main obstacle to bringing about the desired compromise. He is acutely aware of the prevalence of ignorance among the masses and calls for the formulation of a comprehensive, enlightened educational policy to be developed and implemented by the future democratic government.[36]

The author also addresses the important question of national minorities. He believes that the Ruthenians, as the age-old settlers in Galicia and as the majority of inhabitants in that province, by natural law have the right to be in the position of hosts, but he is quick to point out that they are obliged to recognize the presence of the Poles and other newcomers living in the territory of the former Ruthenian medieval kingdom of Halych. Among the new settlers, in addition to the Poles, the author singles out the Jews, Armenians, and Germans, all of whom, he feels, deserve to be treated with consideration and courteous hospitality, while from them he expects friendship and respect.[37]

The greater part of the author's message rests on solid, logically presented, and carefully crafted arguments, with supportive illustrations ranging from republican Rome to more recent political developments in Western Europe, from Ukrainian political and ecclesiastical history to the nationality question in the United States.[38] Only when he approaches the sensitive issue of one's native language does the author abandon his intellectual restraint and permits himself to enter the realm of emotions, at times expressing thoughts highly reminiscent of the sentiments voiced by the seminarians during the days of the Triad's most intensive activity. The sound of one's native language and the name of one's native land, he notes, has an overpowering, electrifying effect on a listener, an effect that enters one's veins mysteriously as if by a supernatural force, binding a person to the people. He considers any attempt to deny the right to use one's native tongue as an act of oppression inevitably provoking feelings of resentment and hostility. Obviously drawing on his personal experience, he states that education in a foreign tongue produces a deep mental strain on the psyche of a student, who often feels as if "unnatural chains" were binding his heart. Because of past historical and political developments, he notes, a Ruthenian may speak and even think in Polish, but his heart, as if by a retaliatory reflex, gravitates towards Ruthenia.[39] In other words, the outward appearance of assimilation of an educated Ukrainian can be highly deceptive, for in no way does it signify an individual's acceptance of Polish nationality.[40] For all the reasons presented and the supportive arguments listed, the writer counsels that the Poles ought to be on guard, especially at this critical stage in history.

The author is convinced that because the spirit of the Ruthenian nation has been awakened, it can no longer be put to rest. Therefore, those who wish to have the Ruthenian people on their side ought to work towards reinforcing this spirit, channelling it wisely in the direction of moderation. He expresses doubt that it is possible for a well-educated person to be a fanatic, but even if this unwelcome trait occasionally does appear, eventually, he is confident that the mutual interests of both the Ukrainians and the Poles – two nations bound together by the forces of history and political necessity – will eventually bring about a workable, mutually beneficial compromise.

By no means were all the ideas presented in *Słowo przestrogi* unique. As noted earlier, the pamphlet reflected the thoughts and beliefs that pervaded the Polish and Ukrainian underground a decade earlier, and therefore it was only natural that similar views would be repeated in the polemical literature appearing in 1848. Of interest is a series of articles entitled "Słowo o Rusy i jej polityczeskom stanowyszczy" (A word about Rus' and its political position), which appeared in *Dnewnyk Ruskij*, the organ of the pro-Polish *Sobor Rus'ky* edited by the former Triad member Ivan Vahylevych.[41] The writer, identified only by the initials F.H., shares many of the ideas expressed by the author of *Słowo przestrogi*. He also considers fanaticism to be one of the main reasons for the periodic outbursts of antagonism between the Poles and Ukrainians, both in the past and in the present. He is buoyed, however, by the spirit of democracy and cooperation that he sees developing among the Polish and Ukrainian intelligentsia, especially in the lands under the rule of Russia. He calls attention to a recently uncovered conspiracy in Kyiv: the arrest and trial of the members of the Cyril and Methodius Brotherhood in 1847. Because of this development, the author notes, "the tsar became convinced that the Ruthenian spirit had declared war against him, that the number of his opponents had increased significantly." Like the author of *Słowo przestrogi*, the writer is highly critical of those Poles who do not wish to recognize the Ukrainian language as a separate tongue. Singling out a number of modern Ukrainian writers in the Russian-controlled part of Ukraine, beginning with Kotliarevsky and ending with Shevchenko, he notes that the entry of the Ukrainian language into world literature is not far away. He points out that Polish literature does not suffer because of the progress made in the Ukrainian literary endeavour and notes that Poland, by recognizing what was just for the Ukrainians, "will have on its side a nation that ... will shine alongside it [Poland] in the European political firmament." This is so, the author continues, because this nation is represented not by the conservative members of the Greek Catholic hierarchy but by "martyrs for the national cause, among them Shevchenko, Kostomarov, Kulish, and others." Concurring with the views expressed in *Słowo przestrogi*, the author thinks that the most important objective of the democratic movement in Galicia is the reinforcement of national consciousness and education among the common people, so that they can fully comprehend the importance of having a fatherland. He considers it essential to introduce the Ukrainian language into schools as well as into all government institutions. This will enable the Ukrainian people in both empires to form a common bond, and, with time, the example of the Ukrainians and Poles will inspire the Belarusians and Great Russians to follow in their footsteps and demand political freedoms. In the ideas expressed above, and especially in his concluding remarks, this author, too, shows familiarity with the ideological foundations of Young Europe:

> The Poles should take the path of justice and opportunity! Recognizing the separateness of Rus' is just, because it signifies the recognition of the dignity in man. Separateness is possible because fourteen million people desire it and demand it from mankind.... This is the endeavour of literature, our true goal, which cannot be achieved otherwise than by setting each group of people in its proper place. Call forth Rus' in the interests of Rus', Poland in the interests of Poland, and both in their common interest. Then the colossus of the north [Russia] will collapse.... From this vantage point, it does not seem strange that the Poles will act in the interest of Rus'.[42]

The lively discourse in 1848 between the Poles and Ukrainians affirms the fact that the political training acquired under the influence of Young Europe's underground literature in the previous decade did produce an indelible imprint on the world outlook of both groups, but, as the events of 1848 testify, one that was not strong enough to enable the major part of democrats to forge a common bond during the pivotal year of the revolution. What had been true of the events in Galicia in that year was also true of other parts of Eastern Europe, where two nationalities with unequal status were attempting to assert their national rights. On the other hand, it ought to be remembered that what had been important from the point of view of the founder of Young Europe, Giuseppe Mazzini, was not the attainment of victory at a particular moment in history but the determination to continue the struggle for the movement's highest objectives, even in the face of personal disappointments and staggering political defeats. It would not be redundant to repeat for the sake of comparison a ponderous thought from *Słowo przestrogi*: "Whether this [Ukraine's independence] will be realized in the near future or later is of no great significance. Distance in time does not disturb us because what does a century represent from the perspective of a nation's existence?"[43]

In the course of the revolutionary year, Ukrainians of all political affiliations, including the representatives of the conservative Greek Catholic hierarchy, appear to have been politically alert and quite well prepared to search for the most effective way to protect what were viewed as their nation's vital political, social, and cultural interests. The main concern of the Supreme Council in 1848 – the division of the Austrian province of Galicia into Polish and Ruthenian parts – would have had the full support of the Ukrainian liberals if this issue had not stood in the way of reaching an agreement with the Polish democrats. The controversy on this question between the Ukrainians and Poles, an issue that was much publicized in the Galician press and at the Slavic Congress in Prague,[44] presented a serious impediment to a cooperative effort of all the democratic forces. Yet this bitter controversy was not viewed as an irreparable calamity by all, especially by the older generation of observers, who were able to remove themselves from the emotionally laden political atmosphere of the day and look at the developments from a distance. Šafařík, for example, viewed the existence of national antagonisms as a normal and even beneficial process for national development, observing that the Ukrainian-Polish controversy in Galicia in the course of 1848–9 represented a proof of "the awakening of Slavdom in general."[45]

Many of the Polish democrat-revolutionaries who professed to support the high ideals of Young Europe failed to live up to these promises in 1848. This was especially true of the Hungarian liberals, who openly voiced hostility towards the political awakening of the Slavic nations in the Kingdom of Hungary, as well as of the majority of Polish democrats, who, as soon as the opportunity presented itself for gaining the upper hand in Galicia, gave little thought to the pledges made in the preceding decades. Similarly, as in the case of Lelewel and his co-conspirators in Young Poland, one can detect among the Polish liberals of 1848 a lingering hope that the non-Polish nationalities of the former commonwealth could be absorbed painlessly into the fabric of the more advanced Polish culture into which, as in the past, their elites had blended so well. What Lelewel and his likeminded countrymen failed to recognize or refused to acknowledge was the fact that in an age in which not only elites but also the masses were becoming a factor in political affairs, the situation was radically different from the past. As the author of *Słowo przestrogi* points out, there was no way that a Rusyn in the countryside – on whose support the attainment of the objectives of the democratic movement depended – could be persuaded that he was a Pole. Because of this significant socio-political transformation within the society and the continuing influence of Romanticism among the intellectuals, even the more assimilated segment of the non-Polish intelligentsia in Galicia was ready to cultivate and promote the national traditions of the common folk. At this stage of national awakening, to paraphrase the author of the pamphlet discussed above, "a Ruthenian may speak and even think in Polish, but his heart continues to beat for Ruthenia," or, as he aptly notes in another instance, "In the meantime [until we master Ruthenian] we'll be Ruthenians while speaking Polish, just like once the Poles had been Poles while speaking Latin."[46] The author could have positioned himself as a prime example.

In the tortuous course of Polish-Ukrainian relations in the decades to follow, the influence of Young Europe's ideals lingered, even during the period when Mazzini's ideology was becoming rapidly subverted by a new breed of nationalism. The cooperative effort between the Ukrainians and Poles in Galicia during the "new era" at the end of the nineteenth century[47] serves as a testimony to its continuing presence. The efforts aimed at reconciling the two nationalities in the intensely contentious interwar period of the twentieth century is further proof. However, it would be only in the second half of the twentieth century when Poland once again found itself under a "paternal tutelage" of a system even more intrusive and repressive than the autocratic regimes of the preceding era, that the intellectual elites of both nations recognized fully the necessity of working together, acknowledging what the more perceptive political leaders of the 1830s on both the Polish and Ukrainian side already knew: that the mutual interests of the two nations, bound together by the forces of history and political necessity, dictated the formation of a united front for the benefit of both.[48] In 1991 Poland became the first nation to recognize the independence of Ukraine.

Conclusion

East European nationalism rooted in the humanistic ideals of Young Europe was broad in scope and multilayered in content. In it the political, cultural, moral, and universal principles were masterfully brought together into a coherent whole, with each component complementing and reinforcing the other. It was primarily political, because Young Europe placed the idea of self-determination of nations at the forefront of its program, an idea according to which each nationality had the right to lead an independent existence in accordance with the will of the people. The pivotal role played by the members of Young Poland in the establishment of Mazzini's international organization, and subsequently in spreading the ideals of its program in Eastern Europe, contributed significantly to the rapid politization of the emerging intelligentsia in the Slavic world.

This process manifested itself most vividly in the case of Vzájomnosť, the Slovak section of Young Europe, when under Aleksander Vrchovský's and Ľudovit Štúr's dynamic leadership the strictly culture-oriented group of Lutheran seminarians in Bratislava was transformed into a vibrant political organization virtually overnight in the mid-1830s, that is, soon after the first encounter of Czech and Slovak students with the emissaries of Young Europe. In Galicia the passivity of Ukrainian Greek Catholic theology students was shaken to the ground a few years earlier by the thunder of the Polish November uprising, an event that, together with the impact of Young Europe's underground literature, worked in favour of the fact that for the Ukrainian youth in that province, both the cultural and political phases of the national awakening were taking place at the same time.

Young Europe's influence would assert itself a decade later among Ukrainian intelligentsia under Russian rule with the appearance of the first modern Ukrainian political organization, the Cyril and Methodius

Brotherhood in Kyiv, a city in which the spirit of Szymon Konarski, one of Young Europe's most successful emissaries, continued to inspire both Polish and Ukrainian young men and women long after the conspirator's public execution by the tsarist authorities in the spring of 1839.

But in addition to being political, Mazzini's brand of nationalism was also cultural. For the Italian political thinker, the chief purpose – in fact the raison d'être of a state's existence – was to assure the development of the nation's culture and provide adequate safeguards for the preservation of the national spiritual treasures. This aspect of the program had a strong appeal to the intellectual elites in Eastern Europe whose national cultures were marked by years of a continuing decline due to centuries of foreign rule.

Because of the role they played in the establishment of Young Europe as well as in the dissemination of its ideas, it was taken for granted by many Polish political activists that they occupied a position of leadership among the subject nationalities in both Russian and Austrian Empires. Awareness of this pre-eminent status was most strongly expressed by members of the Polish underground in Galicia, where the spirit of the Enlightenment, with its emphasis on rational thought and material progress, lingered somewhat longer than in other parts of post-Napoleonic Europe. Here only a few among the politically active Poles appeared ready to act in the spirit of Young Europe and make meaningful concessions to the Ukrainians, who constituted the majority of the population in the eastern part of the province. The unyielding obstinacy on the nationality question by the local Polish activists was softened, however, by the presence of influential Polish activists from other parts of the dismembered Polish Commonwealth. Occupying top ranks in Young Poland's leadership, such individuals as Seweryn Goszczyński, Lucjan Siemieński, and Ignacy Kulczyński played a key role in preventing frequent political disputes from developing into serious confrontations and strengthened the position of those local Poles who favoured a policy of concessions and cooperation. In accordance with this tradition developed during the 1830s, political differences that would surface between the two national groups during the revolution of 1848 were kept from exploding into open battles. This spirit of finding a modus vivendi, even during situations of high political tensions, continued to guide Ukrainian-Polish relations to the end of the Austrian rule.

Mazzinian nationalism was also universal in the sense that the ultimate political aim of Young Europe was the creation of a free union of independent nation states cooperating with one another for their individual well-being as well as for the benefit of the entire human community. A reflection of this idea, though on a smaller scale, found expression in the political program of the Cyril and Methodius Brotherhood, which envisaged a loose confederation of independent Slavic states working together in conformity with the principles of equality and brotherhood. Among the Czech and Slovak political activists of the 1830s, Jozef Podlipský came up with a similar idea by proposing the creation a federal union of all Slavic nationalities living in the Habsburg lands on the model of the United States.

Lastly, Mazzini's political thought also included a spiritual component by emphasizing the idea that the recovery of authentic national traditions and values was essential for the moral regeneration of a subjugated nation and that, without such spiritual renewal, no meaningful progress in the political, economic, and cultural sense was possible. This aspect of nationalism expressed itself most clearly in the unwritten program of the precursor the Cyril and Methodius Brotherhood, a secret student group in Kyiv, the members of which viewed themselves as the "apostles of the people" in the true Mazzinian sense: through the recovery of the spiritual treasures of their nation's past they hoped to halt the moral decline of their people brought about by centuries of foreign domination. Yet, even though the Kyivan youth's interest in tradition – just as it was among the members of the Ukrainian intelligentsia in Galicia and among the Czech and the Slovak national awakeners – was genuine and deep, the young men did not approach this task as a nostalgic retreat into the distant past but rather, as a British authority on the subject of nationalism has aptly expressed it, "as a means to catapult the nation from present backwardness and divisions to the most advanced stage of social development."[1] In the research notes that the national awakeners have left behind, there is little evidence of idealization of the masses, but their creative works resonate with sentiments of sympathy and compassion for the common folk. This partly accounts for the success of their efforts to win the support of the people and formulate a meaningful program that would benefit their nation in the years to come.

Mazzinian nationalism embodied both the traditional and modern, the national and universal, the political and cultural, the worldly and spiritual. Thus it was embraced with enthusiasm by the youthful, well-educated, forward-looking intelligentsia of the subject nationalities ruled by the conservative regimes of the Habsburgs and the Romanovs. Because of the dedication and thoroughness with which the majority of national awakeners approached the study of the customs, habits, and spiritual beliefs of their people, to them the twentieth century constructivist notions such as the "invention of tradition" would have sounded absurd. Similarly, in view of the seriousness with which they applied themselves to the study of historical and linguistic documentary sources through which they were tracing the path of their people's historical past, the idea of a nation as an "imagined community" would have had an alien sound. In their zeal to learn about the past and bring about a better future, they may have resorted to an occasional exaggeration or could have drawn an erroneous conclusion, but without question they were convinced that the people who represented the subject matter of their investigation possessed certain unique qualities and traits that entitled them the right to be called a nation.

One element found missing in the Mazzinian concept of a nation is the twentieth-century social Darwinist notion of racial exclusiveness or "ethnic purity." What mattered in determining one's national identity or allegiance from the point of view of Young Europeans was not so much the purity of one's family lineage or race but the spirit of the milieu that moulded an individual's personality and shaped an individual's world outlook. A good example of this liberal and very personal approach to one's identity is the case of Joachim Lelewel, the head of Young Poland, who, in spite of his multiethnic background on both sides of the family tree, considered himself a genuine Pole and was viewed as such by his colleagues and followers. It is worth repeating that Mazzini's devoted co-conspirators and trusted intimate friends throughout his long and difficult years of political exile were two Italians of Jewish background from northern Italy.

To sum up, Young Europe's ideas served as a powerful impetus in the process of the political awakening of the emerging intelligentsia among the Slavic nationalities during the 1830s and 1840s. The role of the Poles as disseminators of Young Europe's program was of primary importance in the establishment of solid foundations for modern nationalism based on the Mazzinian ideals of brotherly love and humane relations among nations. Mazzini's deep-seated belief in the duty of all democrats to promote the principles of Young Europe's covenant, particularly in Eastern Europe, where the potential for national democratic revolutions he believed was the strongest, provided the principal driving force for the politicization of thought among the Western and Eastern Slavs who, with the exception of the Poles, if left to their own resources, were not prepared during the 1830s to embark on the road of national liberation. Once the ideas of Young Europe were injected into their midst, very quickly, in addition to their fascination with the linguistic affinities of the Slavic tongues and preoccupation with Eastern European antiquities, the young intelligentsia placed political ideals and aims at the top of its program. Young Europe's emissaries, consisting mainly of patriotically charged participants of the November revolution, played the role of an important catalyst in the transformation of what could have been a slowly developing form of cultural nationalism into an explicitly political one.

The 1830s – the period of Young Europe's most intensive drive for revolutionary action – paved the ground for the national renaissance that exploded in the next decade. Mazzini's somewhat naïve yet firm conviction that the national animosities plaguing Europe were mainly the products of imperial rivalries among autocratic regimes as well as the abandonment of the Christian principle of brotherly love by modern societies, appealed to the young members of the intelligentsia in Eastern Europe – in many instances tied closely to religious professions – and smoothed the way for cooperation among them, even though the road towards attaining Young Europe's lofty ideals would be long and tortuous, yet not without promising signs of progress.

A good example of a cooperative effort in the spirit of Young Europe during the second half of the nineteenth century was the support rendered to Polish insurgents by their Slavic neighbours during their anti-Russian uprising of 1863. In it, the Ukrainian volunteers constituted the largest group among the non-Polish participants.[2] Of the more prominent Ukrainians who lost their lives in this second nineteenth-century anti-Russian revolution was Andrii Potebnia, the brother of the prominent Ukrainian linguist Oleksander. An officer in the Russian army, Andrii Potebnia was one of the few members of the East European political underground who, during his travels abroad, had direct ties with Mazzini.[3]

The Italian leader's confidence in the revolutionary potential of the Slavic peoples of Eastern Europe never waned. As noted earlier, even in his advanced years Mazzini attempted to persuade a young British poet-translator, Harriet Hamilton King, to learn Polish, because he firmly believed that the Slavic nations were destined to become the dominant power in Europe and that eventually "these younger people would regenerate the 'older' nations of Europe."[4]

Without question, the politicization of nascent nationalism among the Slavs would have taken place even without the dissemination of Young Europe's ideas, but the process would have been slower, and the impact of social Darwinism, with its stress on the natural right of the strong to dominate the weak, and its emphasis on a continuing struggle as an accepted manner of human existence, would have been significantly more pronounced. The attitude of tolerance towards the minorities that was characteristic of the Ukrainian national rebirth under the guiding hand of Mykhailo Hrushevsky during the

revolution of 1917–21, the readiness to find a platform for cooperation with the Ukrainian National Republic by the Polish leader of that
period, Josef Pilsudski, as well as the spirit of humanism pervading the
Czechoslovak Republic under the leadership of Thomas G. Masaryk
were, to a great degree, the results of the deeply imbedded ideas of
Young Europe among the leaders of the Slavic nations at the beginning
of the twentieth century. The political elites in those years still remembered that the first wave of modern nationalism that entered Eastern
Europe was of the Mazzinian brand: unequivocally democratic and
profoundly humanistic. After seventy years of Communist rule during
which every form of nationalism had been systematically equated with
Fascism,[5] the idea of "nationalism with a human face" has been erased
from the realm of the possible, even in scholarly discourse. A good sign
of a more balanced approach towards this question in Eastern Europe
has been the appearance in Ukraine of a monograph commemorating
the 200th anniversary of the Italian thinker's birth in 2005.[6] A revival of
Mazzinian studies in Poland, a country with a history of solid scholarly
works on this subject during the interwar period, is still to come.

Notes

Introduction

1 For surveys of the period, see Michael Broers, *Europe after Napoleon: Revolution, Reaction, and Romanticism, 1814–1848* (Manchester, NY: Manchester University Press, 1996); Jacques Droz, *Europe between Revolutions, 1815–1848* (New York: Harper & Row, 1967); Martyn Lyons, *Post-revolutionary Europe, 1815–1856* (Basingstoke, UK: Palgrave Macmillian, 2006).

2 For biographies of Metternich, see Alan Palmer, *Metternich: Councillor of Europe* (London: Phoenix Giant, 1997); Wolfram Siemann, *Metternich: Stratege und Visionär: eine Biografie* (München: C.H. Beck, 2016).

3 For a discussion of the revolutions of 1830, see Clive H. Church, *Europe in 1830: Revolution and Political Change* (London: Allen & Unwin, 1983); John M. Merriman, ed., *1830 in France* (New York: New Viewpoints, 1975).

4 For a description of these events, see Els Witte, Jan Craeybeck, and Alain Meyen, *Political History of Belgium: From 1830 Onwards* (Brussels: Academic and Scientific Publishers, 2009).

5 Between 1772 and 1795 the Polish-Lithuainian Commonwealth was partitioned by its three neighbouring powers, Russia, Prussia, and Austria. For a good discussion of this subject, see Piotr S. Wandycz, *The Lands of Partitioned Poland, 1795–1918* (Seattle: University of Washington Press, 1984); I.A. Betley, *Poland in International Relations 1830–31* (S – Gravenhage: Mouton, 1960); Charles Morley, "The European Significance of the November Uprising," *Journal of Central European Affairs* 11 (January 1952): 407–19.

6 For these events, see Stefan Kieniewicz, Andrzej Zahorski, and Władysław Zajewski, *Trzy Powstania Narodowe: Kościuszkowskie, Listopadowe, Styczniowe*, ed. Władysław Zajewski (Warsaw: Książka i Wiedza, 1992); F. Leslie, *Polish Politics and the Revolution of November 1830* (London: University of London Athlone Press, 1956); Piotr S. Wandycz, *The Lands*

of Partitioned Poland, 1795–1918 (Seattle: University of Washington Press, 1974). See also chap. 2, n2.

7 For a brief but very good discussion of this event, see Marc Raeff, *The Decembrist Movement* (Englewood Cliffs, NJ: Prentice Hall, 1966).

8 On the rule of Nicholas I, see Nicholas V. Riasanovsky, *Nicholas I and Official Nationality in Russia, 1825–1855* (Berkeley: University of California Press, 1967); Sidney Monas, *The Third Section: Police and Society in Russia under Nicholas I* (Cambridge, MA: Harvard University Press, 1961); Bruce W. Lincoln, *Nicholas I: Emperor and Autocrat of All the Russias* (Bloomington: Indiana University Press, 1989).

9 Andrzej Walicki, *Philosophy and Romantic Nationalism: The Case of Poland* (Notre Dame, IN: University of Notre Dame Press, 1989); Walicki, *The Slavophile Controversy: The History of a Conservative Utopia in Nineteenth-Century Russian Thought* (Oxford: Clarendon, 1975); Walicki, *Russia, Poland and Universal Regeneration: Studies on Russian and Polish Thought of the Romantic Epoch* (Notre Dame, IN: University of Notre Dame Press, 1991); Walicki, *The Enlightenment and the Birth of Modern Nationhood: Polish Political Thought from Noble Republicanism to Tadeusz Kosciuszko* (Notre Dame, IN: University of Notre Dame Press, 1989); Walicki, *Mesjanizm Adama Mickiewicza w perspektywie porównawczej* (Warsaw: IfiS, 2006).

10 John Hutchinson, *The Dynamics of Cultural Nationalism: The Gaelic Revival and the Creation of the Irish Nation State* (Boston: Allen & Unwin, 1987); Anthony D. Smith, *The Ethnic Origins of Nations* (Oxford: Basil Blackwell, 1986).

11 Benedict Anderson, *Imagined Communities: Reflections on the Origins and Spread of Nationalism* (London: Verso, 2006); Miroslav Hroch, *Social Preconditions of National Revival in Europe* (New York: Columbia University Press, 2000); Ernest Gellner, *Nations and Nationalism* (Ithaca, NY: Cornell University Press, 1983); E.J. Hobsbawm, *Nations and Nationalism since 1780: Programme, Myth, Reality* (Cambridge: Cambridge University Press, 1990).

12 For a brief but very good critical analysis of the constructivist school of thought, see Andrzej Walicki, "Ernest Gellner and the 'Constructivist' Theory of Nation," in *Cultures and Nations of Central and Eastern Europe: Essays in Honor of Roman Szporluk*, ed. Zvi Gitelman, Lubomyr Hajda, John-Paul Himka, and Roman Solchanyk, 611–17 (Cambridge, MA: Harvard University Press, 2000).

13 *Ruthenians* (*Rusyny* in local usage) was the official name of the Ukrainians in the Habsburg domains. In the writings of the Ukrainian intelligentsia in the two empires during the period under consideration, both terms referred to the same nation. They will be used interchangeably in this study.

14 Edyta M. Bojanowska, *Nikolai Gogol: Between Ukrainian and Russian Nationalism* (Cambridge, MA: Harvard University Press, 2007), 16.

15 Roman Szporluk, "Ukraine: From an Imperial Periphery to a Sovereign State," in *Russia, Ukraine, and the Breakup of the Soviet Union* (Stanford, CA: Hoover Institution Press 2000), 367.

16 On the historical background of Galicia, see Chris Hann and Paul Robert Magocsi, *Galicia: A Multicultured Land* (Toronto: University of Toronto Press, 2005); and Paul Robert Magocsi, *Galicia: A Historical Survey and Bibliographical Guide* (Toronto: University of Toronto Press, 1983). For a good survey and analysis of the relations between Poles and Ukrainians in Galicia under Austrian rule, see Ivan Lysiak Rudnytsky, "The Ukrainians in Galicia under Austrian Rule," in *Austrian History Yearbook* 3, pt 2 (1967): 394–429. Piotr S. Wandycz, "The Poles in the Habsburg Monarchy," in *Austrian History Yearbook* 3, pt 2 (1967): 261–86; and Henryk Wereszczycki, "The Poles as an Integrating and Disintegrating Factor," in *Austrian History Yearbook* 3, pt 2 (1967): 287–313.

17 Feodosii Steblii, "Vyznachna pam'iatka ukraïns'koï politychnoï dumky seredyny XIX stolittia: 'Slovo perestorohy' Vasylia Podolyns'koho," in *Zapysky Naukovoho Tovarystva im. Shevchenka* (Zapysky NTSh) 228 (1994), 434–87:453. Even though the author uses the term *Ruthenian*, it is clear from the context of this essay that he refers to the Ukrainian people living in both empires.

Chapter 1

1 Giuseppe Mazzini, quoted in Joanna Ugniewska, *Giuseppe Mazzini: historia jako narodowa terapia* (Wrocław: Wydawnictwo Polskiej Akademii Nauk, 1986), 102.

2 Mazzini's recollections can be found in *Life and Writings of Joseph Mazzini* (hereafter cited as Mazzini, *Writings*), new ed., 6 vols (London: Smith, Elder, 1890–1), 1:34. In his penetrating study of Mazzini's life and thought, the American author Roland Sarti questions the Italian leader's claim that the idea of a new organization was born as early as his imprisonment at Savona. See his *Mazzini: A Life for the Religion of Politics* (Westport, CT, 1997), 40. In addition to Sarti's excellent work, numerous studies on Mazzini's life, political thought, and revolutionary work have appeared in Italian, English, Polish, and other languages since the last decades of the nineteenth century. Among those published in English in recent decades, in addition to Sarti's study, are Denis Mack Smith, *Mazzini* (New Haven, CT: Yale University Press, 1994); William Roberts, *Prophet in Exile: Joseph Mazzini in England, 1837–1868* (New York: Peter Lang, 1989); Marcella Pellegrino Scuffle, *Victorian Radical and Italian Democrats* (London: Boydell, 2014); Gaetano Salvemini, *Mazzini* (Stanford: Stanford University Press, 1957); Salvo Mastellone, *Mazzini and Marx* (Westport,

CT: Praeger, 2003); Simon Levis Sullam, *Giuseppe Mazzini and the Origins of Fascism*, Italian and Italian American Studies, ed. Stanislao G. Pugliese, trans. Sergio Knipe and Oona Smyth (Basingstoke: Palgrave Macmillan, 2015); Enrico Dal Lago, *William Lloyd Garrison and Giuseppe Mazzini: Abolition, Democracy, and Radical Reform* (Baton Rouge: Louisiana State University Press, 2013) (electronic resource). Among the older biographies of note are Edward E.Y. Hales, *Mazzini and the Secret Societies: The Making of a Myth* (New York: Kennedy, 1956); Emilie Venturi Ashurst, *Joseph Mazzini: A Memoir* (London: King, 1877); Harriet King Bolton, *The Life of Mazzini* (London: Dent, 1902); Harriet King Bolton, *Letters and Recollections of Mazzini* (London: Longmans Green, 1912); Giuseppe Mazzini, *Note autobiografiche*, ed. Mario Menghini, 2nd ed. (Florence: F. le Monnier, 1944). Also of interest are recent collections of essays: Nick Carter, *Britain, Ireland and the Italian Risorgimento* (Houndmills, Basingstoke, Hamphshire: Palgrave Macmillan, 2015); Christopher A. Bayly and Eugenio F. Biagini, eds, *Giuseppe Mazzini and the Globalization of Democratic Nationalism 1830–1920* (Oxford: Oxford University Press, 2008). A selection of Mazzini's writings on nationalism can be found in Stefano Recchia and Nadia Urbinati, eds, *A Cosmopolitanism of Nations: Giuseppe Mazzini's Writings on Democracy, Nation Building, and International Relations* (Princeton, NJ: Princeton University Press, 2009).

3 Mazzini, *Note autobiografiche*, 25–6; Giuseppe Mazzini, *Edizione Nazionale, Scritti editi ed inediti di Giuseppe Mazzini (1906–90)*, (hereafter cited as *EN SEI*), 106 vols (Imola: Cooperativa Tipografico; Editrice Paolo Galeati, 1906–90), 77:33.

4 *EN SEI*, 1:215.

5 *Fede e avvenire* was first published in French as *Foi et avenir* in 1835. It appeared in Italian shortly thereafter. For the Italian version I used *Fede e avvenire ed altri scritti*, ed. Luigi Salvatorelli (Rome: Giulio Einaudi, 1945). An English translation of the essay is contained in Joseph Mazzini, *The Duties of Man and Other Essays* (London: J.M. Dent, 1936), 141–94. The phrase "European in substance, national in form" can be found on p. 180. For other essays by Mazzini I consulted *Essays: Selected from the Writings, Literary, Political and Religious, of Joseph Mazzini*, ed. William Clarke (London: Walter Scott, 1887).

6 On Mazzini's influence on Marx, see Mastellone, *Mazzini and Marx*.

7 The questions of internationalism, cosmopolitanism, and nationalism in Mazzini's thought are discussed by Nadia Urbinati, "The Legacy of Kant: Giuseppe Mazzini's Cosmopolitanism of Nations"; and by Maurizio Isabella, "Mazzini's Internationalism in Context: From the Cosmopolitan Patriotism of the Italian Carbonari to Mazzini's Europe of Nations," both in Bayly and Biagini, *Giuseppe Mazzini*, 11–36 and 37–58.

8 Eugen Kuehnemann, ed., *Herders Werke*, pt 4, s. 3, *Ideen zur Philosophie der Geschichte der Menschheit*, 677, in Joseph Kürschner, ed., *Deutsche National-Litteratur*, 77 (Stuttgart: Union Deutsche Verlagsgessellschaft, n.d.). Quoted in *Nationalism in Eastern Europe*, ed. Peter F. Sugar and Ivo J. Lederer (Seattle: University of Washington Press, 1969), 14. For an excellent discussion of Herder's philosophy, see John K. Noyes, *Herder: Aesthetics against Imperialism* (Toronto: University of Toronto Press, 2015).

9 Quoted in Sugar and Lederer, *Nationalism in Eastern Europe*, 14.

10 *EN SEI*, 3:299.

11 Mazzini, "Faith and the Future," 178.

12 Mazzini's ideas on these questions are contained in a collection of essays translated into English by Stefano Recchia. See Recchia and Urbinati, *Cosmopolitanism of Nations*.

13 Sarti, *Mazzini*, 50–1; Stefania Sokołowska, *Młoda Polska: Z dziejów ugrupovań demokratycznych wielkej emigracji* (Wrocław: Zakład narodowy imienia Ossolińskich, Wydawnictwo Polskiej Akademii Nauk, 1972), 60.

14 *EN SEI*, 2:45–6.

15 *EN SEI*, 2:53–4.

16 See Szymon Konarski, *Dziennik z lat 1831–1834* (Wrocław: Zakład Narodowy im. Ossolińskich, 1973), especially 277, 314. Konarski was no stranger to the idea of an irregular army fighting on behalf of a nation's independence. Similar ideas were expressed by the Polish eighteenth-century hero Thaddeus Kosciuszko. Alex Storozynski, *The Peasant Prince: Thaddeus Kosciuszko and the Age of Revolution* (New York: St Martin's, 2009). See especially chapter 12, "Kosciuszko's Rebels: Peasant Scythemen, a Burgher Militia, and a Jewish Cavalry."

17 *EN SEI*, 5:49–50.

18 Sarti, *Mazzini*, 63–4.

19 *EN SEI*, 5:33.

20 *EN SEI*, 2:45.

21 Cited in Joanna Ugniewska, *Giuseppe Mazzini: historia jako narodowa terapia* (Wrocław: Wydawnictwo Polskiej Akademii Nauk, 1986), 118.

22 *EN SEI*, 2:68.

23 Mazzini, *Writings*, 1:34, quoted in F. Gunther Eyck, "Mazzini's Young Europe," *Journal of Central European Affairs* 17 (1958): 358.

24 *Edizione Nazionale*, 5:16. Quoted in Eyck, "Mazzini's Young Europe," 358.

25 *La Giovine Italia*, ed. Mario Menghini, in *Biblioteca Storica del Risorgimento*, 6 vols (Rome, 1902–5), 2:225. Quoted in Eyck, "Mazzini's Young Europe," 358.

26 *Giovine Italia*, 1:36.

27 Sarti, *Mazzini*, 64.

28 On the question of women, see Mazzini, *Duties of Man and Other Essays*,
    especially 62–4; see also *Mazzini's Letters to an English Family*, 3 vols
    (London: John Lane, 1920–2), 1:33–4.
29 On Maria Mazzini, see Bianca Montale, *Maria Drago Mazzini* (Genoa:
    Comune di Genova, 1955); Itala Cremona Cozzolino, ed., *Maria Mazzini
    e il suo ultimo carteggio* (Florence: La Nuova Italia, 1939); Carlo Cagnacci,
    Giuseppe Mazzini e i fratelli Ruffini (Porto Maurizio: Tipografia Berio, 1893).
30 Sarti, *Mazzini*, 53.

Chapter 2

1 Witold Łukaszewicz, "Wpływ masonerii, karabonaryzmu i Józefa
   Mazziniego na polski ruch rewolucyjny w latach poprzedzających
   Wiosnę Ludów (1831–1847)," in *Wiosna Ludów w Europie*, pt 2, *Zagadnienia
   ideologiczne*, ed. Natalia Gąsiorowska (Warsaw: Państwowy Instytut
   Wydawniczy, 1951), 370.
2 A large proportion of the 8,000–10,000 émigrés consisted of Polish
   elites and gentry. Among them were: Prince Adam Jerzy Czartoryski,
   leader of the Polish Government-in-Exile in Paris (with embassies in
   London and Istanbul); the prominent historian and politician Joachim
   Lelewel; national bards and writers, including Adam Mickiewicz, Juliusz
   Slowacki, Cyprian Kamil Norwid, Jozef Bohdan Zaleski, and others.
   See Lubomir Gadon, *Wielka emigracja w pierwszych latach po powstaniu
   listopadowym* (Paris: Księgarnia Polska, 1960); Slawomir Kalembka,
   Towarzystwo Demokratyczne Polskie w latach 1832–1846 (Toruń: Panstwowe
   Wydawnictwo Naukowe, 1966); Witold Łukaszewicz and Wladyslaw
   Lewandowski, *Postępowa Publicystyka Emigracyjna 1831–1846: wybor
   źródel* (Wrocław: Wydawnictwo Polskiej Akademii Nauk, 1961).
3 Walicki, *Philosophy and Romantic Nationalism*, 80.
4 Sokołowska, *Młoda Polska*, 4. The book, which appeared in 1832 in Paris,
   was soon translated into French. It had a profound impact on Mazzini,
   and many of its ideas found reflections in his soon-to-be-published *Fede e
   avvenire*.
5 Ibid., 15. For a detailed discussion of this period, see also Adam Lewak,
   *Od związków węglarskich do Młodej Polski: Dzieje emigracji i legjonu polskiego
   w Szwajcarji w r. 1833–1834* (Warsaw: E. Wende i Spólka, 1920).
6 Ugniewska, *Giuseppe Mazzini*, 74.
7 Friedrich Meinecke, *Cosmopolitanism and the National State* (Princeton, NJ:
   Princeton University Press, 1970), 10.
8 Walicki, *Philosophy and Romantic Nationalism*, 69.
9 Of particular inerest in this context are the thoughts of the Russian liberal Piotr Struve, *Patriotika: Politika, kul'tura, religiia, sotsializm; sbornik*

statei za piat' let, 1905–1910 gg. (St Petersburg: D.E. Zhukovskii, 1911). For a summary of these ideas and a discussion of this question, see also Anna Procyk, *Russian Nationalism and Ukraine: The Nationality Policy of the Volunteer Army during the Civil War* (Edmonton: Canadian Institute of Ukrainian Studies, 1995), 14–16.

10 Mazzini's first published literary essay was "On Dante's Love of Country" written in 1826, when he was barely twenty-one. See Sarti, *Mazzini,* 32–3.

11 See, e.g., his correspondence with the Ashurst family, in Mazzini, *Mazzini's Letters to an English Family.*

12 Witold Łukaszewicz, "Wpływ masonerii," 370.

13 Ibid.

14 Aleksandr I. Herzen, *Byloe i Dumy* (Leningrad: OGIZ, 1946), 589, 594; Adam Lewak, "Ideologia polskiego romantyzmu politycznego a Mazzini," *Przegląd Historyczny* 37 (1948): 311–21, here 318; Łukaszewicz, "Wpływ masonerii," 381; Jerzy Jędrzejewicz, *Zwycięstwo Pokonanych: Opowieść o Stanisławie Worcellu* (Warsaw: Instytut Wydawniczy Pax, 1974), 461–5.

15 Summaries of the Savoy campaign in English can be found in Sarti, *Mazzini,* 47–80; Smith, *Mazzini,* 7–11.

16 Kałembka, *Towarzystwo Demokratyczne Polskie v latach 1832–1846,* 20; Sokołowska, *Młoda Polska,* 62–3.

17 G. Mazzini to J. Lelewel, 9 May 1833, quoted in Lewak, *Od związków węglarskich,* 140–1.

18 Sokołowska, *Młoda Polska,* 63.

19 During Napoleon's Russian campaign, Antonini was taken prisoner. After he was freed, he chose to remain in the Russian-dominated Kingdom of Poland, and during the revolution of 1830–1 he fought with distinction on the side of the Polish patriots. Sokołowska, *Młoda Polska,* 14, 29.

20 Paul Harro-Harring, *Memorie sulla "Giovine Italia" e sugli ultimi avvenimenti di Savoia* (Milan: Societa Editrice Dante Alighieri, 1913).

21 Sokołowska, *Młoda Polska,* 62–5. On these events, see Lewak, *Od związków węglarskich,* especially 85–102. Italian-Polish contacts during this period are also discussed in Giovanna Tomassucci, "Mazzini e la Polonia, 'Sorella Combattente,'" in *Il Mazzinianesimo nel Mondo,* ed. Giuliana Limiti (Pisa: Instituto Domus Mazziniana, 1996), 2:367–462. See especially 373–80.

22 On Konarski, see Konarski, *Dziennik;* Łukaszewicz, *Szymon Konarski;* H. Moscicki, *Szymon Konarski* (Warsaw: Państwowy Inst. Wydawniczy, 1949); Stanisław Szpotański, *Konarszczyzna i Lud Polski: przygotowania powstańcze w Polsce w 1835–1839 roku* (Cracow: Książka, 1926).

23 "Z dzienniczka Sz. Konarskiego," ed. M. Wierzchowski, *Mowią Wieki* 11 (1959): 19–22. Quoted in Sokołowska, *Młoda Polska,* 92–3.

24 Konarski, *Dziennik*, 277, 314.

25 "Quatrieme Anniversaire de la mort de Simon Konarski celebré a Londres le 27 fevrier 1843," as reported in *Orzeł Bialy* 10, 31 March 1843, 42–4, cited in Łukaszewicz, "Wpływ masonerii," 349–50.

26 Lewak, *Od związków węgliarskich*, 91.

27 The Polish involvement in the Savoy campaign is discussed in Lewak, *Od związków węgliarskich*, 89–102; Sokołowska, *Młoda Polska*, 63–76.

28 Łukaszewicz, "Wpływ masonerii," 379.

29 *Orzeł Bialy*, 20, 31 August 1842, quoted in Łukaszewicz, "Wpływ masonerii," 346.

30 Zwierkowski to J. Lelewel, Tours, 26 October 1834, quoted in Łukaszewicz, "Wpływ masonerii," 294. On this subject, see Stefan Kieniewicz, "La pensée de Mazzini et le mouvement national slave," in *Atti del Convegno Mazzini e l'Europa*, 109–23 (Rome: Acccademia dei Lincei, 1974); Lewak, "Ideologia polskiego romantyzmu," 311–21.

31 Zwierkowski to Lelewel, 26 October 1834.

32 J. Zaliwski to W. Piętkiewicz, Galicia, 3 August 1833, Lewak, *Od związków węglarskich*, appendix, 128–9.

33 Regarding the Zaliwski expedition, see Łukaszewicz, "Wpływ masonerii," 294.

34 Wilhelm Marr, *Das junge Deutschland in der Schweiz* (Leipzig, 1846), 68. Quoted in Eyck, "Mazzini's Young Europe," 357.

35 Mazzini, *Scritti*, 3:386, in "Alla Gioventù Italiana," quoted in Eyck, "Mazzini's Young Europe," 360.

36 Quoted in Sarti, *Mazzini*, 80.

37 See "Due note al Discorso del Krempowiecki intorno alla Rivoluzione Polacca," in *EN SEI*, 3:161–5.

38 See chap. 1, n4.

39 Łukaszewicz, "Wpływ masonerii," 311.

40 See, e.g., Giuseppe Mazzini, "Adam Mickiewicz," *EN SEI*, 94:3–43; G. Maver, "Mazzini and Mickiewicz," in *Adam Mickiewicz, 1855–1955. Międzynarodowa Sesja Naukowa Polskiej Akademii Nauk 17–20 kwietnia 1956*, ed. Kazimierz Wyka and Jadwiga Rużyło Pawłowska, 212–25 (Wrocław: Zaklad Narodowy im. Ossolińskch, 1958).

41 Lewak, "Ideologia polskiego romantizmu," 316.

42 King, *Letters and Recollections of Mazzini*, 56.

43 Mikołaj Mazanowski, *Józef Bohdan Zaleski: Życie i dzieła, zarys biograficzny* (St Petersburg: Nakładem Księgarni K. Grendyszyńskiego, 1901), 54. The author quotes Zaleski's letter of 8 April 1869 to Wladyslaw Mickiewicz, in which he describes the close cooperation between himself and the great Polish bard during the writing of *Księgi*.

44 Vladimir A. Frantsev, *Pol'skoe slavianovedenie kontsa XVIII i pervoi chet-verti XIX st.* (Prague: Tipografia "Politiki," 1906), 309 and clx; Henryk Batowski, *Przyjaciele Słowianie* (Warsaw: "Czytelnik," 1956), 43, 45, 51, 55; Józef Bodhan Zaleski, *Pisma Józefa Bohdana Zaleskiego* (St Petersburg, 1852), 2:201; Mazanowski, *Józef Bohdan Zaleski*, 76–7; Tetiana Dovzhok, "Adam Mitskevich ta 'ukraïns'ka shkola' (do problemy pol's'ko-ukraïns'koho pohranychchia," in *Adam Mitskevych i Ukraïna: Zbirnyk naukovykh prats'*, ed. Rostyslav Radyshevsky and H.D. Verves, 94–111 (Kyiv: Vydavnytstvo "Biblioteka Ukraïntsia, 1999).

45 V.V. Adadurov, "Memorandumy pol's'kykh avtoriv pochatku XIX st. iak dzherelo uiavlen' imperatora Napoleona I ta ioho uriadovtsiv stosovno pivdenno zakhidnykh okraïn Rosiiskoï imperiï," *Ukraïnskyj istorychnyi zhurnal* 2 (2008): 158, 162.

46 Ibid.

47 Ibid., 162–3.

48 Mazzini, *Fede e avvenire ed altri scritti*, 21. Mazzini's familiarity with the works of Bohdan Zaleski and Seweryn Goszczyński, Polish romantic writers who wrote about the Ukrainian Cossack's love of freedom, is noted by Giovanna Tomassucci, "Romantyzm polski w pismach G. Mazziniego," in *Contributi Italiani al XII Congresso Internazionale degli Slavisti*, ed. Francois Esvan, 541–42 (Naples: Associazione Italiana degli Slavisti, 1998).

49 Quoted in Ugniewska, *Giuseppe Mazzini*, 101. From the point of view of the future international upheaval of oppressed peoples, Ukraine would appear very well suited to the role of an initiator-leader, because the Ukrainians, while manifesting, on numerous occasions in history, a strong determination to fight for liberty, were free from expressing a desire to rule over others.

50 *EN SEI*, 1:180. Quoted in Eyck, "Mazzini's Young Europe," 367n42.

51 For an excellent and well-documented study of the process through which Josef Václav Frič came to this realization, see Zdeněk V. David, "Frič, Herzen, and Bakunin: The Clash of Two Political Cultures," *East European Politics and Societies* 12, no. 1 (Winter 1998): 1–30.

52 Mazzini, *Fede e avvenire*, 22.

53 The title "uncrowned king of Poland" was invented for Czartoryski by Władysław Zamoyski. This appellation was ridiculed by the majority of liberal émigrés, including some of Czartoryski's own followers. Czartoryski himself was rather unhappy with it and accepted it only half-heartedly. Pertinent information on the nationality policy of Czartoryski's political circle can be found in Marceli Handelsman, *Ukraińska polityka ks. Adama Czartoryskiego przed wojną krymską* (Warsaw, 1937); Handelsman,

Francja – Polska, 1795–1845: Studja nad dziejami myśli politycznej (Warsaw: Gebethner i Wolff, 1926).

54 Mickiewicz, e.g., believed that the Lithuanian people, constituting the majority of the inhabitants in the territory in which he was born, represented a nationality too small to form a viable nation and thus were not destined to have an independent state. A decade later the English liberal thinker John Stuart Mill, in his conversations with Mazzini, expressed similar thoughts with respect to the future of the Irish.

55 The official name, given at birth, of both of these intimate, lifelong friends was Józef Bohdan Zaleski. For reasons of clarity, the poet will be referred to by the name by which he is commonly known in literature, Bohdan Zaleski. His namesake, a distinguished soldier of the Napoleonic wars, a participant in the November Revolution and the anti-Russian Zaliwski campaign, and, subsequently in emigration, a confidant of Lelewel, will be referred to as Józef Zaleski.

56 S. Pigoń, *Zręby Nowej Polski w publicystyce Wielkiej Emigracji* (Warsaw, 1939), 12–13. Cited in Walicki, *Philosophy and Romantic Nationalism*, 70.

57 For a brief but very good biographical sketch of Terlecki, see Ivan L. Rudnytsky, "Hipolit Vladimir Terlecki," in *Essays in Modern Ukrainian History*, 143–72 (Edmonton: Canadian Institute of Ukrainian Studies, 1987).

58 See V. Bazilevskii (V. Bogucharskii), *Gosudarstvennye prestupleniia v Rossii v XIX v.* (St Petersburg, 1906), 29; Volodymyr Mijakovs'kyj, "Shevchenko in the Brotherhood of Saints Cyril and Methodius," in *Taras Ševčenko 1814–1861: A Symposium*, ed. Volodymyr Mijakovskyj and George Y. Shevelov (S-Gravenhage: Mouton, 1962), 27; O. Hermaize, "Rukh dekabrystiv i ukraïnstvo," *Ukraïna* 6 (1925): 33.

59 In spite of its original limited scope, the slogan proved to be of timeless significance. It was emblazoned on a banner on Red Square in August 2008 by political activists protesting Russia's invasion of Georgia, and four decades earlier in August 1968 the slogan "*Za vashu i nashu svobodu*" was unfurled by Soviet dissidents protesting the invasion of Czechoslovakia.

60 For a thorough and very well-documented description of these developments, see Sokołowska, *Młoda Polska*, 127–63. See also chapters 4 and 5.

61 Liakhova, "Ukraïns'kyj lyst Mykoly Hoholia"; George S.N. Luckyj, *Between Gogol' and Ševčenko: Polarity in the Literary Ukraine: 1798–1847*, Harvard Series in Ukrainian Studies, vol. 8 (Munich: Wilhelm Fink Verlag, 1971), 118. For an excellent discussion of Gogol's attachment to Ukrainian history and culture during his early career, see Edyta M. Bojanowska, *Nikolai Gogol: Between Ukrainian and Russian Nationalism* (Cambridge, MA: Harvard University Press, 2007).

62 Dyonizya Poniatowska, *Listy Dyonizyi Poniatowskiej do Bohdana i Józefa Zaleskich*, 2 vols (Cracow: G. Gebethner i Spólka, 1900), 1:13.

63 For details of this relationship, see *Listy Dyonizyi Poniatowskiej*; Mazanowski, *Józef Bohdan Zaleski*; Józef Tretiak, *Bohdan Zaleski na tulactwie: 1831–1838: życie i poezya. Karta z dziejów emigracyi polskiej*, 2 vols (Cracow: Nakładem Akademii Umiejętnosci, 1913), especially 2:282–3, 290.

64 Quoted in Tretiak, *Bohdan Zaleski*, 2:278–9.

65 Ibid.

66 Ibid., 2:279.

67 Ibid., 2:270.

68 Sokołowska, *Młoda Polska*, 76–9.

69 Ibid., 68; Lewak, *Od związków węglarskich*, 85–6.

70 Łukaszewicz, "Wpływ masonerii," 291–4. Correspondence regarding these events can be found in Adam Lewak, *Giuseppe Mazzini e l'emigrazione polacca. Lettere inedite* (Casale: Tipografia cooperativa, 1925); also in Joachim Lelewel, *Listy emigracyjne Joachima Lelewela*, vol. 1, ed. Helena Więckowska (Cracow: Nakład Polskiej Akademii Umiejętnosci, 1848).

71 Sokołowska, *Młoda Polska*, 93.

72 G. Mazzini to Melegari, Lausanne, 28 February 1834, *EN SEI*, 9:216–17.

73 Ibid., 240, 243–4. Young Poland's Central Committee consisted of five members: Stolzman, Dybowski, K. Zaleski, Gordaszewski, and Staniewicz, although not all sources are in agreement that Staniewicz was a member. See Sokołowska, *Młoda Polska*, 78–9.

74 Even though a number of copies of the pact exist, the original has been lost. On Young Europe, see Eyck, "Mazzini's Young Europe"; Hans Gustav Keller, *Das "Junge Europa," 1834–1836; Eine Studie zur Geschichte der Völkerbundsidee und des nationalen Gedankens* (Zurich: Max Niehaus Verlag, 1938). For a very good and more recent discussion of Young Europe, see Roland Sarti, "Giuseppe Mazzini and Young Europe," in Bayly and Biagini, *Giuseppe Mazzini*, 275–98. Young Europe and related documents were also presented in Sokołowska, *Młoda Polska*, 77–84. For the Pact of Brotherhood and the Charter of Young Europe, see *EN SEI*, 4:3–21.

75 Sokołowska, *Młoda Polska*, 78–9.

76 Ibid., 80–1.

77 Eyck, "Mazzini's Young Europe," 361n21.

78 *EN SEI (Epistolario*, III), 10:101–2.

79 *EN SEI (Politica*, III), 4:37–41.

80 An undated letter quoted in Eyck, "Mazzini's Young Europe," 362–3n25.

81 Quoted in Eyck, "Mazzini's Young Europe," 364n31.

82 Eduard Scriba (*Pirate*) to Hermann von Rauschenplatt (*Kater*), 19 January 1835, Staatsarchiv Zürich, Faszikel, 187, quoted in Eyck, "Mazzini's Young Europe," 362.

83 Mazzini's letter of 30 August 1833, *ENSEI*, 5:480. See also Lewak, *Giuseppe Mazzini*, 32–40, 42–6. The bulk of Mazzini's correspondence with the Polish leader is contained in Joachim Lelewel, *Listy emigracyjne Joachima Lelewela*, ed. H. Więckowska, 5 vols (Cracow: Nakład Polskiej Akademii Umiejętnosci, 1948).
84 Quoted in Ugniewska, *Giuseppe Mazzini*, 102.
85 Ibid.
86 Ibid.
87 Łukaszewicz, "Wpływ masonerii," 300.
88 Sokołowska, *Młoda Polska*, 94–6.
89 Ibid., 101.
90 Lelewel to W. Piętkiewicz, Brussels, 21 November 1834, in Lelewel, *Listy*, 1:301, quoted in Sokołowska, *Młoda Polska*, 102.
91 Sokołowska, *Młoda Polska*, 96.
92 Quoted in ibid., 107.
93 Łukaszewicz, "Wpływ masonerii," 300.

Chapter 3

1 J. Gruss, writing about his former classmate František Cyril Kampelík, the Czech political and cultural activist during the 1830s and 1840s, in *Obzor*, 1889, 239. Quoted in František Komárek, *František Cyril Kampelík: Obraz životopisný* (Hradec Králové: Bratři Peřinú, 1895) 28.
2 Łukaszewicz, "Wpływ masonerii," 302–4; Sokołowska, *Młoda Polska*, 112–15.
3 Sokołowska, *Młoda Polska*, 114.
4 Łukaszewicz, "Wpływ masonerii," 304.
5 Konarski, *Dziennik*, 223; quoted in H.I. Marakhov, *Sotsial'no-politicheskaia bor'ba na Ukraine v 20-40-e gody XIX veka* (Kyiv: "Vyshcha Shkola," Izdatel'stvo pri Kievskom Gosudarstvennom Universitete, 1979), 80.
6 J. Lelewel to J. Zaleski, January 1834, in Lelewel, *Listy*, 1:239–44. Excerpts of the letter are quoted in Sokołowska, *Młoda Polska*, 96–7.
7 Besides Józef Zaleski and Bohdan Zaleski, the signatories of the appeal, dated 29 October 1833, were A. Mickiewicz, K. Różicki, and I. Domeyko. See Zaleski, *Korespondencja*, 1:50–2. Quoted in Sokołowska, *Młoda Polska*, 95.
8 Józef Tretiak, *Bohdan Zaleski na tulactwie: 1831–1838*, 2 vols (Cracow: Nakładem Akademii Umiejętnosci, 1913), 1:282–83, 290, 300; Vasyl' H. Shchurat, *Vybrani pratsi z istoriï literatury* (Kyiv: Vydavnytstvo Akademiï Nauk Ukraïnskoï RSR, 1963), 272; Sokołowska, *Młoda Polska*, 97.
9 For references to these contacts, see Tretiak, *Bohdan Zaleski na tulactwie*, 282–3, 290.

10 On this subject see Andrzej Nowak, *Między carem a rewolucją. Studium politycznej wyobraźni i postaw Wielkiej Emigracji wobec Rosji 1831–1849* (Warsaw: Wydawnictwo Instytutu Historii PAN i Warszawska Oficyna Wydawnictwa Gryf, 1994); Nowak, *Jak rozbić rosyjskie imperium? Idee polskiej polityki wschodniej 1733–1921* (Warsaw: Warszawska Oficyna Wydawnictwa Gryf, 1995).

11 Jędrzejewicz, *Zwycięstwo Pokonanych*, 446.

12 Ibid.

13 Polacy w Brukseli do rodaków, inc.: "Starodawna Polska od czasu, jak się Rzeczpospolita ukonstytuowała...," Bruksela 29 XI 1834, Bruksela 1834, 2; *Nowa Polska*, 1835, polak. 13/14, 293–4. Quoted in Sokołowska, *Młoda Polska*, 111.

14 Adadurov, "Memorandumy po's'kykh avtoriv," 154–71.

15 This city, called Lwów in Polish, Lemberg in German, and Lviv in Ukrainian, was the capital of the Austrian province of Galicia. Like Prague, in the province of Bohemia, it was known for the multinational composition of its inhabitants.

16 Quoted in Sokołowska, *Młoda Polska*, 133. Manuscripts of both of these appeals can be found in Biblioteka Narodowa, 6572, k. 22, 20; copy of the appeal to the Ukrainian clergy (duchowenstva ruskiego) Biblioteka Jagiellońska, papiery po K. Zaleskim, 7159, k. 63. Publications of these appeals are located in Biblioteka Polska in Paris. See Sokołowska, *Młoda Polska*, 133–4. Similar appeals were addressed to Lithuanians, and some thought was given to addressing an appeal to the Russians.

17 Sokołowska, *Młoda Polska*, 133–4.

18 Ivan Krevets'kyi, "Fal'shuvannia metryk dlia pol's'kykh povstantsiv z 1830–1831 rr. (Prychynok do kharakterystyky halyts'ko-rus'koho dukhovenstva pershoï polovyny XIX st.)," *Zapysky Naukovoho Tovarystva im. Shevchenka* 77 (1907): 107–13 (hereafter cited as *Zapysky NTSh*). The Austrian authorities were cooperating with the Russians in accordance with the pledges of the "Holy Alliance" and in the interests of the three partitioning powers.

19 Kyrylo Studyns'kyi, *L'vivs'ka dukhovna seminariia v chasakh Markiiana Shashkevycha 1829–1843* (Lviv, 1916), xcvi–xcvii, xvi–cxi, cxxvi–cxxvi, cli, ccvii–ccix, ccxxix–ccxx, 333–37; Studyns'kyi, "Pol's'ki konspiratsiï sered rus'kykh pytomtsiv i dukhovenstva v Halychyni v rokakh 1831–1846," *Zapysky NTSh* 80 (1907): 53–108; 82 (1908): 87–177; Jan Kozik, *The Ukrainian National Movement in Galicia: 1815–1849* (Edmonton: Canadian Institute of Ukrainian Studies, 1986), 38; Hryhorii I. Herbil's'kyi, *Peredova suspil'na dumka v Halychyni: 30-i, seredyna 40-kh rokiv XIX stolittia* (Lviv: Vydavnytstvo L'vivs'koho Universytetu, 1959), 139–48.

20 Lelewel to J. Zaleski, Brussels, 15 March 1835; Lelewel, *Listy*, 1:319–20, quoted in Sokołowska, *Młoda Polska*, 133–5. On Józef's Zaleski's transit

through Galicia, see the biographies of his friend, Bohdan: Tretiak, *Bohdan Zaleski na tulactwie*, 1:1–10; Mazanowski, *Józef Bohdan Zaleski*, 52–3.

21 Sokołowska, *Młoda Polska*, 147.

22 On this question of special interest, see the views expressed by the Russian liberal Piotr B. Struve, in *Russkaia mysl'*, especially "Chto takoe Rossiia," January 1911, 175–8; and his "Obshcherusskaia kul'tura i ukrainskii partikularizm: Otvet ukrainstvu," January 1912, 65–86. The question of liberalism and the nationality question is discussed at length in my book *Russian Nationalism and Ukraine*. See especially 27–31 and 165–75.

23 Sokołowska, *Młoda Polska*, 127–9.

24 Ibid., 129–30.

25 Ibid., 131.

26 Ibid., 132.

27 According to the treaty of Vienna of 1815, the city enjoyed, at least nominally, a free status, even though the police authorities of the three partitioning powers monitored the political activities, especially with respect to the swelling émigré community from the three partitioned parts of historical Poland.

28 Excerpts from the letter are cited in Sokołowska, *Młoda Polska*, 135; Marakhov, *Sotsial'no-politicheskaia bor'ba na Ukraine*, 80.

29 Tsentral'nyi derzhavnyi istorychnyi arkhiv Ukraïny v Kyievi (TsDIA Ukraïny, Kyiv), fond 442, op. 786, 1836, d. 22, l. 1 (hereafter cited as TsDIA Ukraïny); Marakhov, *Sotsial'no-politicheskaia bor'ba na Ukraine*, 79.

30 See chapter 5.

31 Lukazsewicz, *Wpływ masonerii*, 304; Sokołowska, *Młoda Polska*, 148; Moscicki, *Szymon Konarski*, 46–7; Szpotański, *Konarszczyzna i Lud Polski*, 44–5.

32 Sokołowska, *Młoda Polska*, 147.

33 Ibid.

34 A summary of Łukaszewicz's biography can be found in Václav Žáček, *Čechové a Poláci roku 1848: Studie k novodobým politickým stykům česko-polským* (Prague: Nákl. Slovanského ústavu a Slovanského výboru Česko-Slovenska v komisi nakl. "Orbis," 1947), 160–6.

35 Václav Žáček, *Z revolučných a politických poľsko slovenských stykov v dobe premarcovej* (Bratislava: Vydavateľstvo akademie vied, 1966), 35. On František Kampelík, see Komárek, *František Cyril*. For a brief biographical sketch of Amerling, see Jilji V. Jahn, *Karel Slavoj Amerling: Obraz Života a Práce* (Prague: F. Šimáček, 1893).

36 Of special interest on this subject are the following works: Jozef Butvin, "Tajny politicky spolok Vzájomnosť (1837–1840)," in *Sborník Filozofickej Fakulty Univerzity Komenského* (Bratislava: Slovenské pedagogické naklateľstvo, 1963), 14:1–37; Butvin, "Zjednocovanie snahy v slovenskom narodnom hnutí v 30-ych rokoch 19. stor.," *Historické studie* 8

(1963): 7–67; Vladimír Matula, "The Conception and the Development of Slovak National Culture in the Period of National Revival," *Studia Historica Slovaca* 17 (1990): 153–93; Matula, "Slovanská Vzájomnosť – Národnooslobodzovacia ideologia Slovenskeho narodneho hnutia (1835–1849)," *Historický Časopis* 8, no. 2 (1969): 248–64; Matula, "Snahy o prehlbenie demokratickej linie Slovenských narodných novín a formovanie revolučného programu slovenského narodného hnutia (1845–1848)," *Historický Časopis* 6 (1958): 202–23; Žáček, *Čechové a Poláci*, vol. 1. For the Ukrainian national awakening in Galicia, see Studyns'kyi, *L'vivs'ka dukhovna seminariia*; Studyns'kyi, "Pol's'ki konspiratsiï sered rus'kykh pytomtsiv"; Kozik, *Ukrainian National Movement in Galicia*; Herbil's'kyi, *Peredova suspil'na dumka*.

37 Lesław Łukaszewicz Kampelíkovi Františku Cyrilovi, letters dated 1 February, 8 May, and 22 May 1835. Památník Narodního Písemnictví, Kampelík F.C. 34–9; 13/86. Literární Archiv Památníku Narodního Písemnictví v Praze.

38 Robert Sak, *Rieger: Konzervativec nebo liberál?* (Prague: Academia, 2003), 26–7.

39 The mountain may have acquired this second appellation, in the same manner as the Czech and Slovak activists were adopting names of ancient Slavic heroes and saints as their middle names: Slavoj adopted by Amerling, Cyril by Kampelík, Boleslavín by Vrchovský, etc. In their correspondence, it was usually this middle, "adopted" name that was used. The mountain was also known for attracting lightening during storms.

40 Žáček, *Čechové a Poláci*, 162; Butvin, "Tajný politický spolok Vzájomnosť," 4.

41 In 1834 Łukaszewicz visited the two cities on a false passport made in the name of Józef Grzymalski. Žáček, *Čechové a Poláci*, 162.

42 Łukaszewicz uses the name *Czerwonorusyn* (Red Ruthenian), an archaic name applied to the inhabitants of the medieval province of Galicia called in Polish *Czerwona Rus'*.

43 For *Czerwona Rus'* (Red Ruthenia) see n42.

44 Łukaszewicz to Kampelík, 1 February 1835.

45 This is a reference to the title of a well-known work by Ján Kollár, an influential advocate of Slavic cultural unity and reciprocity among the Czech and Slovak national awakeners. See Ján Kollár, *Slávy dcéra* (Prague: Mladá Frtonta, 1961).

46 Łukaszewicz to Kampelík, 8 May 1835.

47 According to a recent biography of Mickiewicz, the poet was urged to write a work on Jan Žižka six years earlier, during his visit to Prague in 1829. It appears that the Polish poet never worked on this theme or, if he did, never finished the poem. Years later he explained that "a hero who projects himself from the single perspective of hate and revenge

appeared to [him] as but an episode, not a finished whole." What appealed to the Polish bard – and this view would have been shared by Mazzini – were: "Only *deeds* or *words* and *thoughts* that engender deeds are what we call politics, action. Such deeds are struggle, victory, or martyrdom; such words were, for example, first the words of the Gospels, then of those who emulate them: the words of the Koran, the words of Wycliffe, Hus, Luther, Saint Simon." Both quotations from Roman Robert Koropecky, *Adam Mickiewicz: The Life of a Romantic* (Ithaca, NY: Cornell University Press, 2008), 124, 205. During his brief visit to Prague, Mickiewicz met Čelakovský and Hanka. With the latter he kept in touch when he was preparing his lectures for the Collège de France in Paris. Ibid., 124. There is no evidence that Bohdan Zaleski worked on the theme of Žižka.

48 See Smith, *Mazzini*, 7.

49 Quoted in Sokołowska, *Młoda Polska*, 139–40. The Charter of the Association of the Polish People can be found in Handelsman, *Francja – Polska, 1795–1845*, 183–5; the charter is discussed in Łukaszewicz, *Wpływ masonerii*, 306.

50 See, e.g., Stefan Kozak, *Ukraińscy spiskowcy i mesjaniści: Bractwo Cyryla i Metodego* (Warsaw: Pax, 1990), 86; the works of Herbil's'kyi and Kozik.

51 In his advanced years Kampelík was corresponding with one of the leading figures of the Ukrainian renaissance in Galicia, Yakiv Holovats'kyi, the brother of his old friend from his student days in Vienna, Ivan Holovasts'kyi. See Kampelík's correspondence in Literární Archiv Památníku Národního Písemnictví v Praze.

52 Quoted in Komárek, *František Cyril*, 18. The letter was written to Tomáš Burian, a professor of Czech language at the Military Academy in Vienna.

53 Ibid.

54 Kampelík uses the name Budym, the Slavic name for Buda, the capital of the Kingdom of Hungary, known today as Budapest.

55 Samuel Medvecký, "Rozpomienky na Sama Chalupku," *Slovenskè pohľady* 7, no. 10 (1887): 235–9.

56 For a detailed description of the beginnings of these Polish-Czech-Slovak political encounters, see Žáček, *Z revolučných a politických poľsko sloven-ských stykov v dobe premarcovej*, especially 19–43.

57 "Alexander Boleslavín Vrchovský (1812–1865)," a typewritten copy of Vrchovský's autobiographical letter attached to "Životopisy vedúcich členov tajného spolku Vzájomnosť (A.B. Vrchovský, P.V. Ollík, M.M. Hodža)," a manuscript typed by Ján Béder in Aleksander B. Vrchovský Papers, Literarný Archiv Matice Slovenskej v Martine-Archiv Slovenského Národného Muzea (LAMS-ASNM) Martin, Slovak Republic.

See also Ján Béder, "Vlastné životopisy vedúcich členov tajného spolku Vzájomosť (Vrchovský – Ollík – Hodža)," *Slovenská Literatúra: Časopis Slovenskej Akadémie Vied* 6 (1959): 91–9. For a biographical sketch of Vrchovský, see J.D. Buchta, "A.B. Vrchovský: ideológ mladého Slovenska," *Hlas Ľudu*, 29 January 1983; see also Eva Fordinálová, "'Sivá eminencia' Slovenskej romatickej generácie," *Hlas Ľudu*, 27 October 1992; Žáček, *Z revolučných a politických*, 29–4.

58 Quoted in Matula, "Slovanska Vzájomnosť," 252.

59 Quoted in Ján Béder, "Kollárova koncepcia Slovanskej Vzájomnosti a Mladé Slovensko," *Historický Časopis* 8, nos 2–3 (1960): 245.

60 Vrchovský's letters to *Spoločnosť* and fragments of his writings have been edited by Pavol Vongrej, "Z tvorby Alexandra Boleslavína Vrchovského," in *Literatúrny archív*, 138–53 (Martin: Matica Slovenská, 1987). Excerpts from drafts of the letters have been quoted in the cited articles by Béder and Matula. "Centrum gravitates" is a frequently quoted phrase from Vrchovský's letter to Václav Satopluk Štulc; see Jan Béder, "Spoločnosť česko-slovenská a slovanský ústav v Bratislave v rokoch 1835–1840," *Zborník štúdií a prác Vysokej školy pedagogickej v Bratislave* 1 (1957): 9. Štúr's activities at the Lutheran lyceum in Bratislava both before and after his collaboration with Vrchovský are discussed by Karol Rosenbaum, "Ľudovit Štúr na evanjelickom lýceu v Bratislave v rokoch 1829–1836," in *Ľudovit Štúr v súradniciach minulosti a súčasnosti*, ed. Imrich Sedlák, 15–27 (Martin: Matica Slovenská, 1997); and by Imrich Sedlák, "Ľudovit Štúr a slovenské študenské hnutie," in *Ľudovit Štúr v súradniciach minulosti a súčasnosti*, ed. Imrich Sedlák (Martin: Matica Slovenská, 1997), 15–27 and 28–55.

61 Vrchovský, from Vienna, to *Spoločnosť*, in Bratislava, 15 April 1935, in Vongrej, "Z tvorby Alexandra Boleslavína Vrchovského," 146–7. A quotation from a draft of a letter to Ľudovít Štúr and the Association, ibid., 9.

62 From a letter of 15 April 1835 to Ľudovít Štúr, Béder, ibid.

63 Vongrej, "Z tvorby Alexandra Boleslavína Vrchovského"; also quoted in Matula, "Slovanska Vzájomnosť," 252.

64 Béder, "Spoločnosť," 10–11.

65 Vrchovský from Vienna to "Drahým bratrům našim, členům národního spolku slovanského v Prešporku," April 1835, ibid., 9.

66 See cited articles by Béder "Spoločnosť"; and Matula, "Slovanska Vzájomnosť."

67 Béder, "Spoločnosť," 10–11.

68 Quoted in Béder, "Spoločnosť Česko-slovanská," 32.

69 *Nove Slovo*, 8 April 1982, "Boleslavínovi Vrchovskému."
Kto sa pod tou, pod košatou,
Lipou modlí,

Lipou modlí,
Lipou modlí?
A kto na ňu upiera svoj
Pohľad orlí,
Pohľad orlí,
Pohľad orlí?
Jeho pohľad plný túžby
Čerí lístky,
Čerí lístky,
Čerí lístky -
A váň listkov bozkáva ho,
Je mu blízky,
Je mu blízky,
Je mu blízky.
Vej, vetríček: viej si lipu
uctiť Slavín,
uctiť Slavín,
uctiť Slavín:
ajhľa, veď tam kľačí brat náš
Boleslavín,
Boleslavín, Boleslavín.

70 Peter Petro, *A History of Slovak Literature* (Montreal and Kingston: McGill-Queen's University Press, 1995), 60.

71 Peter Brock, *The Slovak National Awakening: An Essay in the Intellectual History of East Central Europe* (Toronto: University of Toronto Press, 1976), 70n57.

72 Béder, "Spoločnosť Česko-Slovenská a Slovanský Ústav," 8. Even though other authors have written on this subject, Béder's work is the most comprehensive and the most thoroughly documented. He examined the archive of Spoločnosť i Česko-slovanský Ústav deposited in the archive of the Slovak National Museum (LAMS-ASNM) in Martin. According to his notes, the minutes of the meetings of *Spoločnosť* and of the institute are contained in four books: the first two under the title *Pametníci* and the last two *Dejini hodín výkonných*. He also examined other documentary sources, including the most important correspondence between the leading figures of the movement. He refers to them as "Young Slovaks" and to the movement as "Young Slovakia." Of special interest are the letters of L. Štúr, B. Vrchovský, A.H. Škultéty, J.M. Hurban, B.P. Červenák, P.V. Ollík, J. Kuzmany, Ct. Zoch, S. Chalupka, M.M. Hodža, T.H. Hroš, and others. See Béder, "Spoločnosť," 7n18.

73 Štefan Krčméry, *Výber z diela III: Stopäťdesiať rokov slovenskej literatury* (Bratislava: Slovenské vydavateľstvo krásnej literatúri, 1954), 60; Milan

Pišút, *Počiatky básnickej školy Štúrovej* v *Bratislavě* (Bratislava: Práce Učené společnosti Šafaříkovy, 1938) 25:30. On this question see also Andrej Mráz, *Dejiny slovenskej literatúry* (Bratislava: Slovenská akadémia vied a umení, 1948), 137–8.

74 Žáček, *Čechové a Poláci*, 165–6.

75 Łukaszewicz to Kampelík, 8 May 1835.

76 Jakub Malý, *Zpomínky a úvahy starého vlastence* (Prague: J.S. Skrejsovský, 1872), 78–9. See also Miloslav Matoušek, *Život a působení Dr. F.C. Kampelíka* (Prague: Alois Svoboda, 1947), 44–5; Novotný, *František Cyril Kampelík*, 44–5.

77 It was well known that Metternich considered Mazzini the chief enemy of the status quo in Europe. The mere fact of belonging to his organization was declared by the Austrian minister to be an act of treason punishable by death. See Smith, *Mazzini*, 7; Satri, *Mazzini*, 63.

78 Václav Žáček, *Cesty českých studentů na Slovensko v době Předbřeznové: Paměti a dokumenty*, Svazek I (Brno: Brnenská tiskárna, 1948), 37. See also J. Novotný, *O bratrské družbě Čechů a Slováků za národního obrození: kapitoly z dějin vzájemných vztahů Čechů a Slováků v národním hnutí do roku 1848* (Prague: Štátni náklad politické literatury, 1959).

79 Matula, "Slovanská Vzájomnosť," 248.

80 Ibid., 253–4.

81 Vladimir Matula, "Mladé Slovensko a Juhoslavania," in *Československo a Juhoslavia*, 106–45 (Bratislava: Vydateľstvo Slovenskej akadémie vied, 1968).

82 Zdeněk Hájek, "Stýky Jakiva a Ivana Holovackých s Josefem Podlipským a Františkom Kampelíkom," in *Franku Wollmanovi k sedmdesátinám: Sborník prací* (Prague: Státní pedagogické nakladatelství, 1958), 218.

83 Ibid., 226.

84 Ján Béder, "Nástup Generácie Mladé Slovensko," *Sovenská Literatúra* 7, no. 1 (1960): 46–9; see also Béder, "Spoločnosť Česko-slovanska a Slovanský Ústav," 26–31; and Elena Várossová, *Slovenské obrodenecké myslenie: jeho zdroje a základné idey* (Bratislava: Vydavateľstvo Akadémie vied, 1963).

85 Brock, *Slovak National Awakening*, 30.

86 Béder, "Spoločnosť Česko-slovanska," 48–9; Brock, *Slovak National Awakening*, 29.

87 Quoted in Vladimír Matula, "Lyceum a Lipa Slovanská," in *Nad Tatrou sa blýska* (Bratislava: Veda, Vydavateľstvo Slovenskej akademie vied, 1994), 77.

88 See chapter 6.

89 Brock, *Slovak National Awakening*, 32–3.

90 For these and related developments, see chapters 4 and 5.

Chapter 4

1 From a letter of the Greek Catholic seminarian Mykola Kmytsekevych to a Polish friend, Kazimierz J. Turowski, written in the early 1830s and quoted in Vasyl' Shchurat, *Na dosvitku novoï doby: Do vidrodzhennia Hal[yts'koï]. Ukraïny* (Lviv: Z Drukarni Naukovoho Tovarystva im. Shevchenka, 1919), 140. See also Mykhailo Tershakovets', "Materialy i zamitky do istoriï natsional'noho vidrodzhennia Halyts'koï Rusy v 1830 ta 1840 rr.," *Ukraïns'ko-rus'kyi arkhiv ist.-filosof. Sektsii Nauk. Tovarystva im. Shevchenka* 3 (1907): 22–3.
2 The full text of the "Charter of the Association of the Polish People" (21 July 1835), can be found in *Przegląd Historyczny* 60 (1969): 351–62.
3 The other members of the council were Franciszek Bobiński, Romauld Giedrojc, Henryk Bogusz, Teofil Januszewicz, Teofil Zebrawski, Ludwig Milkowski, and Leon Zienkowicz. Giller, *Historia powstania Narodu Polskiego*, pt 3, 462; Limanowski, *Histoiria*, 1:335; Łukaszewicz, "Wpływ masonerii," 306.
4 J. Lelewel to W. Zwierkowski, Brussels, 20 August 1835, in Lelewel, *Listy*, 1:351.
5 Sokołowska, *Młoda Polska*, 155; Łukaszewicz, "Wpływ masonerii," 309.
6 Łukaszewicz, "Wpływ masonerii," 308; Sokołowska, *Młoda Polska*, 155.
7 Henryk Bogdański, "O tajnych politycznych związkach w Galicii od roku 1832 do roku 1841," in *Pamiętniki spiskowców i więźniów galicyjskich w latach 1832–1846*, ed. Karol Lewicki (Wroclaw: Zaklad imienia Ossolińskich, 1954), 3–69, 55–6.
8 Łukaszewicz, "Wpływ masonerii," 307. Besides Lviv, local branches were established in Kolomyia and Stanyslaviv (today: Ivano-Frankivs'k), Przemyśl, Sambir, Zolochiv, and Sanok.
9 It appears from the memoirs of Julian Horoszckiewicz, *Notatki z życia* (Wroclaw: Zaklad Narodowi im. Ossolinskich, 1957) that the author is not aware of the organization's international connection. The same is true of the reminiscences of Andrzej Józefczyk, "Wspomnenia ubiegłych lat," in *Pamiętniki spiskowców i więźniów galicyjskich w latach 1832–1846*, ed. Karol Lewicki, 122–37 (Wroclaw: Zaklad imienia Ossolińskich, 1954).
10 The other active members in the organization were Tomasz Rajski, Ignacy Żegota Kulczyński, Stanisław Malinowski, and Jan Szczepanowski. All of them with the exception of Kulczyński had held positions in local *Carbonari* operations. Konarski was represented on the council by Marian Podhoreński. See Boleslaw Łopuszański, *Stowarzyszenie Ludu Polskiego (1835–1841)* (Cracow: Wydawnictwo Literackie, 1975), 87–101.
11 Sarti, *Mazzini*, 60.
12 Ibid.

13 Out of a total of 3,113,320 inhabitants in the twelve districts in the eastern part of Galicia, 71 per cent were Ukrainians; 20.4 per cent were Poles; 7.9 per cent were Jews; 0.6 per cent were Germans; 0.1 per cent were undetermined. Kozik, *Ukrainian National Movement in Galicia*, 17.

14 A literal translation of the title "Poslanie Ukraince" would read: "A message to a Ukrainian woman," but it is clear from the context of the poem that the author is addressing Ukraine as a nation. See Seweryn Goszczyński, *Dzieła zbiorowe Seweryna Goszczyńskiego* (Lviv: Nakladem Księgi Altenberga, 1911), 1:161. The poem was written in Paris, shortly after Goszczyński fled abroad from Lviv.
POSLANIE UKRAINCE
Ukrainko, wdzięczność tobie,
Wdzięczność dla twojej piosenki!
Jak żebym w kochanym grobie
Znajome posłyszal jęki ...
Ale boleśna pieśń twoja:
Jest ona więźnia jęczeniem.
A więc, Ukrainko moja,
Odśpiewam ci pocieszeniem.
Jak to ciężko, kogo pchnięto
Więdnąć między obcą rzeszą,
Komu od serca odjęto
Wszystko, czem się ludzie cieszą!
Jak to milo, komu wiara
Tyle napoju udzieli
Że ze wspólnego puhara
I bliżniego rozweseli!
Paris, 1839.

15 Sokołowska, *Młoda Polska*, 102–3.

16 Zygmunt Wasilewski, *Seweryn Goszczyński w Galicyi: Nieznane pamiętniki, listy i utwory, 1832–1842* (Lviv: Słowo Polskie, 1902), 132–3.

17 Zorian Dołęga Chodakowski, *O Slowiańszczyznie przed chrześcijaństwem, oraz inne pisma i listy*, ed. Julian Maslanka (Warsaw: Państwowe Wydawnicwo Naukowe, 1967), 26. The author published his works under the pseudonym Zorian Dołęga Chodakowski.

18 Ia. Holovatsky to O. Bodiansky, 26 July 1846, in Fedir Savchenko, ed., *Zakhidnia Ukraïna v lystuvanni Holovats'koho z Bodians'kym, 1843–1876*, 5 (Kyiv: "Kyïv-Druk," 1930); Kozik, *Ukrainian National Movement in Galicia*, 23.

19 See Henryk Bogdański, *Pamiętnik: 1832–1848*, ed. Antoni Knot (Cracow: Wydawnictwo Literackie, 1971), 71; Łopuszański, *Stowarzyszenie Ludu Polskiego*, 122–3, 133–4; Klemens Mochnacki [Mokhnatsky], "Pamiętnik spiskowca i nauczyciela 1811–1846," in *Pamętniki spiskowców i więźniów*

galicyjskich v latach 1832–1846, ed. Karol Lewicki, 138–57 (Wrocław: Zaklad im. Ossolińskich, 1954).

20 Shchurat, *Na dosvitku,* 117–19. Studyns'kyi, *L'vivs'ka dukhovna seminariia,* 168.

21 Stefan Kieniewicz, *Konspiracje galicyjskie 1831–1848* (Warsaw: Książka i Wiedza, 1950), 92–3; Julian Horoszkiewicz, *Notatki z życia* (Wroclaw: Zaklad Narodowi im. Ossolińskich, 1957), 51–193; Adam Świątek, *Gente Rutheni, natione Poloni: Z dziejów Rusinów narodowości polskiej w Galicii* (Cracow: Księgarnia Akademicka, 2014), 167.

22 Stefan Kieniewicz, cited in Świątek, 155.

23 Roman Kyrchiv, *Markiianove Suzir'ia: Ti, koho probudyv, "voodushevyv" i poviv za sobouu Markiian Shashkevych* (Lviv: Vydavnytstvo L'vivs'koï Politekhniky, 2012), 32–4.

24 Łopuszański, *Stowarzyszenie Ludu Polskiego,* 139–43.

25 Kyrchiv, *Markiianove Suzir'ia,* 48–52; Łopuszański, *Stowarzyszenie Ludu Polskiego,* 223–4.

26 Kyrchiv, *Markiianove Suzir'ia,* 67–89.

27 See chapter 2.

28 Bogdański, *Pamiętnik,* 71.

29 Mochnacki, "Pamiętnik spiskowca i nauczyciela 1811–1848," 138–57.

30 Łopuszański, *Stowarzyszenie Ludu Polskiego,* 224.

31 *Slovo,* 1861, no. 5:1–2. See also Mykhailo Tershakovets', "Do zhyttiepysu Markiiana Shashkevycha," in *Zapysky NTSh* 105 (1911): 111–15; and 106 (1911): 77–134.

32 Bogdański, *Pamiętnik,* 72; Lopuszański, *Stowarzyszenie Ludu Polskiego,* 224.

33 Bogdański, *Pamętnik,* 72–3, 292–5. On Hordynsky, see Studyns'kyi, *L'vivs'ka dukhovna seminariia,* 181–8; and Shchurat, *Na dosvitku,* 117–19.

34 Shchurat, *Na dosvitku,* 118.

35 Ibid.

36 The only names that Hordynsky mentioned at the trial were of those individuals who were either already deceased or who, like Napoleon Nowicki, had found a safe haven abroad.

37 Shchurat, *Na dosvitku,* 117.

38 Studyns'kyi, *L'vivs'ka dukhovna seminariia,* 181–8.

39 Shchurat, *Na dosvitku,* 117; Lopushański, *Stowarzyszenie Ludu Polskiego,* 136.

40 Bogdański, *Pamiętnik,* 72.

41 Łopuszański, *Stowarzyszenie Ludu Polskiego,* 135.

42 Ibid., 126–7.

43 Studyns'kyi, *L'vivs'ka dukhovna seminariia,* 61; Swiątek, *Gente Rutheni, natione Poloni,* 168.

44 The Špilberk prison was in the Austrian province of Moravia, today within the territory of the Czech Republic.

45 Bogdański, *Pamętnik,* especially 71–3, 292–5. See also Shchurat, *Na dosvitku,* especially "Chorna knyha," 114–28.

46 It is of interest to note that in the abridged version of Bogdański's memoirs, "O tajnych politycznych związkach," in *Pamiętniki* the editor Karol Lewicki chose to "abridge" the sentence describing Hordynsky by omitting the phrase "of all who came to know him." In the abridged version, Hordynsky is described as an individual "capable of winning the respect of his subordinates"! Bogdański, "O tajnych politycznych związkach," 9. In 1935 when the abridged version was published, the social-Darwinist brand of nationalism became the dominant force in Polish politics and thought. It was difficult for some Poles, Karol Lewicki among them, to acknowledge that a Greek Catholic priest had been capable of earning the respect of "all who came to know him." On the basis of Bogdański's detailed reminiscences, there is no question in the reader's mind that in Galicia, Hordynsky was the best-educated man among the conspirators. He spoke six languages, in prison he spent the days by translating Plato's *Dialogues,* and to the delight of his cellmates, gave lessons in classical languages. Among his "students" was Leslaw Lukaszewycz, one of the top leaders of the Association of the Polish People when its headquarters were located in Cracow. See Bogdański, *Pamętnik,* especially 71–2, 292–6.

47 Łopuszański, *Stowarzyszenie Ludu Polskiego,* 141.

48 Bogdański, *Pamętnik,* 71–2, 292–6.

49 Bogdański, *Pamętnik,* 293.

50 According to the proposal, the name of the organization was to be changed to the Association of the Polish and Ruthenian People. Korecki and his group of supporters in the council claimed that there was no valid reason for the proposed change. See Shchurat, *Na porozi,* 141; and Shchurat, *Vybrani pratsi,* 266; Łopuszański, *Stowarzyszenie Ludu Polskiego,* 87–9, 101, 231–2; Józef Krajewski, *Tajne związki polityczne w Galicyi, od r. 1833 do r. 1841. Według niewydanych źródeł rękopiśmiennych, oraz aktów sądowych i gubernialnych* (Lviv: Nakł. Słowa Polskiego, 1903), 85.

51 Łopuszański, *Stowarzyszenie Ludu Polskiego,* 231–2. Regarding some unpleasant encounters Hordynsky had with Korecki, see 87–101; and Bogdański, "O tajnych politycznych związkach," 39.

52 Kyrchiv, *Markiianove Suzir'ia,* 48–83.

53 Studyns'kyi, *L'vivs'ka dukhovna seminariia,* 121–2, 152–4, 159–60.

54 Bogdański, "O tajnych politycznych związkach," 72.

55 Ibid.

56 Lopushański, *Stowarzyszenie Ludu Polskiego,* 135.

57 Shchurat, *Na dosvitku,* 118.

58 *Zoria Halyts'ka* 88 (1850): 542, quoted in Kozik, *Ukrainian National Movement in Galicia,* 58. The author of the article is anonymous, but

after an analysis of its style, Jan Kozik, a Polish authority on this period, observes that "the contents and certain formulations in the article suggest that the author may have been Mykola Ustyianovych," a contemporary and a friend of Markian Shashkevych. My examination of the article's style and content, in particular the sentiments expressed, leads me to believe that it was the author of the 1848 publication, entitled *Słowo przestrogi*, which is discussed at length in chapter 7.

59 On the "Ruthenian Triad," see Feodosii Steblii, V.I. Horyn', and O. Kupchyns'kyi, eds, *Rus'ka triitsia v istoriï suspil'no-politichnoho rukhu i kul'tury Ukraïny* (Kyiv: Naukova dumka, 1987); Włodzimierz Mokry, *"Ruska Trójca": Karta z dziejów życia literackiego Ukraińców w Galicji w pierwszej połowie XIX wieku* (Cracow: Wydawnictwo Uniwersytetu Jagiellońskiego: Fundacja Świętego Włodzimierza, 1997).

60 Kozik, *Ukrainian National Movement in Galicia*, 37–8.

61 The literature on Markian Shashkevych is very rich. Among the works used for this study: Mykhailo Tershakovets', "Do zhyttiepysu Markiana Shashkevycha," *Zapysky NTSh* 105 (1911): 92–115; and 106 (1911): 77–134. A brief but good review of Shashkevych's political views can be found in Feodosii Steblii, "Markian Shashkevych – provisnyk nezalezhnosty sobornoï Ukraïny," *Visnyk Naukovoho Tovarystva im. Shevchenka* 45 (2011): 9–13 (hereafter cited as *Visnyk NTSh*); Volodymyr Hnatiuk, *Natsional'ne vidrodzhennia avstro-uhors'kykh ukraïntsiv (1772–1880 rr.)*, ed. Feodosii Steblii, 2nd ed. (Lviv: Instytut Ukraïnoznavstva im. I. Krypiakevycha NAN Ukraïny, 2006). See also articles in *Shashkevychiiana*, n.s., vyp. 1–2 (Instytut Ukraïnoznavstva im. I. Krypiakevycha NAN Ukraïny, 1996), especially Peter Brock, "Ivan Vahylevych (1811–1866) ta ukraïns'ka natsional'na identychnist'," 389–416; Jaroslav Rozumnyj, ed., *Markiian Shashkevych na Zakhodi* (Winnipeg: Instytut-zapovidnyk Markiiana Shashkevycha, 2007).

62 Even though the authorship of Istoriia Rusov has not been determined, Archbishop Heorhii Konysky, Vasyl Poletyka, and Oleksander Bezborodko are often cited as the most likely authors. For an excellent discussion of this work, see Serhii Plokhy, *The Cossack Myth: History and Nationhood in the Age of Empires* (Cambridge: Cambridge University Press, 2012).

63 Oleksandr Dz'oban. "Shashkevychiiana u fondakh viddilu rukopysiv l'vivs'koï naukovoï biblioteky (LNB) im. V. Stefanyka NAN Ukraïny," in *Shashkevychiiana*, n.s., vyp. 5–6 (Lviv: Instytut Ukraïnoznavstva im. I. Krypiakevycha NAN Ukraïny, 2004), 285; Shchurat, *Na dosvitku*, 56–61, 122–3; Iakov Golovatskii [Iakiv Holovats'kyi], "K istorii galitsko-ruskoi pismennosti (Neskol'ko zamechanii na pis'mo I. Vagilevicha k M.P. Pogodinu)," *Kievskaia starina* (1883): 646–7; Bogdański, "O tajnych politycznych związkach," 15.

64 Shchurat, *Na dosvitku*, 122–3.
65 Steblii, "Markiian Shashkevych – provisnyk," 9–13, 11.
66 Oleh Kupchyns'kyi, "Zabuti imena v ukraïnskii nautsi ta kul'turi: Ivan Zakhar Avdykovs'kyi," *Visnyk NTSh* 42 (2009): 45–52.
67 Golovatskii, "K istorii galitsko-ruskoi pismennosti," 657.
68 Quoted in Kozik, *Ukrainian National Movement in Galicia*, 59, from Iakiv Holovats'kyi, "Pam'iat' Markiianu Shashkevychu," in *Vinok Rusynam na obzhynky* (Vienna, 1846), pt 1, 57.
69 See Petro Shkrabiuk, "M. Pavlyk – spadkoiiemets' ideï 'Rus'koï Triitsi,'" in *Shashkevychiana*, n.s., vyp. 1–2 (1996): 74–82. See 82n54.
70 The literature on the significance of these publications is very rich. A good summary in English of the events related to *Zoria* and *Rusalka Dnistrovaia* can be found in Kozik, *Ukrainian National Movement in Galicia*, 66–71.
71 Quoted in Kozik, *Ukrainian National Movement in Galicia*, 47.
72 Ibid.
73 Wasilewski, *Seweryn Goszczyński w Galicyi*, 112; Łopuszański, *Stowarzyszenie Ludu Polskiego*, 228.
74 "Protokoly, donesennija, lysty, 1834–1843," Lviv, Istorychnyi Arkhiv, fond 451, spr. 390, 1836–1848. See, especially, "Protokoly rozsliduvannia sprav seminarystiv, zvynuvachenykh v porushenni dystsypliny; dopovidni zapysky ta lystuvannia z Hreko-katolyts'koiu mytropolychoiu konsystoriieiu z ts'oho pytannia." The conspiratorial activities of the seminarians are well documented in both Ukrainian and Polish studies. See, especially, Studyns'kyi, *L'vivs'ka dukhovna seminariia*; Studyns'kyi, "Pol's'ki konspiratsiï sered rus'kykh pytomtsiv i dukhovenstva v Halychyni v rokakh 1831–1846," *Zapysky NTSh* 82 (1908): 87–177; Tershakovets', "Materialy i zamitky do istoriï natsional'noho vidrodzhennia Halyts'koï Rusy v 1830 ta 1840 rr."; Krajewski, *Tajne związki*; Zygmunt Zborucki, *Proces studentów samborskich 1837–1839* (Lviv: Universytet Jana Kazimierza we Lwowie, 1927); M. Andrusiak, "Ukraiński ruch narodowy i konspiracja polska w Galicji," *Biuletyn polsko-ukrainski* 5, no. 6 (1936); Kieniewicz, *Konspiracje Galicyjskie*.
75 Studyns'kyi, "Pol's'ki konspiratsiï," 113.
76 Ibid., 87–114.
77 Ibid., 152.
78 Iurii Kmit, "Prychynky do istoriï rus'koho dukhovnoho seminariia u L'vovi 1837–1851 r.," *Zapysky NTSh* 91 (1909): 151–8.
79 For details on the arrests, interrogations, and imprisonment, see Bogdański, *Pamiętnik*, 211–65; Shchurat, *Na dosvitku*, 114–28.
80 Studyns'kyi, "Pol's'ki konspiratsiï," 88.
81 It was a member of this group, Vasyl Podolynsky, who in 1848 wrote or co-authored a brochure that raised, among other matters, the question

of Ukraine's independence. See V. Podoliński [Vasyl' Podolyns'kyi],
Słowo przestrogi (Sanok, 1848). The brochure was written in Polish, as
it was addressed to the Poles as a word of caution (*Słowo przestrogi*)
regarding their relations with the Ukrainians. For a reprint and a
Ukrainian translation of this borchure as well as a discussion of the ideas
contained in it, see Feodosii Steblii, "Vyznachna pam'iatka ukraïns'koï
politychnoï dumky seredyny XIX stolittia – 'Slovo perestorohy' Vasylia
Podolyns'koho," *Zapysky NTSh* 228 (1994): 434–87. See also a discussion
of the content of this brochure in chapter 7.

82 Studyns'kyi, "Pol's'ki konspiratsiï," 88–9; Studyns'kyi, *L'vivs'ka dukhovna
    seminarija*, clvi–vlxxxi. The death sentences were subsequently commuted
    to lengthy terms of imprisonments.

83 Krajewski, *Konspiracje Galicyjskie*, 131; Studyns'kyi, "Pol's'ki konspirat-
    siï," 88–9.

84 Studyns'kyi, *L'vivs'ka dukhovna seminariia*, ccxxix.

85 *EN SEI*, 12:233.

86 Kozik, *Ukrainian National Movement in Galicia*, 32.

87 On this and related issues, see Sak, *Rieger: Konzervativec nebo Liberál?*,
    54–5.

88 Bogdański, *Pamiętnik*, 435–6.

89 Horoszkiewicz, *Notatki z życia*, 55.

90 Kasper Cięglewicz, "Żyvot, prace i cierpienia," *Gazeta Narodowa* (Lviv),
    nos 227–33 (1886) no. 28:1. The reminiscences were completed shortly
    before the author's death. Julian Horoszkiewicz, a good friend and a
    fellow-conspirator, provided some additional details about Cięglewicz's
    life. See Julian Horoszkiewicz, *Notatki z życia* (Wroclaw: Zaklad Narodowi
    im. Ossolinskich, 1957). From the author's autobiographical sketch, it
    is clear that Cięglewicz was a Roman Catholic and that his background
    was Polish. He was born in the village of Horodenka in the Pokuttia
    region of East Galicia on 6 January 1807. Because, according to the
    Gregorian calendar, this is the feast of the Epiphany, he was baptized
    Kasper Melchior Balthazar, in honour of the "three kings." His parents
    were Mateusz Cięglewicz and Katarzyna (née Abrahamowicz). Perhaps
    because he knew the Ukrainian language and because of his involvement
    in the enlightenment work among the Ukrainian masses, he has often
    been presented in some recent scholarly works as a Ukrainian who chose
    to adopt Polish nationality. See, e.g., Mar'ian Mudryi, "*Gente Rutheni* v
    pol's'kii tsentral'nii radi narodovii 1848 roku," *Zapysky NTSh* 256 (2008):
    244–87. A similar erroneous conclusion has been made about Cięglewicz's
    mentor, Ignacy Żegota Kulczyński, a landowner from Volynia, who
    fled to Galicia because of his involvement in the November upris-
    ing. Like Goszczyński, Kulczyński managed to establish a temporary

residence in Galicia. As a leading member of the Executive Committee of the Association of the Polish People in Lviv and as Konarski's trusted associate, Kulczyński never pretended to have Ukrainian roots. Throughout his stay in Galicia he was instrumental in encouraging young Poles to work on behalf of the Ukrainian people in the spirit propagated by Young Poland. He had direct contact with the Konarski movement in the territories controlled by Russia. On Kulczyński, see also Horoszkiewicz, *Notatki z życia*, especially 54–141.

91 Cięglewicz, *Gazeta Narodowa*, no. 228:1. A study of Kulczyński and Cięglewicz during this period can be found in Włodzimier Borys, "Z dziejów walk o wyzwolenie narodowe i społeczne w Galicji w pierwszej połow-inie XIX w.: Ignacy Kulczyński w świetle zeznań Juliana Horoszkiewicza i Kaspra Cięglewicza," in *Przemyskie Zapiski Historyczne*, 4–5:223–30 (Przemyśl: Polskie Towarzystwo Historyczne, Oddzial w Przemyślu, 1987).

92 "Koby buty waszym tiniom, nisbym wam u slidy
Nisbym wsiuda pered wamy obraz waszoj bidy,
A toj obraz tak kierwawy jak Chrystos rozpiatyj,
Szczo na kryzu musiw hirko za ludej wmeraty." Cięglewicz,
Gazeta Narodowa, no. 229:1.

93 Ibid., no. 230:1.

94 Aleksander Vrchovský Archive, M113, B15, Matica Slovenská, Archiv Lit-eratury, Martin.

95 Quoted in Kozik, *Ukrainian National Movement in Galicia*, 41.

96 Cięglewicz, *Gazeta Narodowa*, no. 230:1.

97 Wacław z Oleska, *Pieśni polskie i ruskie ludu galicyjskiego z muzyką in-strumentowaną przez Karola Lipińskiego* (Lviv, 1833), xliii. Cited in Kozik, *Ukrainian National Movement in Galicia*, 35–56.

98 Cited in Hryhorii Herbil's'kyi, *Rozvytok prohresyvnykh idei v Halychyni u pershii polovyni XIX st.: (do 1848 r.)* (Lviv: Vyd-vo L'vivs'koho Univer-sytetu, 1964), 227.

99 Cited in Kozik, *Ukrainian National Movement in Galicia*, 41–2.

100 Cited in Adam Świątek, ed., *Gente Rutheni, natione Poloni: z dziejów Rusinów narodowosci polskiej w Galicji*. (Cracow: Księgarnia Akademicka, 2014), 155.

101 Yakiv Holovatsky to Osyp Bodiansky, 4 December 1844, quoted in Kozik, *Ukrainian National Movement in Galicia*, 37.

102 From a letter of the Greek Catholic seminarian Mykola Kmytsekevych to a Polish friend, Kazimierz J. Turowski, written in the early 1830s and quoted in Shchurat, *Na dosvitku*, 140. See also Tershakovets, "Materialy i zamitky," 22–3.

103 Kozik, *Ukrainian National Movement in Galicia*, 29–30.

104 Lopuszański, *Stowarzyszenie Ludu Polskiego*, 103.

105 See chapter 5.
106 Bogdański, "O tajnych politycznych związkach," 39.
107 Ibid., 39–43.

Chapter 5

1 Adam Mickiewicz's response to Adam Czartoryski in 1842, when the prince referred to the poet as Poland's foremost genius and national prophet. Quoted in Rostyslav Radyshevs'kyi, "Velykyi piligrim i prorok," in *Adam Mitskevych i Ukraïna* (Kyiv: Biblioteka Ukraintsia, 1999), 36.

2 Tsentral'nyi derzhavnyi istorychnyi arkhiv Ukraïny v Kyievi (hereafter cited as TsDIAUK; Kyiv, Ukraine), fond 442, op. 785, spr. 2, ark. 239, 241, 244; see also Mykola Varvartsev, *Dzhuzeppe Madzini: madzinizm i Ukraïna* (Kyiv: Universytets'ke vydavnytstvo PULSARY, 2005), 145.

3 Wacław Łasocki, *Wspomnienie z mojego życia*, 2 vols (Cracow: Nakladem Gminy Stołecznego Królewskiego Miasta Krakówa, 1933), 1:76–81.

4 Szymon Konarski to Joachim Lelewel, from Lithuania, 23 September 1836, and 4 April 1837, in Łukaszewicz, *Szymon Konarski*, 214–15.

5 Ibid., 215–16.

6 Ibid., 126–7.

7 For the impact of Konarski's movement on students, see Maciej Łowicki, *Duch Akademji Wileńskiej: z czasów Szymona Konarskiego pamiętnik ucznia Wileńskiej Akademji Medyczno-Chirurgicznej (D-ra M. Łowickiego): Z czasów Szymona Konarskiego pamiętnik ucznia Wileńskiej Akademji Medyczno-Chirurgicznej* (Wilno: Zorza, 1925).

8 H.A. Serhiienko, "Diial'nist' 'Soiuzu pol's'koho narodu' na Ukraïni 1835–1839 rr.," *Ukraïns'kyi istorychnyi zhurnal* 12 (December 1969): 82.

9 Varvartsev, *Dzhuzeppe Madzini*, 153.

10 Information regarding Konarski's personal life and underground activities as the leader of the conspiracy is contained in Łukaszewicz, *Szymon Konarski*.

11 G.I. Marakhov, *Sotsial'no-politicheskaia bor'ba na Ukraine v 50-60-e gody XIX veka* (Kyiv: Izdatel'stvo pri Kievskom gosudarstvennom universitete izdatel'skogo obedineniia "Vyshcha shkola," 1981), 45.

12 Information regarding the Ukrainian members of the secret organization at the University of Kyiv is found in TsDAUK, fond 442, op. 794, spr. 159. In the documents and letters Oleksander Chornyi is referred to at times as Chernyi or Chernykh. See also *Kyrylo-Mefodiïvs'ke tovarystvo*, 3 vols, ed. P.S. Sokhan', I.L. Butych, L.Z. Gistsova, H.I. Marakhov, V.H. Sabrei, H. Ia. Serhiienko, Ie. S. Shabliovsky, and F.P. Shevchenko (Kyiv: Naukova dumka, 1990), 2:650n150; Varvartsev, *Dzhuzeppe Madzini*, 152; Mikula

Varvarcev [Mykola Varvartsev], "La diffusione del pensiero mazziniana in Ucraina nell'Ottocento," in *Il Mazzinianesimo nel Mondo*, ed. Giuliana Limiti, 474–5 (Pisa: Istituto Domus Mazziniana, 1996).

13 Information regarding this circle can be found in Jan Tabis, "Polskie rewolucyjne organizacje studenskie na Universytecie Kijowskim," in *Szkice z dziejów stosunków polsko-ukraińskich*, ed. Antoni Podraza, 21–7 (Cracow: Wydawnictwo Literackie, 1968); S.S. Simonov, "Oseredok 'Soiuzu pol's'koho narodu' w Kyïvs'komu Universyteti," *Visnyk Kyïvs'koho Universytetu* 4 (1961): 96; Łukaszewicz, *Szymon Konarski*, 132–3.

14 Łasocki, *Wspomnienie*, 1:151–2.

15 Ibid.

16 Tabis, "Polskie rewolucyjne organizacje," 21–4.

17 Mikula Varvarcev [Mykola Varvartsev], "La diffusione," 478.

18 Tabis, "Polskie rewolucyjne organizacje," 22–4. See also P.D. Sielecki, "Zapiski (1821–1846)," *Kyïvs'ka staryna* (1884): 2–9.

19 The other active members at the secret group at the University of Dorpat and the Medical Academy who were interrogated by the police when the organization was uncovered in 1838 were: Apolinary Kiersnowski, Aleksander Zdrodowski, Franciszek Giedgowd, Adolf Ostromecki, Jozef Bogusławski, Jozef Strzemski, Wladyslaw Zawisza, Adam Medeksza, Eryk Szwejkowski, Michal Soltanow, Walenty Podgórski, Wladyslaw Jeleński, Stanisław Falkowski, Julian Walicki, and Jan Wierzbicki. For details, see Łukaszewicz, Szymon *Konarski*, 133; Bronisław Zaleski, Cajetan Cieszkowski, Wiesław Caban, and Ryszard Matura, eds, *Bronisława Zaleskiego i Kajetana Cieszkowskiego nieznane relacje o powstaniu styczniowym* (Kielce: Wyższa Szkoła Pedagogiczna im. Jana Kochanowskiego w Kielcach, 1997), 27; Johannes Remy, *Higher Education and National Identity: Polish Student Activism in Russia 1832–1863* (Helsinki: Suomalaisen Kirjallisuuden Seura, 2000), 142–8.

20 Łukaszewicz, *Szymon Konarski*, 133–4.

21 Szymon Konarski to Joachim Lelewel, 23 September 1836, in ibid., 214–15.

22 Łukaszewicz, *Szymon Konarski*, 137.

23 This was the official name of the secret police department established during the reign of Nicholas I.

24 Tabis, "Polskie rewolucyjne organizacje," 23–4.

25 TsDIAUK, fond 470, op. I, 230–2, 1838–1839. The names of the Polish women on the list in the possession of the police were handwritten in Cyrillic. Not all are legible. Transliteration from the list follows: except for Solomia Bekue, who is identified as an acquaintance of Evva Felinskaya from Kremenets, all other women are listed by surnames only: Zaleska, Malynovska, Kitska, Yelovitska, Ledukhovska, and Ozharovska. The

informer, a certain Pavlina Vilgopolska, accused the women of belonging to a secret women's organization tied to Konarski, who was known to her by the name of Yanush.

26 Zaleski et al., *Bronisława Zaleskiego*, 26n28.

27 *Kyrylo-Mefodiïvs'ke tovarystvo*, 2:650.

28 They were: Antoni Janiszewski, Stanisław Winnicki, Jan Zrzodlowski, Arystarkh Sosnovsky, Ksaverij Pietraszkiewicz, Edward Milewski, Oleksander Chornyi, Wladysław Jurkowski, Seweryn Szymański, Jan Lubowicki, and Julian Osiecimski. Tabis, "Polskie rewolucyjne organizacje," 25. The original leader of the group, Gordon, threatened by arrest, fled the country. His position was taken over by Stanisław Winnicki.

29 *Kyrylo-Mefodiïvs'ke tovarystvo*, 2:650; Tabis, "Polskie rewolucyjne organizacje," 26. With the exception of Konarski and the top four conspirators, all death sentences were commuted to life imprisonment or service in the army.

30 Zaleski et al., *Bronisława Zaleskiego*, 26n31.

31 *Kyrylo-Mefodiïvs'ke tovarystvo*, 2:650; Tabis, "Polskie rewolucyjne organizacje," 21–6. See also the documentation in n10, above.

32 Varvarcev [Varvartsev], "La diffusione," 474–5; *Kyrylo-Mefodiïvs'ke tovarystvo*, 2:650.

33 TsDIAUK, fond 274, op. 1, spr. 22; fond 442, op. 794, spr. 235. See also A.I. Bortnikov, "Kirillo-Mefodicheskoe obshchestvo i pol'skoe natsional'no-osvoboditel'noe dvizhenie," in *Razvitie kapitalizma i natsional'niye dvizheniia v slavianskikh stranakh*, ed. V.I. Freidzon (Moscow: Izdatel'stvo "Nauka," 1970), 189.

34 Quoted in Varvarcev [Varvartsev], "La diffusione," 475.

35 Ibid.

36 Quoted in Lewak, "Ideologia polskiego romantyzmu," 312.

37 Łasocki, *Wspomnienie z mojego życia*, 1:76–81.

38 Varvarcev [Varvartsev], "La diffusione," 478–80.

39 For a discussion based on reports of the tsarist police about foreign literature reaching Odesa from Marseilles and Brussels during Konarski's underground activities, see Varvartsev, *Dzuzeppe Madzini*, 152–5.

40 F.I. Steblii, O.A. Kupchyns'kyi, and N.F. Vradii, eds, *"Rusalka Dnistrova," Dokumenty i materialy* (Kyiv: Naukova dumka, 1989), 142–3, 485.

41 Žáček, *Čechové a Poláci*, 148. The police agencies of Austria and Russia cooperated closely, especially with respect to underground activities that could be tied to the Polish underground.

42 Sacher-Masoch to Sedlnitsky, 24 July 1840, quoted in ibid., 150.

43 Łopuszański, *Stowarzyszenie Ludu Polskiego*, 35.

44 Žáček, *Čechové a Poláci*, 135.

45 Regarding the investigation and trial, see ibid., 139–48; Jan Novotný, *František Cyril Kampelík* (Praha: Melantrich, 1975), 71–5.

46 Zdeněk Fišer, "Zpráva Brnenského Policejního Reditele z Roku 1840 o Moravskych Vlastencích," *Zpravodaj Muzea Kroměřžiska* 2 (1992): 1–5.

47 Łopuszański, *Stowarzyszenie Ludu Polskiego*, 108. *František Cyril Kampelík* (Praha: Melantrich, 1975).

48 On these developments in Galicia, see Krajewski, *Tajne związki polityczne*; Zygmunt Zborucki, *Proces studentów samborskich 1837–1839* (Lviv, 1927); Andrusiak, "Ukraiński ruch narodowy"; Kieniewicz, *Konspiracje Galicyjskie*; Bogdański, *Pamiętnik*, 290–5; Łopuszański, *Stowarzyszenie Ludu Polskiego*, 108.

49 On Hordynsky, see Studyns'kyi, *L'vivs'ka dukhovna seminariia*, 181–8; Bogdański, *Pamiętnik*, 292–6.

50 Łopuszański, *Stowarzyszenie Ludu Polskiego*, 180–1.

51 Bogdański, *Pamiętnik*, 292–6.

52 Łukaszewicz died in 1855 at the age of forty-six. See Žáček, *Čechové a Poláci*, 181. See also Zdeněk Hájek, *Polský revolucionař na Špilberku* (Brno: Globus, 1932); Giller, *Historia powstania narodu polskiego*, pt 3, 399.

53 Malý, *Zpomínky*, 78–9.

54 J. Gruss, *Obzor*, 1889, 239, quoted in Komárek, *František Cyril Kampelík*, 28.

55 On this question, see Žáček, *Cesty českých studentů*, especially 9–37. See also Novotný, *O bratrské družbe Čechů a Slovaků*.

56 Medvecký, "Rozpomienky," 235–9.

Chapter 6

1 According to documents, the official name of the secret organization has been Slavic Society of Saints Cyril and Methodius (Slov'ians'ke tovarystvo sv Kyryla i Metodiia). However, in a preponderant majority of scholarly works and encyclopedias, the most commonly used designation is Cyril and Methodius Brotherhood. It will be this title that will be used in this study.

2 Mykola Kostomarov, "Spohad pro dvokh maliariv," quoted in Pavlo Zaitsev, *Taras Shevchenko: A Life*, ed. and trans. George Luckyj (Toronto: University of Toronto Press, 1988), 122.

3 *Kyrylo-Mefodiïvs'ke tovarystvo*, 2:507.

4 Panteleimon Kulish, *Khutorna poeziia* (Kyiv: Naukova Dumka, 1994), 361.

5 Ibid.

6 See chapter 5.

7 See chapter 1.

8 On this subject, see: M. Vozniak, *Kyrylo-Metodiïvs'ke Bratstvo* (Lviv: Nakladom fondu "Uchitesia, braty moï," 1921); Zenovii Hurevych, *"Moloda Ukraïna: Do vos'mydesiatykh rokovyn Kyrylo-Metodiïvs'koho Bratstva* (Kharkiv: Derzhavne vydavnytstvo Ukraïny, 1928); Józef Goląbek,

Bractwo Sw. Cyryla i Metodego w Kijowie (Warsaw: Nasza Przyszłość, 1935); Dennis Papazian, "N.I. Kostomarov and the Cyril-Methodian Ideology," *Russian Review* 29 (1970): 59–73; George S.N. Luckyj, *Young Ukraine: The Brotherhood of Saints Cyril and Methodius in Kiev, 1845–1847* (Ottawa: University of Ottawa Press, 1991); P.A. Zaionchkovskii, *Kirillo-Mefodievskoe obshchestvo (1846–1847)* (Moscow: Izdatel'stvo Moskovskogo Universiteta, 1959); V. Semevskii, "Kirillo-Mefodi-evskoe obshchestvo, 1846–1847," *Russkoe bogatstvo* 5–6 (1911): 5:98–127; 6:29–67; Thomas M. Prymak, *Mykola Kostomarov: A Biography* (Toronto: University of Toronto Press, 1996); Dmytro Doroshenko, *Mykola Ivanovych Kostomarov* (Kyiv: Ukraïns'ka nakladnia, 1920); Marta Bohachevs'ka [Martha Bohachevsky], "U dzherelakh novitnikh politychnykh idei: Kyrylo-Metodiïvs'ke Bratstvo," *Biuleten' "Obnova": Zhurnal Tovarystv Ukraïns'kykh Studentiv Katolykiv (Periodicum Societatum Ukrainorum Studentium Catholicorum)* (May–June 1958): 13–29.

9   On student corporations and Polish clandestine associations at the University of Dorpat, see Karl Siilivask, ed. *History of Tartu University: 1632–1982*, trans. Ants Aaver (Tallinn: Perioodika, 1985), 91–3, 164–5; Remy, *Higher Education and National Identity*, 140–8. On Mykola Hulak, see Valerii Marchenko, "Mykola Hulak," *Suchasnist'* 4, 5 (1982): 117–36; Hurevych, *Moloda Ukraïna*, 18–19.

10   For the testimonies of O.M. Petrov, Kostomarov, and Kulish, see *Kyrylo-Mefodiïvs'ke tovarystvo*, vol. 1; and of Andruzsky, vol. 2.

11   Bortnikov, "Kirillo-Mefodicheskoe obshchestvo," 186.

12   For Petrov's report, see *Kyrylo-Mefodiïvs'ke tovarystvo*, 1:25–7.

13   Hurevych, *Moloda Ukraïna*, 90.

14   L.K. Polukhin, *Formuvannia istorychnykh pohliadiv M.I. Kostomarova: Do krytyky burzhuazno-pomishchyts'koï istoriohrafiï na Ukraïni* (Kyiv: Vydavnytstvo AN URSR, 1959), 59–69.

15   See chapter 3.

16   Ibid.

17   Prymak, *Mykola Kostomarov*, chapter 1, especially 6–14.

18   Volodymyr Mijakovs'kyj, "Ševčenko in the Brotherhood of Saints Cyril and Methodius," in *Taras Ševčenko 1814–1861: A Symposium*, ed. Volodymyr Mijakovs'kyj and George Y. Shevelov ('S-Gravenhage: Mouton, 1962), 32; Miiakovs'kyi [Mijakovs'kyj], "Kostomarov u Rivnomu," *Ukraïna* 12 (1925): 28–66; Miiakovs'kyi [Mijakovs'kyj], "Knyha pro Kyrylo-Metodiïvs'ke Bratstvo," *Suchasnist'* 3 (1963): 85–96.

19   *Kyrylo-Mefodiïvs'ke tovarystvo*, 1:250–8.

20   See the comparison of Mickiewicz and Kostomarov in Dmitry Čiževsky [Dmytro Chyzhevs'kyj], "Mickiewicz and Ukrainian Literature," in *Adam Mickiewicz in World Literaturee: A Symposium*, ed. Waclaw Lednicki, 409–63

(Berkeley: University of California Press, 1956); Stefan Kozak, "Knyhy
Bytia Ukraïns'koho narodu Mykoly Kostomarova i Księgi narodu i pielgrzymstwa Polskiego Adama Mickiewicza," *Slavia orientalis* 1 (1973):
177–88; Zaionchkovskii, *Kirillo-Mefodievskoe obshchestvo*, 9–12.

21 *Kyrylo-Mefodiïvs'ke tovarystvo*, 1:300. Both Bohdan Zaleski and Michał
Czajkowski, as noted earlier, are known as writers belonging to the
Ukrainian school of Polish literature. In the emigration, Czajkowski
was connected not with Young Poland but with the Polish conserv-
ative circle under the leadership of Prince Czartoryski, a political
group that in its nationality program also attempted to win the sup-
port of the Ukrainians. For a very good summary of Czajkowski's
colourful life, with a special focus on the Ukrainian question, see
Ivan L. Rudnytsky, "Michał Czajkowski's Cossack Project during the
Crimean War: An Analysis of Ideas," in Ivan L. Rudnytsky, *Essays in
Modern Ukrainian History*, 173–86 (Edmonton: Canadian Institute of
Ukrainian Studies, 1987).

22 *Kyrylo-Mefodiïvs'ke tovarystvo*, 1:150–2.

23 Ibid. Cyril and Methodius were two medieval monks from Salonika, who
are credited with spreading Christianity among the Slavic peoples.

24 The appeals "Braty ukraïntsi!" and "Bratiia velikorossiane i poliaky!,"
ibid., 1:170–2.

25 Occasional depictions of the Germans and Turks as aggressors and
imperialists in the writings of the Russian Slavophiles most likely
provided the basis for the critical evaluation of these two nations by the
members of the Cyril and Methodius Brotherhood.

26 See Mazzini's correspondence with Lelewel in chapter 2.

27 See chapter 5.

28 Shchurat, *Vybrani pratsi*, 325–30.

29 Taras H. Shevchenko, "Khudozhnyk," in *Povisti*, ed. O.P. Sinichenko,
441–534 (Kyiv: Derzhavne vydavnytstvo khudozhn'oï literatury, 1964).
See also Paweł Zajcew [Pavlo Zaitsev], "Dwie postacie polskie w powieściach T. Szewczenki," *Biuletyn Polsko-Ukraiński* 8 (1935): 82.

30 Because of Soviet historians' lack of knowledge about Young Europe and
their shoddy scholarship on the Konarski conspiracy, Bronislaw Zaleski is
consistently referred to as a Polish exile sent to Siberia because of his participation in the November uprising of 1830. At that time Bronislaw was
barely ten years old!

31 Iulian Belina-Kendrzhyts'kyi [Bielina-Kędrzycki], "U Shevchenka v
Kyievi, 1846," in *Spohady pro Tarasa Shevchenka* (Kyiv: Vydavnytstvo
khudozhn'oï literatury "Dnipro," 1982), 153–9; Mijakovs'kyj,
"Shevchenko in the Brotherhood," 34–5.

32 *Kyrylo-Mefodiïvs'ke tovarystvo*, 1:6.

33   Panteleimon Kulish, "Avtobiohrafiia," in *Sami pro sebe: Avtobiohrafiï vydatnykh ukraïntsiv XIX-ho stolittia*, ed. Iurii Luts'kyi [George S.N. Luckyj] (Woodstock, MD: Ukraprint, 1989), 33 and 36. See also the correspondence between Kulish and Grabowski in Kulish, *Panteleimon Kulish: Lysty*, vol. 1, 1841–1850 (Kyiv: Krytyka, 2005).

34   In the police records Grabowski was listed as a member of Konarski's secret organization. Though subjected to police interrogations, the Polish writer was not arrested but continued to be under police observation at least until September 1840. See TsDIAK Ukraïny, fond 442, op. 790, spr. 14, ark. 1–21. On this subject, see also Volodymyr Miiakovs'kyi, "Shevchenko i Kostomarov," in *Zarubizhne Shevchenkoznavstvo (z materialiv UVAN)*, pt 2 (Kyiv: Khronika, 2011), 307–9.

35   Tretiak, *Bohdan Zaleski na tulactwie*, 2:279. See also chapter 2, nn60–3.

36   Kulish, "Avtobiohrafia," 35. One of Świdziński's manuscripts on a historical subject would be found by the police among Kostomarov's papers during the young historian's arrest.

37   See chapter 2.

38   Mykola I. Kostomarov, "Avobiografiia N.I. Kostomarova, zapisannaia N.A. Bilozerskoi," *Russkaia mysl'* 5 (1885): 185–223; 6 (1885): 20–43. In this first printing of Kostomarov's autobiography, the author identifies the head-mistress as the widow of the "well-known Polish poet Bohdan Zaleski." In later printings of the autobiography, no references to the poet are made. See Alina Kostomarova, "Nikolai Ivanovich Kostomarov," in *Avtobiografiia N.I. Kostomarova*, ed. V. Kotel'nikov (Moscow: Zadruga, 1922), 64–5.

39   Tretiak, *Bohdan Zaleski na tulactwie*, 1:55–6; Mazanowski, *Józef Bohdan Zaleski*, 53, 63–4; Sokołowska, *Młoda Polska*, 97. After the November uprising, before fleeing to France in 1833, Józef Zaleski spent some time in eastern Galicia, not only to take part in the preparations for the Zaliwski campaign against Russia, but also in order to establish underground channels of communications with his wife, who remained home. Józef Zaleski was more than ten years older than Bohdan, and his age corresponds more or less to that of the "widow" Zaleska, who, according to Kostomarov's reminiscences, was about sixty at the time of his employment at the *pension* in 1845. Bohdan was only eighteen and single when he left Ukraine. In Paris the poet married Zofia Rosengardt in 1846, just a few months before Kostomarov's arrest, and continued to live in France until his death in 1886. See also Poniatowska, *Listy Dyonizyi Poniatowskiej do Bohdana i Józefa Zaleskich*.

40   Kostomarova, "Nikolai Ivanovich Kostomarov," 64–5.

41   *Kyrylo-Mefodiïvs'ke tovarystvo*, 1:300.

42   Ibid., 1:500n165.

43   See chapter 5.

44 Of special interest in this instance is Zenovii Hurevych's work *"Moloda Ukraïna"* (Young Ukraine), written to commemorate the eightieth anniversary of the founding of the Cyril and Methodius Brotherhood. By tracing a connection between the Ukrainian political organization and Young Europe through the Konarski movement, the author concludes, "Similar to its older sister, Young Italy, promoting the slogan 'God and the people,' our young Ukraine by declaring the rule of God and the people, ideologically belongs to that bourgeois organization that is known in history as Young Europe." Hurevych, *"Moloda Ukraïna,"* 112. Shortly after its publication in 1928, the book was banned and its young author and his mentor, M. Yavorsky, were sent to Siberia. What must have upset the Soviet authorities in particular was that Hurevych stressed the impact of the Konarski movement and minimized the influence of Russian social thought on the ideology of the Cyril and Methodius Brotherhood. See especially *"Moloda Ukraïna,"* 88. The fate of the two scholars had a strong impact on Soviet research in connection with the Cyril and Methodius Brotherhood. A Russocentric orientation became the rule.

45 Doroshenko, *Mykola Ivanovych Kostomarov*, 24. This point of view is supported by the research works of Shchurat, *Vybrani pratsi*, 242–350; and Mijakovs'kyj, "Ševčenko in the Brotherhood," 32–6.

46 Stefan Kozak, *Ukraińscy spiskowcy i mesjaniści*, 86.

47 See chapters 4 and 5.

48 *Kyrylo-Mefodiïvs'ke tovarystvo*, 1:6–7.

49 Hipolit Terlecki, *Słowo Rusina ku wszech braci szczepu słovianskego o rzeczach słowiańskich* (Paris, 1849).

50 Mazanowski, *Józef Bohdan Zaleski*, 54.

51 Similarities between the texts are discussed in Handelsman, *Ukraińska polityka ks. Adama Czartoryskiego pred wojną krymską*, 124–6.

52 For a thorough discussion of the background during which the poem had been written as well as a good analysis of its content, see Ivan Bryk, "Shevchenkova poema 'Ivan Hus,'" *Zapysky NTSh* 119–20 (1917), 95–168; 126–7 (1918), 223–58.

53 *Kyrylo-Mefodiïvs'ke tovarystvo*, 1:105.

54 Eyck, "Mazzini's Young Europe," 361.

55 See Fedir Turchenko, "Stanovlennia svitohliadu," in *Mykola Mikhnovs'kyi: Suspil'no-politychni tvory*, ed. Ihor Hyrych, Fedir Turchenko, and Oleh Protsenko, 8–63 (Kyiv: Smoloskyp, 2015).

56 Bryk, "Shevchenkova poema," 119–20: 99.

57 Mykhailo Mol'nar, *Taras Shevchenko u chekhiv ta slovakiv* (Prešov: Slovenské pedagogické nakadateľstvo, 1961), especially 61–71; Mykola Neverly [Mikuláš Nevrlý], "Retseptsiia Husa v ukraïns'kii literaturi," *Duklia* 1 (2003): 36–41; Iosyf Shelepets', "Shevchenkiv virsh 'Shafarykovi'

iak pokhvala Shafarykovi," *Duklia* 2 (2007): 23–5. Josef Václav Frič's translation of the dedication to Šafařik was published in the American Czech journal *Zvoy* (no. 6 [1863]).

58 Josef V. Frič, *Ivan Mazepa: Tragedie v 5 Dějstvich* (Prague: Tiskem Rohlička a Sieverse, 1865).

59 Malý, *Zpomínky*, 7–9, 68.

60 Quoted in Shchurat, *Vybrani pratsi*, 303; Hurevych, 90. Members of the Cyril and Methodius Brotherhood were aware that at their roots they were tied to the Konarski underground. See the interrogation of H.L. Andruzsky, in *Kyrylo-Mefodiïvs'ke tovarystvo*, 2:507.

Chapter 7

1 "Słowo o Rusi i jej polityczeskom stanowyszczy," *Dnewnyk Ruskij*, 25 October 1848, 33.

2 For a detailed discussion and documentation of the issues summarized in this section, see chapters 3 and 4.

3 Kto za pravdu horí v svätej obeti,
kto za ľudstva práva život posvätí,
kto nad krivdou biednych slzu vyroní:
tomu moja pieseň slávou zazvoní.
Keď zahrmia delá, orol zaveje,
za slobodu milú kto krv vyleje,
pred ohnivým drakom kto vlasť zacloní:
tomu moja pieseň slávou zazvoní.
Kto si stojí slovu, čo priam zhŕkne svet,
komu nad statočnosť venca v nebi niet,
koho dar nezvedie, hrozba neskloní:
tomu moja pieseň slávou zazvoní.
Pán Boh šľachetnosti nebo vystavil,
večné on pre podlosť peklo podpálil;
kto ctí pravdy božskej božské zákony:
tomu moja pieseň slávou zazvoní.

4 I became acquainted with Štúr's poem at the age of nine or ten in central Slovakia, when our music teacher (an organist at the Lutheran Church) was preparing our school for the annual commemoration of Czechoslovak independence. The words of this poem, declaimed during every national holiday, and the haunting melody of the hymn heard on special occasions during the six years I spent in that country as an accidental resident, left such a strong imprint on my mind that they still resonate in my memory. The same applies to the poetry of Štúr and the works of his contemporaries, which were memorized and recited at national holidays,

even when communism was already entrenched in Czechoslovakia. At the time I could not have known that my teachers were the ideological great-grandchildren of Slovaks active in Vrchovský's *Vzájomnoť.*

5 See chapter 2.

6 Here one can mention anthologies, such as Kampelík's *Květy* and journals like Oheral's *Morava* among the Czechs. For the Slovaks, of note were Vrchovský's compendium *City vděčnosti mladých synů Slovenska* and Štúr's *Slovenskje narodňje novini* (The Slovak national newspaper) with its literary supplement *Orol tatraňski* (The Tatran eagle).

7 J. Gruss, *Obzor*, 1889, 239, quoted in Komárek, *František Cyril Kampelík*, 28.

8 See the first part of chapter 4.

9 The uprising of February 1846 in Kraków, led by Jan Tyssowski and Edward Dembowski, was an attempt to incite a revolution against the three partitioning powers to regain Poland's independence. The uprising was centred in the city of Kraków and lasted about nine days. It ended in victory of the Austrian army. For details see Marian Tyrowicz, *Jan Tyssowski i Rewolucja 1846 r. w Krakowie: Dzieja porywu i pokuty* (Kraków: Krajowa Agencja Wydawnicza, 1986).

10 *Rusalka Dnistrovaia* (Ruthenische Volks-Lieder) (Budym [Budapest]: Pysmom Korol. Vseuchylyshcha Peshtańskoho, 1937). A rare original copy of this anthology can be found in the library of the Shevchenko Scientific Society in New York. See also Steblii, "Markiian Shashkevych," 12.

11 Kozik, *Ukrainian National Movement in Galicia*, 69.

12 Mykola Ustianovych was one of the closest associates of the deceased Triad's leader, Markian Shashkevych. Because of Ustianovych's liberal political convictions and pro-Polish sympathies in 1848, Bishop H. Yakhymovych, in order to prevent problems with the Austrian authorities, transferred the democratically inspired and politically active priest from his parish to a remote monastery. Ibid., 184–5.

13 For an excellent, well-documented analysis of the revolutionary events of 1848 in eastern Galicia, see ibid., 177–368.

14 Quoted in ibid., 196.

15 *Zoria Halytska*, 15 May 1848.

16 Studyns'kyi, "Pol's'ki konspiratsiï sered rus'kykh pytomtsiv," 89–90. See also Oleh Turii, "Natsional'ne i politychne polonofil'stvo sered Hreko-Katolyts'koho Dukhovenstva Halychyny pid chas revoliutsiï 1848–1849 rokiv," *Zapysky NTSh* 228 (1994): 183–206. It is interesting to note that in the mid-1830s Skomorovsky, together with the members of the Triad, was on a list of seminarians suspected of harbouring sympathies for Russia. See Kozik, *Ukrainian National Movement in Galicia*, 47.

17 Kozik, *Ukrainian National Movement in Galicia*, 337.

18 See the information pertaining to nn 21 and 40 in chapter 4.

19 *Dziennik Narodowy*, nos 39, 55; no. 67:279 (1848).

20 Kasper Cięglewicz, *Rzecz Czerwonoruska 1848 roku* (Lviv, 1848).

21 As noted earlier, in 1838 Goszczyński fled to France, while Kulczyński committed suicide.

22 Quoted in Kozik, *Ukrainian National Movement in Galicia*, 358.

23 As already noted, in 1838 Vasyl Podolynsky, together with seminarians Venedykt Kushchykevych and Marian Lapchynsky, formed a radical clandestine group called "Vilni Halychany" (Free Galicians). He was also a member of the "Sons of the Fatherland," a sub-group of "Young Sarmatia," an organization of which Mykola Hordynsky was also a member. For a biographical sketch of Podolynsky as well as the full text of *Słowo przestrogi*, see Steblii, "Vyznachna pam'iatka ukraïns'koï politychnoï dumky seredyny XIX stolittia."

24 The only known written record left by Hordynsky is the already cited biographical sketch that he prepared during his trial in 1842. In it he writes about his great fascination with the democratic ideals of republican Greece and Rome during his student years, his deep interest in history and philosophy of the classical world, and his subsequent recruitment to the Polish underground in the early 1830s, including his role in the Association of the Polish People and eventual participation in "Young Sarmatia." As noted above, in addition to being a prefect, Hordynsky taught philosophy and theology at the Greek Catholic Seminary in Lviv between 1830 and 1837.

25 "Young Sarmatia" was a splinter group of the association, which suspended its activities in 1838.

26 In the second half of 1848 Podolynsky was on his way to join the revolutionary cause of Lajos Kossuth, the leader of Hungary's struggle for independence, but was arrested before he could join the struggle.

27 Podolynsky's father was a priest in Bylychi, a village in the Sambir district. Hordynsky's birthplace, Hordynia, was located in the same district.

28 See chapter 4.

29 Throughout the essay the author uses the term *Ruthenian*, even though it is clear from the content that he is referring to the Ukrainian people living on territories of both empires.

30 Steblii, "Vyznachna pam'iatka," 453.

31 Ibid., 455.

32 See Bogdański, *Pamietnik*, 292–5.

33 Ibid.

34 In the Polish original it is clear that the author refers to the the concept of a "philosopher king" found in the the "Allegory of the Cave" in Plato's *Republic*. Steblii, "Vyznachna pam'iatka," 462. This nuance is lost in the Ukrainian translation of the pamphlet. Ibid., 481. The translation was

made during the Soviet period when not too many scholars were well versed in the subtleties of Plato's philosophy.

35 See Steblii, "Vyznachna pam'iatka," for Polish original, 462; for Ukrainian translation, 481.

36 We know from Bogdański's memoirs that Hordynsky has shown deep concern with an enlightened educational policy both for the Ukrainian elite and for the masses. See chapter 4.

37 Bogdański, *Pamietnik*, 445.

38 It is worth remembering that during the 1830s Hordynsky translated Thomas Paine's *Rights of Man*. See Shchurat, *Na dosvitku*, 118.

39 Ibid., 459.

40 Hordynsky would be a prime example of having the traits of an assimilated Ukrainian, considering the fact that he attended a Polish gymnasium and university and spent a great part of his life in close proximity to Polish political activists.

41 *Dnewnyk Ruskij*, 4 October 1848, no. 6, 21–3; 11 October 1848, no. 7, 25–7; 18 October 1848, no. 8, 29–31; 25 October 1848, no. 9, 33.

42 *Dnewnyk Ruskij*, 25 October 1848, no. 9, 33.

43 Podoliński, *Słowo przestrogi*; Steblii, "Vyznachna pam'iatka," 453.

44 For a very good summary of the Slavic Congress in Prague, see Kozik, *Ukrainian National Movement in Galicia*, 215–36.

45 Vladimír Hostička, "Ukrajina v názorech české obrozenecké společnosti do roku 1848," *Slavia* 33, no. 4 (1964): 558–78.

46 Steblii, "Vyznachna pam'iatka," 454.

47 For a brief but very good summary of Polish-Ukrainian relations during the second half of the nineteenth century and the first half of the twentieth, see Rudnytsky, "Polish-Ukrainian Relations," in *Essays in Modern Ukrainian History*, 63–76.

48 Among the strongest voices in favour of reconciliation during this period had been Jerzy Giedroyc (1906–2000), a politician and journalist, founder and editor of the Paris-based Polish émigré journal *Kultura*. It is of interest to note that a century earlier one of the founding members of the Association of the Polish People in Cracow was Romauld Giedroyc.

Conclusion

1 John Hutchinson, "Cultural Nationalism and Moral Regeneration," in *Nationalism*, ed. John Hutchinson and Anthony D. Smith (Oxford: Oxford University Press, 1994), 128–9.

2 Michał Micel, *Spis powstańców 1863 roku więzionych w twierdzy kijowskiej* (Przemysl: Południowo-Wschodni Instytut Naukowy, 1995), 11–12.

3 V. Iu. Franchuk, *Oleksandr Opanasovych Potebnia* (Kyiv: Naukova Dumka, 1975), 10–13. On the participation of Ukrainians and other nationalities in the Polish uprising of 1863, see also Franciszek Rawita-Gawronski, *Rok 1863 na Rusi: Ukraina, Wolyń, Podole* (Lviv: H. Altenberg, 1902–3); and Rawita-Gawronski, *Moje przygody w roku 1863–1864 w Kijowie* (Warsaw, 1922).

4 King, *Letters and Recollections of Mazzini*, 56.

5 A similar attempt in the West to tie Mazzini's nationalism with Fascism has been, at least from the scholarly point of view, unsuccessful. See, for example, Sullam, *Giuseppe Mazzini and the Origins of Fascism*, and the critical reviews of this recent work in scholarly journals.

6 See Varvartsev, *Dzhuzeppe Madzini*.

Bibliography

Archival Materials

Istorychnyi Arkhiv (Lviv, Ukraine). Protocols, Reports, Letters, 1834–1843, fond 451.

Literární Archiv Památníku Narodního Písemnictví v Praze (LAPNPP) (Prague, Czech Republic). František Cyril Kampelík Correspondence and Papers.

Literaturný Archiv Matice Slovenskej v Martine – Archiv Slovenského Národného Muzea (LAMS-ASNM) (Martin, Slovak Republic). Aleksander B. Vrchovský Papers; Spoločnosť Česko-slovanská Archive.

Tsentral'nyi derzhavnyi istorychnyi arkhiv Ukraïny v Kyievi (TsDIAUK) (Kyiv, Ukraine), fonds 274, 442, 470.

Newspapers

Dilo, 1912 (Lviv)
Dnewnyk Ruskij, 1848 (Lviv)
Dziennik Narodowy, 1848 (Lviv)
Gazeta Narodowa, 1886 (Lviv)
Hlas Ľudu 1983, 1992 (Bratislava)
Nové Slovo, 1982 (Bratislava)
Slovenská Literatúra: Časopis Slovenskej Akadémie Vied, 1959 (Bratislava)
Spoločnosť, 1935 (Bratislava)
Zoria Halyts'ka 1848 (Lviv)

Correspondence, Documents, Memoirs, Biographies

Ashurst, Emilie Venturi. *Joseph Mazzini: A Memoir*. London: King, 1877.

Bohdan Zaleski, Józef. *Pisma Józefa Bohdana Zaleskiego* (St Petersburg, 1852).

Bogdański, Henryk. "O tajnych politycznych związkach w Galicii od roku 1832–1841." In *Pamiętniki spiskowców i więźniów galicyjskich v latach*

1832–1846, edited by Karol Lewicki, 3–69. Wrocław: Zaklad imienia Ossolińskich, 1954.

– *Pamiętnik: 1832–1848*, edited by Antoni Knot. Cracow: Wydawnictwo Literackie, 1971.

"Charter of the Association of the Polish People" (21 July 1835). In *Przegląd Historyczny*, 60 (1969): 351–62.

Chodakowski, Zorian Dołęga. *O Slowiańszczyźnie przed chrześcijaństwem, oraz inne pisma i listy*. Edited by Julian Maślanka. Warsaw: Państwowe Wydawnictwo Naukowe, 1967.

Cięglewicz, Kasper. *Rzecz Czerwonoruska 1848 roku*. Lviv, 1848.

– "Żyvot, prace i cierpienia," *Gazeta Narodowa* (Lviv), nos 227–33 (1886).

Goszczyński, Seweryn. *Dzieła zbiorowe Seweryna Goszczyńskiego*. Vol. 1 (Lviv: Nakladem Księgi Altenberga, 1911).

Harro-Harring, Paul. *Memorie sulla "Giovine Italia" e sugli ultimi avvenimenti di Savoia*. Milan: Societa Editrice Dante Alighieri, Albrighi, Segati, 1913.

Herzen, Aleksandr [Aleksandr Gertsen]. *Byloe i dumy*. Leningrad: OGIZ Gosudarstvennoe izdatel'stvo khudozhestvennoi literatury, 1946.

Horoszkiewicz, Julian. *Notatki z życia*. Wroclaw: Zaklad Narodowi im. Ossolinskich, 1957.

Józefczyk, Andrzej. "Wspomnienie ubieglych lat," In *Pamętniki spiskowców i więźniów galicyjskich v latach 1832–1846*, edited by Karol Lewicki, 122–37. Wrocław: Zaklad imienia Ossolińskich, 1954.

King Bolton, Harriet. *Letters and Recollections of Mazzini*. London: Longmans Green, 1912.

– *The Life of Mazzini*. London: Dent, 1902.

Kollár, Ján. *Slávy dcéra*. Prague: Mladá Frtonta, 1961.

Komárek, František. *František Cyril Kampelík: Obraz životopisný*. Hradec Králové: Bratři Peřinú, 1895.

Konarski, Szymon. *Dziennik z lat 1831–1834*. Wrocław: Zakład Narodowy im. Ossolińskich, 1973.

Kulish, Panteleimon. "Avtobiohrafiia." In *Sami pro sebe: Avtobiohrafiï vydatnykh ukraïntsiv XIX-ho stolittia*, edited by George S.N. Luckyj, 23–56. Woodstock, MD: Ukraprint, 1989.

– *Panteleimon Kulish: Lysty*. Vol. 1. 1841–1850. Kyiv: Krytyka, 2005.

Kyrylo-Mefodiïvs'ke tovarystvo, edited by P.S. Sokhan', I.L. Butych, L.Z. Gistsova, H.I. Marakhov, V.H. Sabrei, H. Ia. Serhiienko, Ie. S. Shabliovsky, and F.P. Shevchenko. 3 vols. Kyiv: Naukova dumka, 1990.

Łasocki, Wacław. *Wspomnienie z mojego życia*, 2 vols. Cracow: Nakładem Gminy Stołecznego Królewskiego Miasta Krakówa, 1933–4.

Lelewel, Joachim. *Listy emigracyjne Joachima Lelewela*. Edited by Helena Więckowska. Cracow: Nakład Polskiej Akademii Umiejętnosci, 1948.

Lewak, Adam. *Giuseppe Mazzini e l'emigrazione polacca. Lettere inedite*. Casale: Tipografia cooperativa, 1925.

Lewicki, Karol, ed. *Pamiętniki spiskowców i więźniów galicyjskich v latach 1832–1846*. Wrocław: Zaklad im. Ossolińskich, 1954.

Łowicki, Maciej. *Duch Akademji Wileńskiej: z czasów Szymona Konarskiego pamiętnik ucznia Wileńskiej Akademji Medyczno-Chirurgicznej (D-ra M. Łowickiego): Z czasów Szymona Konarskiego pamiętnik ucznia Wileńskiej Akademji Medyczno-Chirurgicznej*. Wilno: Zorza, 1925.

Łukaszewicz, Witold. *Szymon Konarski 1808–1839*. Warsaw: Książka, 1948.

Łukaszewicz, Witold, and Wladyslaw Lewandowski. *Postępowa Publicystyka Emigracyjna 1831–1846: wybor żródel*. Wrocław: Wydawnictwo Polskiej Akademii Nauk, 1961.

Malý, Jakub. *Zpomínky a úvahy starého vlastence*. Prague: J.S. Skrejsovský, 1872.

Mazzini, Giuseppe [Joseph Mazzini]. *The Duties of Man and Other Essays*. London: J.M. Dent, 1936.

– *Edizione Nazionale, Scritti editi ed inediti di Giuseppe Mazzini (1906–90)*. 106 vols. Imola: Cooperativa Tipografico; Editrice Paolo Galeati, 1906–90.

– *Essays: Selected from the Writings, Literary, Political and Religious, of Joseph Mazzini*. Edited by William Clarke. London: Walter Scott, 1887.

– *Fede e Avvenire ed Altri Scritti*. Edited by Luigi Salvatorelli. Rome: Giulio Einaudi, 1945.

– *Life and Writings of Joseph Mazzini*. 6 vols, new ed. London, 1890–1.

– *Mazzini's Letters to an English Family*. 3 vols. London: John Lane, 1920–2.

– *Note autobiografiche*. Edited by Mario Menghini. 2nd ed. Florence: F. le Monnier, 1944.

Mochnacki, Klemens. "Pamiętnik spiskowca i nauczyciela 1811–1846." In *Pamiętniki spiskowców i więźniów galicyjskich v latach 1832–1846*, edited by Karol Lewicki, 138–57. Wrocław: Zaklad im. Ossolińskich, 1954.

Moscicki, H. *Szymon Konarski*. Warsaw: Państwowy Inst. Wydawniczy, 1949.

Novotný, Jan. *František Cyril Kampelík*. Prague: Melantrich, 1975.

Poniatowska, Dyonizya. *Listy Dyonizyi Poniatowskiej do Bohdana i Józefa Zaleskich*. 2 vols. Cracow: G. Gebethner i Spólka, 1900.

Rawita-Gawronski, Franciszek. *Moje przygody w roku 1863–1864 w Kijowie*. Warsaw, 1922.

– *Rok 1863 na Rusi: Ukraina, Wolyń, Podole*. Lviv: H. Altenberg, 1902–3.

Recchia, Stefano, and Nadia Urbinati, eds. *A Cosmopolitanism of Nations: Giuseppe Mazzini's Writings on Democracy, Nation Building, and International Relations*. Princeton, NJ: Princeton University Press, 2009.

Roberts, William. *Prophet in Exile: Joseph Mazzini in England, 1837–1868*. New York: Peter Lang, 1989.

Sak, Robert. *Rieger: Konzervativec nebo Liberál?* Prague: Akademia, 2003.

Smith, Denis Mack. *Mazzini.* New Haven, CT: Yale University Press, 1994.

Steblii, Feodosii. "Vyznachna pam'iatka ukraïns'koï politychnoï dumky seredyny XIX stolittia: 'Slovo perestorohy' Vasylia Podolyns'koho." In *Zapysky Naukovoho Tovarystva im. Shevchenka* [*Zapysky NTSh*] 228 (1994): 434–87.

Steblii, F.I., O.A. Kupchyns'kyi, and N.F. Vradii, eds. *"Rusalka Dnistrova": Dokumenty i materialy.* Kyiv: Naukova dumka, 1989.

Terlecki, Hipolit. *Słowo Rusina ku wszech braci szczepu słovianskego o rzeczach słowiańskich.* Paris: 1849.

Tomassucci, Giovanna. "Romantyzm polski w pismach G. Mazziniego." In *Contributi Italiani al XII Congresso Internazionale degli Slavisti,* edited by Francois Esvan. Naples: Associazione Italiana degli Slavisti, 1998: 451–570.

Wasilewski, Zygmunt. *Seweryn Goszczyński w Galicyi: Nieznane pamiętniki, listy i utwory, 1832–1842.* Lviv: Słowo Polskie, 1902.

Žáček, Václav. *Cesty českých studentů na Slovensko v době předbřeznové: Paměti a dokumenty,* Svazek I. Brno: Brnenská tiskárna, 1948.

– *Z revolučných a politických pol'sko slovenských stykov v dobe predmarcovej.* Bratislava: Vydavatel'stvo akademie vied, 1966.

Zaleski, Bronisław, Cajetan Cieszkowski, Wiesław Caban, and Ryszard Matura. *Bronisława Zaleskiego i Kajetana Cieszkowskiego nieznane relacje o powstaniu styczniowym.* Kielce: Wyższa Szkoła Pedagogiczna im. Jana Kochanowskiego, 1997.

Books and Pamphlets

Anderson, Benedict. *Imagined Communities: Reflections on the Origins and Spread of Nationalism.* London: Verso, 2006.

Batowski, Henryk. *Przyjaciele Słowianie.* Warsaw: "Czytelnik," 1956.

Bayly, Christopher A., and Eugenio F. Biagini, eds. *Giuseppe Mazzini and the Globalization of Democratic Nationalism 1830–1920.* Oxford: Oxford University Press, 2008.

Bazilevskii, V. [V. Bogucharskii]. *Gosudarstvennye prestupleniia v Rossii v XIX v.* St Petersburg, 1906.

Bilenky, Serhiy. *Romantic Nationalism in Eastern Europe: Russian, Polish, and Ukrainian Political Imaginations.* Palo Alto, CA: Stanford University Press, 2012.

Bohachevsky-Chomiak, Martha. *The Spring of a Nation: The Ukrainians in Eastern Galicia in 1848.* Philadelphia: Shevscheno Scientific Society, 1967.

Bojanowska, Edyta M. *Nikolai Gogol: Between Ukrainian and Russian Nationalism.* Cambridge, MA: Harvard University Press, 2007.

Bradley, John F.N. *Czech Nationalism in the Nineteenth Century.* Boulder, CO: East European Monographs; Distributed by Columbia University Press, 1984.

Brock, Peter. *Nationalism and Populism in Partitioned Poland: Selected Essays.* London: Orbis Books, 1973.

– *The Slovak National Awakening: An Essay in the Intellectual History of East Central Europe.* Toronto: University of Toronto Press, 1976.

Broers, Michael. *Europe after Napoleon: Revolution, Reaction, and Romanticism, 1814–1848.* Manchester, NY: Manchester University Press, 1996.

Cagnacci, Carlo. *Giuseppe Mazzini e i fratelli Ruffini.* Porto Maurizio: Tipografia Berio, 1893.

Carter, Nick, ed. *Britain, Ireland and the Italian Risorgimento.* Houndmills, Basingstoke, Hamphshire: Palgrave Macmillan, 2015.

Church, Clive H. *Europe in 1830: Revolution and Political Change.* London: Allen & Unwin, 1983.

Cremona Cozzolino, Itala, ed. *Maria Mazzini e il suo ultimo carteggio.* Florence: La Nuova Italia, 1939.

Dal Lago, Enrico. *William Lloyd Garrison and Giuseppe Mazzini: Abolition, Democracy, and Radical Reform.* Baton Rouge: Louisiana State University Press, 2013.

Doroshenko, Dmytro. *Mykola Ivanovych Kostomarov.* Kyiv: Ukraïns'ka nakladnia, 1920.

Droz, Jacques. *Europe between Revolutions, 1815–1848.* New York: Harper & Row, 1967.

Franchuk, V. Iu. *Oleksandr Opanasovych Potebnia.* Kyiv: Naukova dumka, 1975.

Frantsev, Vladimir A. *Pol'skoe slavianovedenie kontsa XVIII i pervoi chetverti XIX st.* Prague: Tipografia "Politiki," 1906.

Frič, Josef V. *Ivan Mazepa: Tragedie v 5 dějstvích.* Prague: Tiskem Rohlička a Sieverse, 1865.

Gadon, Lubomir. *Wielka emigracja w pierwszych latach po powstaniu listopadowym.* 2nd ed. Paris: Ksęgarnia Polska, 1960.

Gellner, Ernest. *Nations and Nationalism.* Ithaca, NY: Cornell University Press, 1983.

Giusti, Wolfango. *Mazzini e gli Slavi.* Milano: Instituto per gli studi di politia internazionale, 1940.

Goląbek, Józef. *Bractwo Św. Cyryla i Metodego w Kijowie.* Warsaw: Nasza Przyszłość, 1935.

Hájek, Zdeněk. *Polský revolucionař na Špilberku.* Brno: Globus, 1932.

Hales, Edward E.Y. *Mazzini and the Secret Societies: The Making of a Myth.* New York: Kennedy, 1956.

Handelsman, Marceli. *Francja – Polska, 1795–1845: studja nad dziejami myśli politycznej.* Warsaw: Gebethner i Wolff, 1926.

– *Ukraińska polityka ks. Adama Czartoryskiego pred wojną krymską.* Warsaw: 1937.

Hann, Chris, and Paul Robert Magocsi. *Galicia: A Multicultured Land.* Toronto: University of Toronto Press, 2005.

Herbil's'kyi, Hryhorii. *Peredova suspil'na dumka v Halychyni: 30-i-seredyna 40-kh rokiv XIX stolittia.* Lviv: Vydavnytsvo L'vivs'koho Universytetu, 1959.

– *Rozvytok prohresyvnykh idei v Halychyni u pershii polovyni XIX st.: (do 1848 r.).* Lviv: Vyd-vo L'vivs'koho Universytetu, 1964.

Himka, John-Paul. *Galician Villagers and the Ukrainian National Movement in the Nineteenth Century.* Basingstoke: Macmillan in Association with Canadian Institute of Ukrainian Studies, 1988.

Hnatiuk, Volodymyr. *Natsional'ne vidrodzhennia Avstro-Uhors'kykh ukraïntsiv: 1772–1880 rr.* Edited by Feodosii Steblii, 2nd ed. Lviv: Instytut Ukraïnoznavstva im. I. Krypiakevycha NAN Ukraïny, 2006.

Hobsbawm, E.J. *Nations and Nationalism since 1780: Programme, Myth, Reality.* Cambridge: Cambridge University Press, 1990.

Hoffmannova, Eva. *Karel Slavoj Amerling 1807–1884.* Prague: Melantrich, 1982.

Hroch, Miroslav. *Social Preconditions of National Revival in Europe.* New York: Columbia University Press, 2000.

Hurevych, Zenovii. *"Moloda Ukraïna": Do vos'mydesiatykh rokovyn Kyrylo-Metodiïvs'koho Bratstva.* Kharkiv: Derzhavne vydavnytstvo Ukraïny, 1928.

Hutchinson, John. *The Dynamics of Cultural Nationalism: The Gaelic Revival and the Creation of the Irish Nation State.* Boston: Allen & Unwin, 1987.

Jahn, V. Jilji. *Karel Slavoj Amerling: Obraz Života a Práce.* Preface by František Štolba and Antonín Bĕlohoubek. Prague: F. Šimáček, 1893.

Jędrzejewicz, Jerzy. *Zwycięstwo Pokonanych: Opowieść o Stanisławie Worcellu.* Warsaw: Instytut Wydawniczy Pax, 1974.

Judson, Pieter M. *Exclusive Revolutionaries: Liberal Politics, Social Experience, and National Identity in the Austrian Empire, 1848–1914.* Ann Arbor: University of Michigan Press, 1996.

– *Guardians of the Nation: Activists on the Language Frontiers of Imperial Austria.* Cambridge, MA: Harvard University Press, 2006.

– *The Habsburg Empire: A New History.* Cambridge, MA: Belknap of Harvard University Press, 2016.

Judson, Pieter M., and Marsha L. Rozenblit, eds. *Constructing Nationalities in East Central Europe.* New York: Berghahn Books, 2005.

Kałęmbka, Sławomir. *Towarzystwo Demokratyczne Polskie v latach 1832–1846.* Toruń: Panstwowe Wydawnictwo Naukowe, 1966.

Keller, Hans Gustav. *Das "Junge Europa," 1834–1836: Eine Studie zur Geschichte der Völkerbundsidee und des nationalen Gedankens.* Zurich: Max Niehaus Verlag, 1938.

Kieniewicz, Stefan. *Konspiracje galicyjskie 1831–1848.* Warsaw: Książka i Wiedza, 1950.

Kieniewicz, Stefan, Andrzej Zahorski, and Władysław Zajewski. *Trzy Powstania Narodowe: Kościuszkowskie, Listopadowe, Styczniowe,* edited by Władysław Zajewski. Warsaw: Książka i Wiedza, 1992.

Kizwalter, Tomasz. *O nowoczesności narodu: przypadek polski*. Warsaw: Semper cop., 1999.

Korczok, Anton. *Die griechisch-katholische Kirche in Galizien*. Leipzig: B.G. Teubner, 1921.

Koropeckyj, Roman Robert. *Adam Mickiewicz: The Life of a Romantic*. Ithaca, NY: Cornell University Press, 2008.

Kostomarov, Nikolai [Mykola] I. *Istoricheskie proizvedeniia: Avtobiografiia*. Kyiv: Izdatel'stvo pri Kievskom gosudarstvennom universitete, 1990.

Kozak, Stefan. *Ukraińscy spiskowcy i mesjaniści: Bractwo Cyryla i Metodego*. Warsaw: Instytyt Wydawn. Pax, 1990.

Kozik, Jan. *The Ukrainian National Movement in Galicia: 1815–1849*. Edmonton: Canadian Institute of Ukrainian Studies, 1986.

Krajewski, Józef. *Tajne związki polityczne w Galicyi, od r. 1833 do r. 1841. Według niewydanych źródeł rękopiśmiennych, oraz aktów sądowych i gubernialnych*. Lviv: Nakł. Słowa Polskiego, 1903.

Krčméry, Štefan. *Výber z diela III: Stopäťdesiat rokov slovenskej literatúry*. Bratislava: Slovenské vydavateľstvo krásnej literatúri, 1954.

Kulish, Panteleimon. *Khutorna poeziia*. Kyiv: Naukova dumka, 1994.

Kyrchiv, Roman. *Markiianove Suzir'ia: Ti, koho probudyv, "voodushevyv" i poviv za soboiu Markiian Shashkevych*. Lviv: Vydavnytstvo L'viskoï Politekhniky, 2012.

Leslie, R.F. *Polish Politics and the Revolution of November 1830*. London: University of London Athlone, 1956.

Lewak, Adam. *Od związków węglarskich do Młodej Polski: Dzieje emigracji i legjonu polskiego w Szwajcarji w r. 1833–1834*. Warsaw: E. Wende i Spólka, 1920.

Lewicki, Karol. *Uniwersytet lwowski a powstanie listopadowe*. Lviv: Skład głowny w księgarni A. Krawczyńskiego, 1937.

Limanowski, Bołeslaw. *Historia demokracji polskiej w epoche porozbiorowej*. Warsaw: Wiedza, 1946.

Lincoln, Bruce W. *Nicholas I: Emperor and Autocrat of All the Russias*. Bloomington: Indiana University Press, 1989.

Łopuszański, Bołeslaw. *Stowarzyszenie Ludu Polskiego (1835–1841)*. Cracow: Wydawnictwo Literackie, 1975.

Luckyj, George S.N. *Between Gogol' and Ševčenko: Polarity in the Literary Ukraine: 1798–1847*. Harvard Series in Ukrainian Studies, vol. 8. Munich: Wilhelm Fink Verlag, 1971.

– *Young Ukraine: The Brotherhood of Saints Cyril and Methodius in Kiev, 1845–1847*. Ottawa: University of Ottawa Press, 1991.

Łukaszewicz, Witold. *Szymon Konarski 1808–1839*. Warsaw: Książka, 1948.

Lyons, Martyn. *Post-revolutionary Europe, 1815–1856*. Basingstoke, UK: Palgrave Macmillian, 2006.

Magocsi, Paul Robert. *Galicia: A Historical Survey and Bibliographical Guide*. Toronto: University of Toronto Press, 1983.

Marakhov, G.I. *Sotsial'no-politicheskaia bor'ba na Ukraine v 20-40-e gody XIX veka.* Kyiv: "Vyshcha shkola," Izdatel'stvo pri Kievskom Gosudarstvennom Universitete, 1979.

– *Sotsial'no-politicheskaia bor'ba na Ukraine v 50-60-ie gody XIX veka.* Kyiv: Izdatel'stvo pri Kievskom gosudarstvennom universitete izdatel'skogo obedineniia "Vyshcha shkola," 1981.

Mastellone, Salvo. *Mazzini and Marx.* Westport, CT: Praeger, 2003.

Matoušek, Miloslav. *Život a působení Dr. F.C. Kampelíka.* Prague: Alois Svoboda, 1947.

Mazanowski, Mikołaj. *Józef Bohdan Zaleski: Życie i dzieła, zarys biograficzny.* St Petersburg: Nakładem Księgarni K. Grendyszyńskiego, 1901.

Meinecke, Friedrich. *Cosmopolitanism and the National State.* Princeton, NJ: Princeton University Press, 1970.

Merriman, John M., ed. *1830 in France.* New York: New Viewpoints, 1975.

Micel, Michał. *Spis powstańców 1863 roku więzionych w twierdzy kijowskiej.* Przemysl: Południowo-Wschodni Instytut Naukowy, 1995.

Mokry, Włodzimierz. *"Ruska Trójca": karta z dziejów życia literackiego Ukraińców w Galicji w pierwszej połowie XIX wieku.* Cracow: Wydawnictwo Uniwersytetu Jagiellońskiego: Fundacja Świętego Włodzimierza, 1997.

Mol'nar, Mykhailo. *Taras Shevchenko u chekhiv ta slovakiv.* Prešov: Slovenské pedagogické nakladateľstvo, 1961.

Monas, Sidney. *The Third Section: Police and Society in Russia under Nicholas I.* Cambridge, MA: Harvard University Press, 1961.

Montale, Bianca. *Maria Drago Mazzini.* Genoa: Comune di Genova, 1955.

Mościcki, Henryk. *Szymon Konarski.* Warsaw: Państwowy Inst. Wydawniczy, 1949.

Mráz, Andrej. *Dejiny slovenskej literatúry.* Bratislava: Slovenská akadémia vied a umení, 1948.

Novotný, J. *O bratrské družbě Čechů a Slováků za národního obrození: kapitoly z dějin vzájemných vztahů Čechů a Slováků v národním hnutí do roku 1848.* Prague: Štátni náklad politické literatury, 1959.

Nowak, Andrzej. *Jak rozbić rosyjskie imperium? Idee polskiej polityki wschodniej 1733–1921.* Warsaw: Warszawska Oficyna Wydawnictwo Gryf, 1995.

– *Między carem a rewolucją. Studium politycznej wyobraźni i postaw Wielkiej Emigracji wobec Rosji 1831–1849.* Warsaw: Wydawnictwo Instytut Historii PAN i Warszawska Oficyna Wydawnictwo Gryf, 1994.

Noyes, John K. *Herder: Aesthetics against Imperialism.* Toronto: University of Toronto Press, 2015.

Palmer, Alan. *Metternich: Councillor of Europe.* London: Phoenix Giant, 1997.

Pelech, Orest. "Towards a Historical Sociology of Ukrainian Ideologues in the Russian Empire of the 1830s–1840s." PhD diss., Princeton University, 1976.

Podoliński, B. [Vasyl' Podolyns'kyi]. *Słowo przestrogi.* Sanok, 1848.

Petro, Peter. *A History of Slovak Literature*. Montreal and Kingston: McGill-Queen's University Press, 1995.

Pišút, Milan. *Počiatky básnickej školy Štúrovej v Bratislavě*. Bratislava: Práce Učené společnosti Šafaříkovy, 1938.

Pivano, Livio. *Lamennais e Mazzini*. Turin: Associazione Mazziniana Italiana, 1958.

Plokhy, Serhii. *The Cossack Myth: History and Nationhood in the Age of Empires*. Cambridge: Cambridge University Press, 2012.

Polukhin, L.K. *Formuvannia istorychnykh pohliadiv M.I. Kostomarova: Do krytyky burzhuazno-pomishchyts'koï istoriohrafiï na Ukraïni*. Kyiv: Vydavnytstvo AN URSR, 1959.

Porter, Brian. *When Nationalism Began to Hate*. Oxford: Oxford University Press, 2002.

Procyk, Anna. *Russian Nationalism and Ukraine: The Nationality Policy of the Volunteer Army during the Civil War*. Edmonton: Canadian Institute of Ukrainian Studies, 1995.

Prymak, Thomas M. *Mykola Kostomarov: A Biography*. Toronto: University of Toronto Press, 1996.

Raeff, Marc. *The Decembrist Movement*. Englewood Cliffs, NJ: Prentice Hall, 1966.

Rapport, Mike. *1848, Year of Revolution*. New York: Basic Books, 2009.

Recchia, Stefano, and Nadia Urbinati, eds. *A Cosmopolitanism of Nations: Giuseppe Mazzini's Writings on Democracy, Nation Building, and International Relations*. Princeton, NJ: Princeton University Press, 2009.

Remy, Johannes. *Higher Education and National Identity: Polish Student Activism in Russia 1832–1863*. Helsinki: Suomalaisen Kirjallisuuden Seura, 2000.

Riasanovsky, Nicholas V. *Nicholas I and Official Nationality in Russia, 1825–1855*. Berkeley: University of California Press, 1967.

Roberts, William. *Prophet in Exile: Joseph Mazzini in England, 1837–1868*. New York: Peter Lang, 1989.

Rozumnyj, Jaroslav, ed. *Markiian Shashkevych na zakhodi*. Winnipeg: Instytut-zapovidnyk Markiiana Shashkevycha, 2007.

Rudnytsky, Ivan L. *Essays in Modern Ukrainian History*. Edmonton: Canadian Institute of Ukrainian Studies, 1987.

Sak, Robert. *Rieger: Konzervativec nebo Liberál?* Prague: Academia, 2003.

Salvemini, Gaetano. *Mazzini*. Stanford: Stanford University Press, 1957.

Sarti, Roland. *Mazzini: A Life for the Religion of Politics*. Westport, CT: Praeger, 1997.

Savchenko, Fedir, ed. *Zakhidnia Ukraïna v lystuvanni Holovats'koho z Bodians'kym, 1843–1876*. Kyiv: "Kyïv-Druk," 1930.

Scuffle, Marcella Pellegrino. *Victorian Radical and Italian Democrats*. London: Boydell, 2014.

Shalata, Mykhailo I. *Markiian Shashkevych: Zhyttia, tvorchist' i hromads'ko-kul'turna diial'nist'*. Kyiv: Naukova dumka, 1969.

Shchurat, Vasyl'. *Na dosvitku novoï doby: do vidrodzhennia Hal[yts'koï]. Ukrainy.* Lviv: Z Drukarni Naukovoho Tovarystva im. Shevchenka, 1919.

– *Vybrani pratsi z istoriï literatury.* Kyiv: Vydavnytstvo Akademiï nauk Ukraïns'koï RSR, 1963.

Shevchenko, Taras. *Povisti.* Edited by O.P. Synychenko. Kyiv: Derzhavne vydavnytstvo khudozhn'oï literatury, 1964.

Siemann, Wolfram. *Metternich: Stratege und Visionär: eine Biografie.* Munich: C.H. Beck, 2016.

Siilivask, Karl, ed. *History of Tartu University, 1632–1982.* Translated by Ants Aaver, Ilmar Anvel, Aino Jogi, Ele Kaldjarv, and Krista Kallis. Tallinn: Perioodika, 1985.

Smith, Anthony D. *The Ethnic Origins of Nations.* Oxford: Basil Blackwell, 1986.

Smith, Denis Mack. *Mazzini.* New Haven, CT: Yale University Press, 1994.

Snyder, Timothy. *The Reconstruction of Nations: Poland, Ukraine, Lithuania, Belarus, 1569–1999.* New Haven, CT: Yale University Press, 2003.

Sokołowska, Stefania. *Młoda Polska: Z dziejów ugrupovań demokratycznych wielkej emigracji.* Wrocław: Zakład Narodowy imienia Ossolińskich; Wydawnictwo Polskiej Akademii Nauk, 1972.

Sosnowska, Danuta. *Inna Galizja.* Warsaw: Dom Wydawniczy Elipsa, 2008.

Sperber, Jonathan. *The European Revolutions, 1848–1851.* Cambridge: Cambridge University Press, 1994.

Steblii, Feodosii, V.I. Horyn', and O.A. Kupchyns'kyi, eds. *Rus'ka triitsia v istoriï suspil'no-politichnoho rukhu i kul'tury Ukraïny.* Kyiv: Naukova dumka, 1987.

Storozynski, Alex. *The Peasant Prince: Thaddeus Kosciuszko and the Age of Revolution.* New York: St Martin's, 2009.

Studyns'kyi, Kyrylo. *L'vivs'ka dukhovna seminariia v chasakh Markiiana Shashkevycha 1829–1843.* Lviv, 1916.

Sugar, Peter F., and Ivo J. Lederer, eds. *Nationalism in Eastern Europe.* Seattle: University of Washington Press, 1969.

Sullam, Simon Levis. *Giuseppe Mazzini and the Origins of Fascism.* Translated by Sergio Knipe and Oona Smyth. Italian and Italian American Studies. Edited by Stanislao G. Pugliese. Basingstoke: Palgrave Macmillan, 2015.

Świątek, Adam. *Gente Rutheni, natione Poloni: z dziejów Rusinów narodowości polskiej w Galicii.* Cracow: Księgarnia Akademicka, 2014.

Szpotański, Stanisław. *Konarszczyzna i Lud Polski: przygotowania powstańcze w Polsce w 1835–1839 roku.* Cracow: Książka, 1926.

Teich, Mikuláš, ed. *Bohemia in History.* New York: Cambridge University Press, 1998.

Tretiak, Józef. *Bohdan Zaleski na tułactwie: 1831–1886: życie i poezya. Karta z dziejów emigracyi polskiej.* 2 vols. Cracow: Nakładem Akademii Umiejętnosci, 1913.

Tůma, Karel. *Apoštol svobody.* Prague: Frant. Bačkovský, 1896.

Tyrowicz, Marian. *Jan Tyssowski i Rewolucja 1846 r. w Krakówie: Dzieja porywu i pokuty.* Cracow: Krajowa Wydawnicza, 1986.

Ugniewska, Joanna. *Giuseppe Mazzini: historia jako narodowa terapia*. Wrocław: Wydawnictwo Polskiej Akademii Nauk, 1986.

Várossová, Elena. *Slovenské obrodenecké myslenie: jeho zdroje a základné idey*. Bratislava: Vydavateľstvo Akadémie vied, 1963.

Varvartsev, Mykola. *Dzhuzeppe Madzini: madzinizm i Ukraïna*. Kyiv: Universytets'ke vydavnytstvo Pul'sary, 2005.

Vozniak, Mykhailo. *Kyrylo-Metodiïvs'ke Bratstvo*. Lviv: Nakl. fondu "Uchitesia, braty moï," 1921.

Walicki, Andrzej. *The Enlightenment and the Birth of Modern Nationhood: Polish Political Thought from Noble Republicanism to Tadeusz Kosciuszko*. Notre Dame, IN: University of Notre Dame Press, 1989.

– *Mesjanizm Adama Mickiewicza w perspektywie porównawczej*. Warsaw: IfiS, 2006.

– *Philosophy and Romantic Nationalism: The Case of Poland*. Notre Dame, IN: University of Notre Dame Press, 1994.

– *Russia, Poland and Universal Regeneration: Studies on Russian and Polish Thought of the Romantic Epoch*. Notre Dame, IN: University of Notre Dame Press, 1991.

– *The Slavophile Controversy: The History of a Conservative Utopia in Nineteenth-Century Russian Thought*. Oxford: Clarendon, 1975.

Wandycz, Piotr S. *The Lands of Partitioned Poland, 1795–1918*. Seattle: University of Washington Press, 1984.

Witte, Els, Jan Craeybeck, and Alain Meyen. *Political History of Belgium: From 1830 Onwards*. Brussels: Academic and Scientific Publishers, 2009.

Žáček, Václav. *Čechové a Poláci roku 1848: Studie k novodobým politickým stykům česko-polským*. 2 vols. Prague: Nákl. Slovanského ústavu a Slovanského výboru Česko-Slovenska v komisi nakl. "Orbis," 1947–8.

Zaionchkovskii, P.A. *Kirillo-Mefodievskoe obshchestvo (1846–1847)*. Moscow: Izdatel'stvo Moskovskogo Universiteta, 1959.

Zaitsev, Pavlo. *Taras Shevchenko: A Life*. Edited and translated by George Luckyj. Toronto: University of Toronto Press, 1988.

Zajcew, Pawel [Pavlo Zaitsev]. *Szewczenko i Polacy*. Warsaw: Nakladem Biuletynu Polsko-Ukrainskiego, 1934.

Zborucki, Zygmunt. *Proces studentów samborskich 1837–1839*. Lviv: Uniwesytet Jana Kazimierza we Lwowie, 1927.

Articles

Adadurov, V.V. "Memorandumy pol's'kykh avtoriv pochatku XIX st. iak dzherelo uiavlen' imperatora Napoleona I ta ioho uriadovtsiv stosovno pivdenno-zakhidnykh okraïn Rosiis'koï imperiï." *Ukraïns'kyi istorychnyi zhurnal* 2 (2008): 154–71.

Andrusiak, M. "Ukraiński ruch narodowy i konspiracja polska w Galicji w latach 30-tych i 40-tych XIX w." *Biuletyn Polsko-Ukraiński* 5, no. 6 (1936).

Béder, Ján. "Kollárova koncepcia Slovanskej Vzájomnosti a Mladé Slovensko." *Historický Časopis* 8, nos 2–3 (1960): 243–64.

– "Nástup Generácie Mladé Slovensko." *Slovenská Literatúra* 7, no. 1 (1960): 46–9.

– "Spoločnosť česko-slovenská a slovanský ústav v Bratislave v rokoch 1835–1840." *Zborník štúdií a prác Vysokej školy pedagogickej v Bratislave* 1 (1957): 3–80.

– "Vlastné životopisy vedúcich členov tajného spolku Vzájomnosť (Vrchovský – Ollík – Hodža)." *Slovenská Literatúra: Časopis Slovenskej Akadémie Vied,* Vydavateľstvo Slovenskej Akadémie Vied v Bratislave, Ročník VI, 1959.

Betley, I.A. *Belgium and Poland in International Relations 1830–31.* 'S – Gravenhage: Mouton, 1960.

Bielina-Kędrzycki, Julian. "U Shevchenka v Kyievi, 1846." In *Spohady pro Tarasa Shevchenka,* 153–9. Kyiv: Vydavnytstvo khudozhn'oï literatury "Dnipro," 1982.

Bohachevska, Martha I. "U dzherelakh novitnikh politychnykh idei: Kyrylo-Metodiyivske Bratstvo." *Biuleten "Obnova": Zhurnal Tovarystv Ukrainskykh Studentiv Katolykiv (Periodicum Societatum Ukrainorum Studentium Catholicorum)* May–June (1958): 13–29.

Bortnikov, A.I. "Kirillo-Mefodievskoe obshchestvo i pol'skoe natsional'no-osvoboditel'noe dvizhenie." In *Razvitie kapitalizma i natsional'nye dvizheniia v slavianskikh strankakh,* edited by V.I. Freidzon, 176–93. Moscow: Izdatel'stvo "Nauka," 1970.

Borys, Włodzimier. "Z dziejów walk o wyzwolenie narodowe i społeczne w Galicji w pierwszej połowinie XIX w.: Ignacy Kulczyński w świetle zeznań Juliana Horoszkiewicza i Kaspra Cięglewicza." In *Przemyskie Zapiski Historyczne,* 4–5:223–30. Przemyśl: Polskie Towarzystwo Historyczne, Oddzial w Przemyślu, 1987.

Brock, Peter. "Ivan Vahylevych (1811–1866) ta ukraïns'ka natsional'na identychnist'." In *Shashkevychiana,* n.s., vyp. 1–2. Lviv: Instytut ukrainoznavstva im. I. Krypiakevycha, NAN Ukraïny, 1996, 389–416.

Bryk, Ivan. "Shevchenkova poema 'Ivan Hus.'" *Zapysky NTSh,* 119/20 (Lviv, 1917): 95–168; 126/27 (1918): 223–416.

Buchta, J.D. "A.B. Vrchovský: ideológ mladého Slovenska." *Hlas Ľudu,* 29 January 1983.

Butvin, Jozef. "Tajny politicky spolok Vzájomnosť (1837–1840)." In *Sborník Filozofickej Fakulty Univerzity Komenského,* 14:1–37. Bratislava: Slovenské pedagogické nakladateľstvo, 1963.

– "Zjednocovanie snahy v slovenskom narodnom hnutí v 30-ych rokoch 19. stor." *Historické studie* 8 (1963): 7–67.

Čiževsky, Dmitry [Dmytro Chyzhevs'kyi]. "Mickiewicz and Ukrainian Literature." In *Adam Mickiewicz in World Literature: A Symposium,* edited by Wacław Lednicki, 409–36. Berkeley: University of California Press, 1956.

David, Zdeněk V. "Frič, Herzen, and Bakunin: The Clash of Two Political Cultures." *East European Politics and Societies* 12, no. 1 (Winter 1998): 1–30.

Djakow, W.A. "Polski ruch wyzwoleńczy w latach trzydziestych i szterdziestych XIX stulecia." *Kwartalnik Historyczczny* 84, no. 4 (1977): 977–88.

Dovzhok, Tetiana. "Adam Mitskevych ta 'Ukraïns'ka shkola (do problemy pol's'ko-ukraïns'koho pohranychchia.'" In *Adam Mitskevych i Ukraïna: Zbirnyk naukovykh prats'*, edited by Rostyslav Radyshevsky and H.D. Verves, 94–111. Kyiv: Vydavnytstvo "Biblioteka Ukraïntsia," 1999.

Dz'oban, Oleksandr. "Shashkevychiana u fondakh viddilu rukopysiv l'vivs'koï naukovoï biblioteky (LNB) im. V. Stefanyka NAN Ukraïny." *Shashkevychiana*, n.s., vyp. 5–6. Lviv: Instytut Ukraïnoznavstva im. Krypiakevycha NAN Ukraïny, 2004, 284–93.

Eyck, F. Gunther. "Mazzini's Young Europe." *Journal of Central European Affairs* 17 (1958): 356–77.

Fišer, Zdeněk. "Zpráva Brnenského Policejního Reditele z Roku 1840 o Moravskych Vlastencích." *Zpravodaj Muzea Kroměřžiska* 2 (1992): 1–5.

Fordinálová, Eva. "'Sivá eminencia' Slovenskej romatickej generácie." *Hlas Ľudu*, 27 October 1992.

Golovatskii, Iakov [Iakiv Holovats'kyi]. "K istorii galitsko-ruskoi pis'mennosti (Nieskol'ko zamechanii na pis'mo I. Vagilevicha k M. P. Pogodinu)." *Kievskaia starina*, 1883.

Hájek, Zdeněk. "Stýky Jakiva a Ivana Holovackých s Josefem Podlipským a Františkom Kampelíkom." In *Franku Wollmanovi k sedmdesátinám. Sborník prací*, 213–27. Prague: Státní pedagogické nakladatelství, 1958.

Hermaize, O. "Rukh dekabrystiv i ukraïnstvo." *Ukraïna* 6 (1925): 33.

Hostička, Vladimír. "Pavel Josef Šafařík a Ukrajinci." In *Z dejín československo-ukrajinských vzt'ahov*, 295–318. Bratislava: Vydateľstvo Slovenskej akadémii vied, 1957.

– "Ukrajina v názorech české obrozenecké společnosti do roku 1848." *Slavia* 33, no. 4 (1964): 558–78.

Hutchinson, John. "Cultural Nationalism and Moral Regeneration." In *Nationalism*, edited by John Hutchinson and Anthony D. Smith, 122–33. Oxford: Oxford University Press, 1994.

Isabella, Maurizio. "Mazzini's Internationalism in Context: From the Cosmopolitan Patriotism of the Italian Carbonari to Mazzini's Europe of the Nations." In *Giuseppe Mazzini and the Globalisation of Democratic Nationalism 1830–1920*, edited by Christopher A. Bayly and Eugenio F. Biagini, 37–58. Oxford: Oxford University Press, 2008.

Kieniewicz, Stefan. "La pensée de Mazzini et le mouvement national slave." In *Atti del Convegno Mazzini e l'Europa*, 109–23. Rome: Accademia dei Lincei, 1974.

Kmit, Iurii. "Prychynky do istoriï rus'koho dukhovnoho seminariia u L'vovi 1837–1851 rr." *Zapysky NTSh* 91 (1909): 151–8.

Kostomarov, Mykola I. "Avtobiografiia N.I. Kostomarova, zapisannaia N.A. Bilozerskoi." *Russkaia mysl'* 5 (1885): 185–223; 6 (1885): 20–43.

Kostomarova, Alina. "Nikolai Ivanovich Kostomarov." In *Avtobiografiia N.I. Kostomarova*, edited by V. Kotel'nikov, 64–5. Moscow: Zadruga, 1922.

Kozak, Stefan. "Knyhy bytiia Ukraïns'koho narodu Mykoly Kostomarova i Księgi narodu i pielgrzymstwa Polskiego Adama Mickiewicza." *Slavia orientalis* 1 (1973): 177–88.

Krevets'kyi, Ivan. "Fal'shuvannia metryk dlia pol's'kykh povstantsiv z 1830–1831 rr. (Prychynok do kharakterystyky halyts'ko-rus'koho dukhovenstva pershoï polovyny XIXI st.)" *Zapysky NTSh* 77 (1907): 107–13.

Kupchyns'kyi, Oleh. "Zabuti imena v ukraïns'kii nautsi ta kul'turi: Ivan Zakhar Avdykovs'kyi." *Visnyk Naukovoho Tovarystva im. Shevchenka* 42 (2009): 45–52.

Łepkowski, Tadeusz. "Spoleczne i narodowe aspekty powstania 1831 na Ukraine." *Kwartalnik Historyczny* 64 (1957): 41–65.

Lewak, Adam. "Ideologia polskiego romantyzmu politycznego a Mazzini." *Przegląd Historyczny* 37 (1948): 311–21.

Liakhova, Zhanna. "Ukraïns'kyi lyst Mykoly Hoholia." *Slovo i chas* 12 (2001): 57–65.

Łukaszewicz, Witold. "Wpływ masonerii, karabonaryzmu i Józefa Mazziniego na polski ruch rewolucyjny w latach poprzedzających Wiosnę Ludów (1831–1847)." In *Zagadnienia ideologiczne*. Pt 2 of *Wiosna Ludów w Europie*, edited by Natalia Gąsiorowska, 167–384. Warsaw: Państwowy Instytut Wydawniczy, 1951.

Marchenko, Valerii. "Mykola Hulak." *Suchasnist'* 4–5 (1982): 117–36.

Matula, Vladimír. "The Conception and the Development of Slovak National Culture in the Period of National Revival." *Studia Historica Slovaca* 17 (1990): 153–93.

– "Lyceum a Lipa Slovanská." In *Nad Tatrou sa blýska*. Bratislava: Veda, Vydavatel'stvo Slovenskej akadémie vied, 1994.

– "Mladé Slovensko a Juhoslavania." In *Československo a Juhoslávia*, 106–45. Bratislava: Vydavatel'stvo Slovenskej akadémie vied, 1968.

– "Slovanská Vzájomnosť: Národnooslobodzovacia ideologia Slovenského narodného hnutia (1835–1849)." *Historický Časopis* 8, no. 2 (1969): 248–64.

– "Snahy o prehlbenie demokratickej linie Slovenských narodných novín a formovanie revolučného programu slovenského narodného hnutia (1845–1848)." *Historický Časopis* 6 (1958): 202–23.

Maver, G. "Mazzini and Mickiewicz." In *Adam Mickiewicz, 1855–1955. Międzynarodowa Sesja Naukowa Polskiej Akademii Nauk 17–20 kwietnia 1956*, edited by Kazimierz Wyka and Jadwiga Rużyło Pawłowska, 212–25. Wrocław: Zaklad Narodowy im. Ossolińskich, 1958.

Medvecký, Samuel. "Rozpomienky na Sama Chalupku." *Slovenskè pohl'ady* 7, no. 10 (1887): 235–39.

Miiakovs'kyi [Miiakovsky, Mijakovskyj], Volodymyr. "Knyha pro Kyrylo-Metodiïvs'ke bratstvo." *Suchasnist'* 3 (1963): 85–96.

– "Kostomarov u Rivnomu." *Ukraïna* 12 (1925): 28–66.

– "Ševčehenko in the Brotherhood of Saints Cyril and Methodius." In *Taras Ševčenko 1814–1861: A Symposium*, edited by Volodymyr Mijakovs'kyj and George Y. Shevelov, 9–36. 'S-Gravenhage: Mouton, 1962.

– "Shevchenko i Kostomarov." In *Zarubizhne Shevchenkoznavstvo (z materialiv UVAN)*, pt 2, 296–312. Kyiv: Khronika, 2011.

– "Shevchenko in the Brotherhood of Saints Cyril and Methodius." In *Shevchenko and the Critics 1861–1980*, edited by George S.N. Luckyj, 355–83. Toronto: University of Toronto Press, for the Canadian Institute of Ukrainian Studies, 1980.

Moiseev, Dmitrii S. "Politicheskaia mysl' Dzhuzeppe Madzini," *Voprosy filosofii* 20 (2015): 63–78.

Morley, Charles. "The European Significance of the November Uprising." *Journal of Central European Affairs* 11 (1952): 407–19.

Mudryi, Mari'ian. "*Gente Rutheni* v pol's'kii tsentral'nii radi narodovii 1848 roku." *Zapysky NTSh* 256 (2008): 244–87.

N.M. "Pamiati Nikolaia Ivanovicha Gulaka." *Kievskaia starina* 2 (1900): 261–72.

Nevrli, Mykola [Mikuláš Nevrlý]. "Retseptsiia Husa v ukraïns'kii literaturi." *Duklia* 1 (2003): 36–41.

Papazian, Dennis. "N.I. Kostomarov and the Cyril-Methodian Ideology." *Russian Review* 29 (January 1970): 59–73.

Pfaff, Ivan. "Il movimento nazionale ceco e Risorgimento Italiano (1820–1866)." *Studi storici* 39 (1998): 31–48.

– "Karel Havlíček a italské Risorgimento." *Časopis Národního Muzea* 71, nos 3–4 (2002): 179–93.

Piekut, Stanisław. "Adam Mickiewicz a Józef Mazzini." In *Adam Mickiewicz: Księga w stulecie zgonu*, 151–62. London: Polskie Towarzystwo Naukowe, 1958.

Procyk, Anna. "The Conspiratorial Phase in the Life of František Cyril Kampelík." In *SVU and Its Role in the Era of Globalization: Selected Papers from the Twenty-Sixth World Congress of the Czechoslovak Society of Arts and Sciences*, edited by Zdeněk David, 1:161–71. New York: Publishing House of the Czechoslovak Society of Arts and Sciences, 2013.

– "Giuseppe Mazzini and Eastern Europe." *Do dzherel: zbirnyk naukovykh prats' na poshanu Oleha Kupchynskoho z nahody ioho 70-richchia (Ad Fontes: Studia in honorem Oleh Kupchyns'kyi septuagenario dedicata)*, 450–7. Kyiv-Lviv: Instytut Ukraïnskoï arkheohrafiï ta dzhereloznavstva im Hrushevskoho, 2004.

– "Moloda Evropa i Kyrylo-Metodiïvs'ke bratstvo." *Ukraïns'kyi istoryk* 40 (2003): 275–85.
– "Polish Emigres as Emissaries of the *Risorgimento* in Eastern Europe." *Harvard Ukrainian Studies* 25, no. 1–2 (2001): 7–29.
– "Political Currents among Czech, Slovak and Ukrainian National Awakeners under the Sponsorship of Young Europe." *Kosmas, Czechoslovak and East European Journal* (Spring 2012): 56–74.
– "The Role of Young Europe in the Slavic World." *Kosmas, Czechoslovak and East European Journal* (Spring 2009): 50–8.
Radyshevsky, Rostyslav. "Velykyi piligrim i prorok." In *Adam Mitskevych i Ukraïna*, 26–37. Kyiv: "Biblioteka Ukraïntsia," 1999.
Raikivs'kyi, I. Ia. "Vzaiemyny halyts'kykh i naddniprians'kykh diiachiv u 1830–1840-kh rr." *Ukraïns'kyi istorychnyi zhurnal* 1 (2009): 39–55.
Riall, Lucy. "The Politics of Italian Romanticism and the Making of Nationalist Culture." In *Giuseppe Mazzini and the Globalisation of Democratic Nationalism 1830–1920*, edited by Christopher A. Bayly and Eugenio F. Biagini, 167–86. Oxford: Oxford University Press, 2008.
Rosenbaum, Karol. "Ľudovít Štúr na evanjelickom lýceu v Bratislave v rokoch 1829–1836." In *Ľudovít Štúr v súradniciach minulosti a súčasnosti*, edited by Imrich Sedlák, 15–27. Martin: Matica Slovenská, 1997.
Rudnytsky, Ivan L. "Hipolit Vladimir Terlecki." In *Essays in Modern Ukrainian History*, edited by Peter L. Rudnytsky, 143–72. Edmonton: Canadian Institute of Ukrainian Studies, 1987.
– "Michał Czajkowski's Cossack Project during the Crimean War: An Analysis of Ideas." In *Essays in Modern Ukrainian History*, edited by Peter L. Rudnytsky, 173–86. Edmonton: Canadian Institute of Ukrainian Studies, 1987.
– "The Ukrainians in Galicia under Austrian rule." In *Essays in Modern Ukrainian History*, edited by Peter L. Rudnytsky, 315–52. Edmonton: Canadian Institute of Ukrainian Studies, 1987; also in *Austrian History Yearbook*, vol. 3, pt 2 (1967): 394–429.
Sarti, Roland. "Giuseppe Mazzini and Young Europe." In *Giuseppe Mazzini and the Globalisation of Democratic Nationalism 1830–1920*, edited by Christopher A. Bayly and Eugenio F. Biagini, 275–98. Oxford: Oxford University Press, 2008.
Sedlák, Imrich. "Ľudovít Štúr a slovenské študenské hnutie." In *Ľudovít Štúr v súradniciach minulosti a súčasnosti*, edited by Imrich Sedlák, 28–38. Martin: Matica Slovenská, 1997.
Semevskii, V. "Kirillo-Mefodievskoe obshchestvo, 1846–1847." *Russkoe bogatstvo* 5 (1911): 98–127; 6 (1911): 29–67.
Serhiienko, H.A. "Diial'nist' 'Soiuzu pol's'koho narodu' na Ukraïni 1835–1839 rr." *Ukraïns'kyi istorychnyi zhurnal* 12 (1969): 75–84.
Shchurat, Vasyl'. "Chorna knyha." *Dilo* 134 (1912): 1–2.

Shelepets', Iosyf. "Shevchenkiv virsh 'Shafarykovi' iak pokhvala Shafarykovi." *Duklia* 2 (2007): 23–5.

Shkrabiuk, Petro. "M. Pavlyk – spadkoiiemets' ideï 'Rus'koï Triitsi,'" *Shashkevychiana*, n.s., vyp. 1–2: 74–82. Lviv: Instytut ukraïnoznavstva im. Krypiakevycha NAN Ukraïny, 1996.

Sielecki, P.D. "Zapiski (1821–1846)." *Kyïvs'ka staryna* (1884): 2–9.

Simonov, S.S. "Oseredok 'Soiuzu pol's'koho narodu' w Kyïvs'komu Universyteti." *Wisnyk Kyïvs'koho Universytetu* 4 (1961).

Steblii, Feodosii. "Markiian Shashkevych: provisnyk nezalezhnosty sobornoï Ukraïny." *Visnyk NTSh* 45 (2011): 9–13.

Storozhenko, N. "Kirillo-Mefodievskie zagovorshchiki." *Kievskaia starina* 2 (1906): 135–52.

Struve, Petr. "Chto takoe Rossiia." *Russkaia mysl'* (January 1911): 175–8.

– "Obshcherusskaia kul'tura i ukrainskii partikularizm: Otvet ukrainstvu." *Russkaia mysl'* (January 1912): 65–86.

– *Patriotika: Politika, kul'tura, religiia, sotsializm; sbornik statei za piat' let, 1905–1910 gg.* St Petersburg: D.E. Zhukovskii, 1911.

Studyns'kyi, Kyrylo. "Pol's'ki konspiratsiï sered rus'kykh pytomtsiv i dukhovenstva v Halychyni v rokakh 1831–1846." *Zapysky NTSh* 80 (1907): 53–108; 82 (1908): 87–177.

Szporluk, Roman. "Ukraine: From an Imperial Periphery to a Sovereign State." In *Russia, Ukraine, and the Breakup of the Soviet Union*, 361–94. Stanford, CA: Hoover Institution Press, 2000.

– "The Western Dimension in the Making of Modern Ukraine." In *Contemporary Ukraine on the Cultural Map of Europe*, edited by Larissa M.L. Zaleska Onyshkevych and Maria G. Rewakowicz, 3–17. Armonk, NY: M.E. Sharpe, 2009.

Tabis, Jan. "Polskie rewolucyjne organizacje studenckie na Uniwersytecie Kijowskim." In *Szkice z dziejów stosunków polsko-ukraińskich*, edited by Antoni Podraza, 21–7. Cracow: Wydawnictwo Literackie, 1968.

Tershakovets', Mykhailo. "Do zhyttiepysu Markiiana Shashkevycha." *Zapysky NTSh* 105 (1911): 92–115; 106 (1911): 77–134.

– "Materialy i zamitky do istoriï natsional'noho vidrodzhennia Halyts'koï Rusy v 1830 ta 1840 rr." *Ukraïns'ko-rus'kyi arkhiv* 3 (1907).

Tomassucci, Giovanna. "Mazzini e la Polonia, 'Sorella Combattente.'" In *Il Mazzinianesimo nel Mondo*, edited by Giuliana Limiti, 2:369–462. Pisa: Istituto Domus Mazziniana, 1996.

– "Romantyzm polski w pismach G. Mazziniego." In *Contributi Italiani al XII Congresso Internazionale degli Slavisti*, edited by Francois Esvan, 541–52. Naples: Associazione Italiana degli Slavisti, 1998.

Turchenko, Fedir. "Stanovlennia svitohliadu." In *Mykola Mikhnovs'kyi: Suspil'no-politychni tvory*, edited by Ihor Hyrych, Fedir Turchenko, and Oleh Protsenko, 8–63. Kyiv: Smoloskyp, 2015.

Turii, Oleh. "Natsional'ne i polityczne polonofil'stvo sered
Hreko-Katolyts'koho Dukhovenstva Halychyny pid chas revoliutsiï 1848–
1849 rokiv." *Zapysky NTSh* 228 (1994): 183–206.
Tylusińska-Kowalska, Anna. "Wielcy apostołowie wolności, Mickiewicz i
Mazzini: braterstwo idei i czynu." *Przegląd Humanistyczny* (Warsaw) 49, no.
6 (2005): 13–22.
Urbinati, Nadia. "Mazzini and the Making of the Republican Ideology."
Journal of Modern Italian Studies 17, no. 2 (2012): 183–204.
Varvarcev, Mikula [Mykola Varvartsev]. "La diffusione del pensiero
mazziniana in Ucraina nell'Ottocento." In *Il Mazzinianesimo nel Mondo*,
edited by Giuliana Limiti, 465–509. Pisa: Istituto Domus Mazziniana, 1996.
Vongrej, Pavol. "Z tvorby Alexandra Boleslavína Vrchovského." In *Literatúrny
archív*, 138–53. Martin: Matica Slovenská, 1987.
Walicki, Andrzej. "Ernest Gellner and the 'Constructivist' Theory of Nation."
In *Cultures and Nations of Central and Eastern Europe: Essays in Honor of
Roman Szporluk*, edited by Zvi Gitelman, Lubomyr Hajda, John Paul Himka,
and Roman Solchanyk, 611–17. Cambridge, MA: Harvard University Press,
2000.
Wandycz, Piotr S. "The Poles in the Habsburg Monarchy." In *Austrian History
Yearbook* 3, pt 2 (1967): 261–86.
Wereszczycki, Henryk. "The Poles as an Integrating and Disintegrating
Factor." In *Austrian History Yearbook* 3, pt 2 (1967): 287–313.
Wielomski, Adam. "Prorok 'ich' Europy." *Myśl Polska* (Warsaw) 6 (2006): 1.
Zacek [Žáček], Joseph F. "Nationalism in Czechoslovakia." In *Nationalism in
Eastern Europe*, edited by Peter F. Sugar and Ivo J. Lederer, 166–206. Seattle:
University of Washington Press, 1969.
Zajcew, Pawel [Pavlo Zaitsev]. "Dwie postacie polskie w powieściach T.
Szewczenki." *Biuletyn Polsko-Ukraiński* 8 (1935).

Index

122; Polish underground and, 100–1; as revolutionary recruitment centre, 98; Ruthenian spirit of, 130; students' life at, 102–4, 108, 122–3, 124, 125, 182; Ukrainian studies at, 109–10, 120, 182; underground group at, 101, 102, 103, 122
Grus, J., 149, 180
Guriev, A.D., 66, 142

Hajpelman (Polish underground agent), 133
Hamorak, N., 68
Harro-Harring, Paul, 29, 33
Herder, Johann, 13, 14, 154
Herzen, Alexander, 27, 38
Hildebrandt, Karol, 140
History of the Italian Republics in the Middle Ages (Sismondi), 16
History of the Rus' (Istoriia Rusov), 117
Hobsbawm, Eric J., 8
Hodža, Michal Miloslav, *69*, 91, 93, *174*, 178
Holček, J., *174*
Hollý, Ján, 85, 93; *Cyrilo-Metodiada*, 154
Holovatsky, Ivan, 91
Holovatsky, Yakiv, 91, 100, 110, *115*, 118–19, 124, 130, 184, 218n51
Holy Alliance, 3, 6
Hordynsky, Rev. Mykola: academic career of, 123; arrest and trial of, 104, 106, 124, 148, 183, 224n36; Association of the Polish People and, 104–5; background of, 104, 240n24, 240n27; concern of educational policy, 241n36; conspiratorial work of, 97, 101, 105, 106–7, 109–10, 120, 122, 123–4; education of, 104, 225n46, 241n40; illness of, 148; imprisonment of, 149, 185, 190; Korecki's relations with, 131–2, 182–3; literary works

of, 104, 110; Napoleon Nowicki and, 104; personality of, 106, 225n46; Podolynsky's relation with, 187; police surveillance of, 124; Rector Levytsky and, 109; reputation of, 190; support of Ukrainian studies, 109, 182
Horoszkiewicz, Julian, 126, 228n90
Hotel Lambert, 58
Hrab, Bazylii, 106
Hrechansky, Dezyderii, 101, 107, 109
Hroch, Miroslav, 8
Hronka (Slovak publication), 94
Hroš, T., 91
Hrushevsky, Mykhailo, 200
Hulak, Mykola, 153–4, *157*, 161, 167
Hungary: status of Slavic peoples in, 92, 194
Hunter's hill (Myslivska hora), 73, 217n39
Hurban, Jozef Miloslav, *70*, 84, 91, *174*, 178
Hurevych, Zenovii: "Moloda Ukraina" (Young Ukraine), 237n44
Hus, Jan, 93, 94, 168, 169–70, 171
Hutchinson, John, 8

Independent Ukraine (Mikhnovsky), 170
Instructions for the Teacher of the Ruthenian People, 128
Iwanowska, Felicia, 41, 165

Jabłonowski, Alexander, 163
"Jan Hus" (Shevchenko), 94, 168–71
Jankowski, Ludwik, 41, 164
Januszewicz, Teofil: correspondence of, 66, 76; life in France, 96, 97; native land of, 96; in Young Poland, work of, 65, 68, 76, 87, 95
Jedność Słowiańska (Slavic unity) Masonic lodge, 40
Jelínek, Josef Slavomír, 147